FAVORITE **NEW ENGLAND** RECIPES

ALL NEW! ALL NEW! ALL NEW! ALL NEW!

FAVORITE
NEW ENGLAND
RECIPES

SECOND EDITION

SARA B.B. STAMM

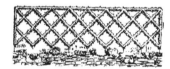

YANKEE BOOKS

CAMDEN · MAINE

JACKET AND TEXT DESIGN BY LURELLE CHEVERIE, ROCKPORT, MAINE

TYPESET BY PROTOTYPE GRAPHICS, INC., NASHVILLE, TENNESSEE

PRINTED AND BOUND BY BOOK PRESS, INC., BATTLEBORO, VERMONT

Library of Congress Cataloging-in-Publication Data

Stamm, Sara B. B.
    All new favorite New England recipes   by Sara B. B. Stamm.
        p.   cm.
    Includes index.
    ISBN 0-89909-318-3
    1. Cookery, American—New England style.   I. Title.
TX715.2.N48S73   1990
641.5974—dc20   90–47022
                                                                CIP

10 9 8 7 6 5 4 3 2 1

For my husband,
JOHN DAVIES STAMM

Contents

Introduction

Since I first compiled this book in 1972 eating habits in New England have changed a bit. Eighteen years ago I never imagined that salmon from Norway and green beans from France would fly through the air every day to the markets of Boston and Portland. The endive from Belgium is as reliable now in New England markets as carrots and turnips from local farms used to be. Herds of Bavarian deer graze in the Berkshires to provide venison year round and goats gambol in the Vermont hills, their milk made into dry white cheese. Reciprocally Maine lobsters fly each day to London and Paris to delight old world palates.

But the more things change the more they stay the same. Yankee cooking remains Yankee and the innovations brought about rapidly by air transportation have been absorbed as naturally as Boston beans absorbed the first molasses that arrived from the West Indies three hundred years ago. Here is a sampling of New England's latest. The traditional recipes continue in use as always—never neglected or forgotten. They mix without any awkwardness with the more exotic flavors of today.

In general, while these recipes may be followed with excellent results, you should feel free to make substitutions as your taste and imagination inspire. The preferences of your family will add changes to a recipe that will make it your own. Fresh butter and cream are wonderful, but margarine with its sweet meadow flavor and its low cholesterol and smooth light yogurt make excellent substitutes. Fresh herbs, or fresh ground pepper contribute subtly to meals. In keeping with present day tastes, I've added main dishes, salads, and desserts that are free of fat and cholesterol. They're delicious!

In searching out the real taste of New England past and present, I've had the greatest help of all from my friends. This big job couldn't have been done without them. Thank you Ann, Connie, Cyndy, Davie, Delphis, Edna, El, Elaine, Elizabeth, Evart, Eve, Freddie, George, Helen, Hyla, Jeanne, Kenneth, Linda, Lisa, Lois, Maria, Marian, Marla, Martin, Mimi, Nan, Narcissa, Pauline, Peter and Steven. A few small local cookbooks have been enormously rich sources of the flavor of New England. Among them are *The First Parish Cookbook*, Sudbury, Massachusetts, *The Little Compton Garden Club Cookbook*, Compton, Rhode Island, *A Lobster in Every Pot*, the Women of the Lobster Industry, University of Maine, *The Somerset Club Cookbook*, Boston, Massachusetts, *The Monadnock Garden*

Club Cookbook, Dublin, New Hampshire, *Watch Hill Cooks,* Watch Hill, Rhode Island, and *Connecticut A La Carte.*

Combining flavors and textures and giving thought to presentation all play a great part in keeping simple meals from being humdrum. The touch of parsley or cherries, or the Thanksgiving turkey's necklace of cranberries—all these flourishes should not be forgotten. Eating is one of the recurring, dependable pleasures of life and eating well together forms a deep bond.

SARA B. B. STAMM
July, 1990

A Boston Sunday Breakfast

orange juice

codfish cakes

eggs goldenrod

crisp bacon

apple muffins

bitter orange marmalade

*strawberries in season, served
whole with powdered sugar*

coffee

Church Supper

Here is a typical, bountiful church supper menu.
Church suppers are served country-style—
plenty of everything, crowding the board. This
is not recommended for weight watchers!

baked ham (clove-studded)

the bean pot

baked macaroni and cheddar cheese

pineapple-cabbage cole slaw

fresh sliced tomatoes with tarragon

watermelon rind pickles

India relish

hot corn bread

Boston cream pie

coffee

tea

St. Patrick's Day Dinner

smoked Irish salmon with capers

*lemon halves tied in net
with watercress "shamrocks"*

thin soda bread sandwiches

Dublin Bay prawns

corned beef with horseradish sauce

colcannon

minted peas

Irish flag salad

hot apple dumplings

brandied apricot sauce

Irish coffee

Fourth of July

Salmon and new green peas are the traditional foods of
the Fourth. If you have a large group or a buffet
party, you may prefer a salmon mousse with green mayonnaise
or old-fashioned boiled salmon with egg sauce.

firecrackers

cold sorrel soup

flash grilled salmon steaks

mustard yogurt sauce with capers

new peas

dilled new potatoes

cucumber salad

*strawberry shortcake with
whipped cream*

Traditional
Thanksgiving Dinner

venison pâté with pickled walnuts

pumpernickel spread with sweet butter

oysters on the half shell

hearts of celery

olives

roast turkey with sausage stuffing

giblet gravy

parsnip soufflé

glazed onions

pear and cranberry relish

buttered mashed potatoes

red cabbage Black Forest

mince pie

pumpkin pie

deep-dish apple pie

hard sauce

fruits

nuts

raisins

Christmas Dinner

smoked turkey with thin
buttered rye bread

celery

olives and mixed salted nuts

cream of oyster soup

roast prime ribs of beef

Yorkshire pudding

horseradish sauce

currant jelly

puree of lima beans and watercress

brussel sprouts

puree of chestnuts

creamed onions

English plum pudding flamed

foamy apricot sauce

Breads and Breakfasts

Traditionally, the Yankee breakfast has been a fine, warm affair, a minor feast that can hold its own with any other meal. Yankees rose early (most of them still do), and the chores that had to be done while breakfast was prepared produced a hearty appetite for fish cakes, baked beans, and pie. Of course, breakfast was something kept over from the day before or something that could be cooked in a reasonably short time.

When I was young, in Vermont, there was a fine-looking man who lived across the street from us. His wife told us that in his whole life he had never missed having a piece of pie for breakfast each morning. We looked upon this fortunate creature with an awe that was not unmixed with envy, for the fine old New England breakfast had disappeared already from our table. Oatmeal, ham, creamed codfish, cornbread—yes; pie—no.

Nowadays, we have reached a compromise in our family. Everyday breakfasts are good—sustaining but simple. But on Saturday and Sunday everything goes. And all of it disappears, too. Family and guests enjoy these weekend occasions. Orange juice and coffee are served to early risers as they appear, and by the time everyone is on hand, the large breakfast is ready. This large, late breakfast also offers a good opportunity for entertaining. Some people call it brunch, and it's a weekend institution that's here to stay.

Homemade Bread

 This is a basic white bread recipe that's been around a long time. This bread is just plain good and makes fine toast.

1 package dry yeast	1 teaspoon salt
1 cup warm (not hot) milk	1 tablespoon granulated sugar
3 tablespoons butter or margarine	3 cups sifted flour

1 In a large, warm bowl, dissolve yeast in milk.

2 Add the butter, salt, and sugar, then sift in the flour until no more can

be worked in with spoon or fingers. Cover lightly and let rise about 2 hours in warm place until the dough is three times its original bulk.

3 Turn out onto a floured board and knead lightly. Coat a bread pan with vegetable spray. Shape and place dough in pan. Cover and let rise again until dough is twice its original size (about 1 hour).

4 Preheat oven to 350°.

5 Bake the bread 40 minutes. When done, remove the bread to cooling rack and rub top lightly with butter.

YIELD: 1 LOAF

Old-Fashioned Vanilla-Flavored White Bread

 Excellent, served thinly sliced with butter and strawberry jam, for tea.

2 packages dry yeast	1 teaspoon (or more) vanilla
2²/₃ cups lukewarm milk	extract
5 cups white flour	2 eggs
³/₄ teaspoon salt	¹/₂ cup granulated sugar
¹/₂ cup melted butter or	1 egg, beaten (optional)
margarine	poppy seeds (optional)

1 Sprinkle dry yeast over milk, stir in, and gradually add 1 cup of the flour. (Mixture should be smooth.) Spread damp towel over bowl and allow to rise in warm (not hot) place.

2 Wait 2 to 3 hours for mixture to double in bulk, then add salt, melted butter, and vanilla.

3 In separate bowl, beat eggs with sugar until light yellow and pour into first mixture. Add remaining flour until dough is kneadable (stiff enough so it does not stick to your hands), then turn out on floured board and knead until velvety-smooth.

4 Coat mixing bowl with vegetable spray or butter and put dough into bowl. Cover with damp towel and let rise again until it doubles in bulk.

5 Punch dough down and turn out again onto floured board. Coat two bread pans with vegetable spray or butter and lightly shape dough into oblongs to fit. Let dough rise in pans 1 hour.

6 Preheat oven to 400°.

7 Bake 15 minutes, then reduce heat to 375° and bake 40 to 60 minutes

more. Bread is done when bottoms give a hollow sound when tapped and toothpick inserted in center comes out dry.

8　Turn loaves out onto cooling racks and rub with butter. Or brush with a beaten egg and sprinkle poppy seeds over loaves.

YIELD: 2 LOAVES

Portuguese Sweet Bread

 These rich yeast loaves with a close, fine texture are reminiscent of the round loaves of sweet Portuguese bread originally found on Nantucket or Cape Cod.

2 cups milk, scalded
1 1/2 cups plus 1 teaspoon granulated sugar
2 tablespoons salt
4 eggs

1/4 cup butter or margarine, melted and cooled
2 packages dry yeast
1/4 cup lukewarm water
8 to 9 cups unbleached flour

1　Preheat oven to 400°. Coat 3 9-inch cake pans with vegetable spray.

2　Pour the milk into a large mixing bowl, add sugar and salt. Cool to lukewarm and whisk in the eggs and butter.

3　Dissolve the yeast in the warm water and sugar. Set aside. Add 4 cups of flour to milk. Add yeast mixture. Beat well. Add remaining flour gradually until the dough is stiff.

4　On a floured board, knead the dough until it is smooth and elastic, about 10 minutes. Form the dough into a ball and place in an oiled bowl. Turn dough to coat, cover the bowl. Put in a warm place to double in bulk, about 2 hours.

5　Divide dough into 3 parts and shape into flattened 8-inch round loaves. Place in pans. Cover; let rise until double in bulk, about 45 minutes.

6　Bake the loaves for 40 minutes, or until a toothpick comes out dry. Cool on racks.

YIELD: 3 LOAVES

Oatmeal Bread

 This recipe may also be used to make rolls. Shape them accordingly.

1 package dry yeast

1 tablespoon granulated sugar

1 cup old-fashioned oatmeal

1/2 cup dark molasses

1 1/4 teaspoons salt

2 tablespoons butter or margarine

2 cups boiling water

3 to 4 cups sifted flour

1 Dissolve yeast in small amount of tap water and sprinkle sugar on top until it rises.

2 In large, warm bowl, mix together oatmeal, molasses, and salt.

3 Dissolve butter in boiling water and add to oatmeal.

4 Sift in the flour until no more can be added. When partly cooled, add yeast and mix well. Let dough rise in warm place free from drafts for almost 2 hours, or until doubled in bulk.

5 Knead on a floured board, coat 2 loaf pans with vegetable spray, and place dough in pans to double a second time.

6 Preheat oven to 350°.

7 Bake about 40 minutes. Remove to cooling rack and rub with butter.

YIELD: 2 LOAVES

Cracked Wheat Bread

 4 cups boiling water

1 cup whole-grain cracked wheat

2 teaspoons salt

1/2 cup dark molasses

4 tablespoons butter or margarine

1 package dry yeast

8 cups (approximately) unbleached flour

1 Pour boiling water over cracked wheat and let stand 3 hours or more (overnight, if you wish).

2 Heat water and wheat to lukewarm and add salt, molasses, and butter.

3 Sift yeast with 2 cups of the flour and stir into cracked wheat mixture. Sift in the remaining flour to make fairly firm, nonsticky dough. Turn out on floured board and knead until smooth and elastic. Coat mixing

bowl with vegetable spray and put dough into bowl. Cover and let rise in warm place until doubled in bulk (about 2 hours).

4 Knead again lightly and divide dough into four parts. Shape into loaves. Coat 4 loaf pans with vegetable spray and place dough in pans. Cover with damp towel and let rise again until doubled in bulk (about 1¼ hours).

5 Preheat oven to 400°.

6 Bake 10 minutes, reduce heat to 350°, and bake 50 minutes more.

7 Remove loaves to cooling rack and brush tops with butter. Loaves may be frozen.

YIELD: 4 LOAVES (ABOUT 1¼ POUNDS EACH)

Wheat Germ White Bread

 A very fine-textured, high-rising bread.

1 package dry yeast	1 cup milk, scalded
1¼ cups lukewarm water	1½ teaspoons salt
1 tablespoon granulated sugar	½ cup honey
1 egg	¼ teaspoon baking soda
6 tablespoons melted butter or	7 cups white flour
margarine	1 cup wheat germ, toasted

1 Sprinkle yeast over ½ cup lukewarm water, stir, and add sugar. Let mixture stand in warm place 45 minutes.

2 Beat in the egg, melted butter, remaining water, scalded milk (milk is scalded when, on being heated, bubbles form around edge of pan), salt, honey, and baking soda. Add flour and wheat germ gradually, until batter is too stiff to beat.

3 Turn dough out onto floured board and knead in remaining flour. Knead until smooth. Coat mixing bowl with vegetable spray, then place dough in bowl. Cover with damp towel. Let stand in warm place (70° to 80°) until dough has doubled in bulk.

4 Punch down dough, knead, and return to greased, covered bowl. Allow dough to double in size again.

5 Punch down again and separate into three loaf-size portions, sealing edges carefully. Coat 3 loaf pans with vegetable spray and place dough in pans. Again, let loaves double in size.

6 Place loaves in cold oven. Set temperature at 400° for 15 minutes, then lower heat to 375° and bake 35 to 45 minutes more.

7 When done, brush loaves with melted butter.

YIELD: 3 LOAVES

Zucchini Bread

 If I have extra zucchini in the garden, I freeze it so I can have this bread year round.

3 cups all-purpose flour	1 teaspoon baking powder
1 cup grated zucchini	1 teaspoon salt
1/3 cup granulated sugar	1/3 cup butter or margarine
3 tablespoons grated Parmesan cheese	1 cup buttermilk
	2 eggs
1/2 teaspoon baking soda	1 tablespoon grated onion

1 Preheat oven to 350°. Coat a 9" x 5" x 3" loaf pan with vegetable spray.

2 Mix together flour, zucchini, sugar, cheese, baking soda, baking powder, and salt. Set aside.

3 Melt the butter and stir into buttermilk.

4 Beat eggs in medium bowl. Add buttermilk mixture and onion. Stir into dry ingredients (the batter will be thick).

5 Spread in prepared pan and bake 1 hour, or until a toothpick inserted into the center comes out clean. Turn out onto wire rack to cool.

YIELD: 1 LOAF

Potato Bread

2 packages dry yeast	1 tablespoon granulated sugar
1/3 cup potato cooking water	3 cups mashed potatoes
1 scant tablespoon salt	5 cups white flour
1 tablespoon shortening	1 cup barley flour

1 Dissolve yeast in lukewarm potato water. Add salt, shortening, sugar, then add mashed potatoes and mix well.

2 Stir in the flour until no more can be added. Place the dough in a dry

bowl coated with vegetable spray. Cover with cloth and set in warm place to rise, about 3 hours.

3 Knead well, divide dough into three parts, and put in loaf pans sprayed with vegetable oil. Let loaves rise again in a warm place until the dough again doubles in bulk.

4 Preheat oven to 375°.

5 Bake 1 hour. Turn onto rack. Rub with butter.

YIELD: 3 LOAVES

Mule Bread for Stubborn People

 This bread is good for toast, good for ham sandwiches or BLTs.

1 bottle (14 ounces) beer, at room temperature	1 teaspoon salt
3 cups self-rising flour	2 tablespoons melted butter or margarine
3 tablespoons granulated sugar	2 tablespoons caraway seeds

1 Preheat the oven to 375°. Coat 9″ x 5″ x 3″ loaf pan with vegetable spray.

2 Mix ingredients together and pour into prepared pan. Allow to rise for 1 hour. Punch down and allow to rise again for another hour.

3 Bake 30 minutes. Brush the top with butter and caraway seeds and bake 10 minutes longer. Cool on wire rack.

YIELD: 1 LARGE LOAF

Norwegian Fisherman's Bread

 This fisherman's bread is supposed to be served with sardines and sour cream. It sounds like a wonderful combination.

bacon fat for greasing skillet	2 teaspoons salt
1 package dry yeast	1 tablespoon granulated sugar
1 cup lukewarm water	1 tablespoon grated lemon rind
2 medium potatoes, peeled and grated	4 cups flour
6 cloves garlic, crushed	1 egg, beaten
	sesame seeds

1 Grease a 10-inch iron skillet or round pan with vegetable spray.

2 In a large bowl, dissolve the yeast in water. Add potatoes, garlic, salt, sugar, and lemon rind and mix well. Gradually add the flour, beating until blended. Cover and let rise about $1^{1}/_{2}$ hours.

3 Punch down the dough and turn into prepared skillet. Let rise again for $^{1}/_{2}$ hour.

4 Preheat oven to 400°.

5 Bake the bread for 30 minutes. Brush bread with the beaten egg and sprinkle with sesame seeds. Bake for 20 minutes more, until golden brown. Turn out onto a wire rack.

YIELD: 1 ROUND LOAF

French Bread

 Twentieth-century Americans have adopted French bread for their own. Made without milk or shortening, it is best eaten—as done in France—shortly after it is baked.

1 package dry yeast	2 teaspoons salt
2 cups lukewarm water	melted butter (for brushing
4 cups sifted flour	loaves)
1 tablespoon granulated sugar	

1 Preheat oven to 400°.

2 Dissolve yeast in 1 cup of the water.

3 Sift together the flour, sugar, and salt and stir in the yeast. Add just enough of the remaining water to hold dough together. Mix until soft and sticky. Cover with clean cloth, place in warm spot, and let rise until double (2 to 4 hours).

4 When dough is high and spongy, punch it down and beat several minutes with floured hands.

5 Divide dough into two parts and shape each part into long loaves. (Roll out dough and roll into tight cylinder, pinching edges together firmly). Coat a baking sheet with vegetable spray. Place loaves on baking sheet, cover, and allow to rise until double in size.

6 Rub bread with butter and bake 1 hour.

YIELD: 2 FRENCH LOAVES

VARIATION — Herb French Bread

Slice French bread $3/4$ inch thick—to the bottom crust but not through it. Preheat oven to 400°. Cream $1/4$ cup butter with 4 tablespoons herbs (parsley with chives or thyme or dill, or tarragon with chives). Brush both sides of each slice with butter mixture. Press bread firmly together, wrap loosely in foil, and heat 10 minutes.

VARIATION — Garlic French Bread

Rub crusty loaf with 1 split clove garlic and proceed as with Herb French Bread.

VARIATION — Cheese French Bread

Mix grated cheese, such as Parmesan, with butter or olive oil and spread on both sides of each slice.

VARIATION — Anchovy French Bread

Add a few mashed anchovies to butter or olive oil and spread on both sides of each slice.

Dill Bread

 Made with unusual ingredients, this is a moist, flavorful loaf that is especially recommended for sandwiches. It is good for ham sandwiches. Poppy seed, caraway, or sesame seed may be substituted for the dill seed or used with it.

1 package dry yeast	2 teaspoons dill seed
$1/4$ cup warm water	1 teaspoon salt
1 cup lukewarm creamed	$1/4$ teaspoon baking soda
cottage cheese	1 egg
2 tablespoons granulated sugar	$2^{1}/4$ to $2^{1}/2$ cups flour
1 tablespoon butter or	butter or margarine for rubbing
margarine, softened	loaf
1 tablespoon finely chopped	
onion	

1 Dissolve the yeast in warm water.

2 In a large bowl, combine cottage cheese, sugar, butter, onion, dill seed, salt, baking soda, and egg. Add to yeast mixture, then gradually add enough flour to make stiff dough, beating well after each addition.

3 Coat mixing bowl with vegetable spray and place dough in bowl. Cover lightly with towel and allow dough to double in bulk.

4 Punch down again, then coat round 2-quart ovenproof casserole (or conventional loaf pan) with vegetable spray. Turn dough into casserole and let it rise again until double in bulk.

5 Preheat oven to 375°.

6 Bake 40 to 50 minutes. Turn onto cooling rack. Rub surface with butter or margarine.

YIELD: 1 LOAF

 ## Bread Hints

In old New England, it was usual to make dough for bread each evening and let it rise overnight. Kneading, a second rising, and baking took place in the morning, and the housewife got up early enough to have the bread ready when the men and children had done the chores and came in to breakfast. Our generation can turn out bread as fine as any produced in the kitchens of long ago. Expertly milled flour and yeast that functions more predictably and more quickly have removed the hazards from breadmaking.

There are many advantages to making bread and rolls at home. First of all, they are infinitely better tasting than the best that you can buy. Commercial breads, although often excellent, have to be adapted to a wide range of tastes, and they must be baked with preservatives to make them keep well. Homemade bread is a great economy, too. And, of course, bread may be varied in dozens of ways by an interesting cook. Most important, bread baking in the oven makes your house smell so good that everyone is happier there. Bread is not hard to make. Even if you have never tried, a couple of loaves will soon make you an expert.

General rules apply to most breads made with yeast, although recipes differ slightly. The type of flour, the amount of shortening, and the amount of time for rising can all vary the formulas a little. But a good loaf is one of medium size with a rounded top and a medium-brown crust free from cracks; the grain is fine and the crumb feels moist and elastic to the touch. Before use in bread dough, milk should be boiled or scalded and then cooled, or your bread may be sour. One teaspoon to one tablespoon of sugar and one teaspoon of salt per loaf is a good general rule when working with yeast. Shortening increases tenderness and improves the keeping quality of bread. Yeast reacts best at a temperature of 80° to 85° (80° within the bread). Be sure to grease the bowl in which you set the dough to rise, and cover it with a damp towel. If no place in your house has this approximate temperature, you can place the pan of dough in a large basin of warm (90° to 95°) water, but be sure to maintain that water temperature during the rising period. An oven heated low and then turned off works well too.

To mix and bake bread in 5 hours, use 1 package of yeast to 2 cups of liquid. The first rising will take 2 to 3 hours, the second 1 to 2 hours, and the baking about 1 hour. A little experience will tell you exactly when each process is right. To test whether the dough has risen properly, make an impression in the dough with your finger; if the impression remains, the rising is complete. The bread is baked when the crust is well browned, shrinks from the sides of the pan, and sounds hollow when tapped. Brush it with butter and turn it out immediately to cool on a rack. When the bread is cool, store it wrapped in waxed paper or cellophane to retain its moisture. Well-wrapped bread freezes well.

Mrs. George Washington's Potato Rolls

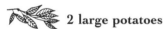

2 large potatoes
1 teaspoon salt
2 tablespoons granulated sugar
3 tablespoons butter or
    margarine
1 1/2 cups potato cooking water

3/4 cup milk, scalded
1 package dry yeast
7 cups (approximately) sifted
    flour
2 tablespoons melted butter or
    margarine

1 Peel and cook the potatoes about 30 minutes, or until tender. Drain, reserving cooking water.

2 Mash hot potatoes, adding salt, sugar, and butter. Beat well. Add potato cooking water and scalded milk and cool until lukewarm. Add yeast and stir in 4 cups of the flour, beating well. Then add remaining flour until dough is stiff enough to knead. Knead on floured board until smooth and elastic. Brush top of dough with melted butter.

3 Coat large bowl with vegetable spray. Place dough in bowl, cover, and let rise slowly (about 5 hours) in warm place until dough has doubled in bulk.

4 Place dough on floured board and pat out to thickness of about 1/2

inch, but do not knead again. Pinch off small pieces and shape into 48 small rolls. Coat baking pans with vegetable spray. Place rolls in pan and allow to rise until more than doubled in bulk.

5 Preheat oven to 400°.

6 Bake 20 minutes, or until done.

YIELD: 48 SMALL ROLLS

Two-Hour Cloverleaf or Parker House Rolls

1 cup milk, scalded
2 tablespoons butter or
   margarine
2 tablespoons granulated sugar
1 teaspoon salt

1 package dry yeast
1 egg yolk, lightly beaten
3 cups sifted bread flour
1 egg white, beaten stiff

1 Combine milk, butter, sugar, and salt in mixing bowl and let cool until lukewarm. Then add yeast, egg yolk, and 1½ cups flour. Stir until smooth. Fold in egg white and remaining flour. Let rise in warm place 2 hours.

2 Coat muffin tins with vegetable spray. Shape dough into 12 to 18 rolls and place in muffin tins. (For cloverleaf rolls, put 3 small balls of dough into each cup.

   For Parker House rolls, cut out rolls with round cutter, elongate each round, and fold over 1 piece butter.) Place on baking sheet. Cover lightly and let rise again 30 minutes.

3 Preheat oven to 350°.

4 Bake 20 minutes.

YIELD: 12 TO 18 ROLLS

Quick Cinnamon Rolls

These rolls can be baked in a 12-muffin tin or all together in a 13-inch Pyrex pie plate. They take a short time to bake and make a good breakfast roll. To save time, you can roll them and place in the pan or pans the night before and refrigerate.

3 cups flour	4 tablespoons granulated sugar
3 teaspoons baking powder	2 teaspoons ground cinnamon
1/2 teaspoon salt	1/2 cup chopped walnuts or
2/3 cup butter or margarine	pecans
1 cup milk	1/2 cup currants or raisins

1 Preheat oven to 400°. Coat muffin tins or pie plate with vegetable spray.

2 Sift together flour, baking powder, and salt. Cut in 1/3 cup of butter so that flour has grainy texture. Add the milk, and mix well.

3 Turn dough out onto a well-floured board and roll into a rectangle approximately 10" x 15" and about 1/4 inch thick.

4 Melt the remaining butter and brush the dough with half of it. Sprinkle with 2 tablespoons of sugar, cinnamon, nuts, and currants.

5 Roll from the long side of the rectangle and cut into 12 pieces.

6 Divide the remaining butter among the muffin tins or butter the pie plate. Sprinkle with remaining sugar.

7 Bake 12 to 15 minutes. Remove from the oven and serve upside down.

YIELD: 12 ROLLS

Pumpkin Biscuits

 This recipe may also be made with squash.

1/2 cup milk, scalded	4 tablespoons butter or
1/2 cup puréed pumpkin (fresh	margarine, softened
or canned)	1/4 package dry yeast
1/4 cup granulated sugar	1/4 cup lukewarm water
1/2 teaspoon salt	2 1/2 cups flour
1/4 teaspoon ground mace	

1 Place the scalded milk in a large bowl and add the pumpkin, sugar, salt, mace, and butter. Cool to lukewarm. Dissolve yeast in lukewarm water and add to pumpkin mixture. Then add flour. Cover, place in warm spot, and allow to rise overnight.

2 Coat baking pan with vegetable spray. Shape the dough into 12 biscuits, place side by side in pan, and allow to double in bulk.

3 Preheat oven to 375°.

4 Bake until golden, about 20 minutes.

YIELD: 12 BISCUITS

Hot Cross Buns

 These are traditionally served during Lent, especially on Good Friday.

1 cup milk, scalded	3 cups flour
1/2 cup granulated sugar	1/2 teaspoon ground cinnamon
3 tablespoons melted butter or margarine	pinch of ground cloves
	1/2 cup currants
1/2 teaspoon salt	1/4 cup chopped citron
1 package dry yeast	2 tablespoons confectioners'
1/4 cup warm water	sugar
2 eggs, well beaten	1 teaspoon milk

1 In large bowl, combine scalded milk, granulated sugar, melted butter, and salt. Dissolve yeast in warm water and add to sugar mixture. Add 1 egg and mix well.

2 Sift together flour, cinnamon, and cloves, then add currants and citron. Mix thoroughly. Cover and let rise in warm place (75° to 85°) until double in bulk.

3 Coat baking pan with vegetable spray. Shape dough into 12 round buns and place close together in pan. Allow to rise again.

4 Preheat oven to 400°.

5 Brush top of each bun with remaining beaten egg. With sharp knife, make a cross on top of each bun. Bake 20 minutes.

6 Remove from oven. Combine confectioners' sugar and milk and put in pastry tube. Squeeze out sugar mixture to make a cross on top of each bun.

YIELD: 12 BUNS

Easy Rolls

 This recipe lets the baker make whatever shape roll he or she wants. The recipe does not use eggs or shortening so the rolls are light and perfect for a "diet" breakfast.

1 cup milk	1 package dry yeast
2½ teaspoons salt	6 cups all purpose flour
1 tablespoon sugar	

1 Scald the milk and add salt and sugar. Set this mixture aside and let cool.

2 Meanwhile, dissolve the yeast in ½ cup of warm water for 10 minutes. Combine the cooled milk, salt, sugar mixture and mix until smooth.

3 Gradually add the flour. Knead the dough well. Place in a warm spot and let rise until almost double in bulk.

4 Shape the dough into rolls of any shape. Place the rolls on a coated baking sheet, cover and let rise again until almost double in bulk.

5 Preheat oven to 275°. Bake for 40 minutes.

6 If storing the rolls, let cool and wrap well. Before serving place on a coated baking sheet and place in a 400° oven for 10 minutes.

YIELD: ABOUT 24 MEDIUM-SIZED ROLLS

Bran Rolls

1 package dry yeast	1 cup bran flour
⅓ cup molasses	1½ cups whole wheat flour
⅓ cup butter	1½ cups white flour
1 egg, beaten	¾ cup raisins
1 tablespoon salt	

1 Dissolve the yeast in ¼ cup lukewarm water. Add the molasses. Boil 1½ cups water and melt the butter in it. Let the mixture cool to luke-warm and add the lightly beaten egg and salt. Add the yeast.

2 In a large bowl, mix the flours and raisins. Stir in the yeast mixture and beat very hard for three minutes.

3 Let the dough rise in a warm place, covered with a towel, until double in bulk. Form into rolls. Let rise again.

4 Preheat oven to 375°.

5 Bake rolls on coated baking pan 25 minutes.

YIELD: ABOUT 24 MEDIUM-SIZED ROLLS

Popovers

 It is not hard to make high, puffy popovers—in fact, given one lesson, a child can do it. Their appearance is impressive and always seems to produce a gasp of joy. Serve them with plenty of butter and jam for breakfast, or split them and fill them with creamed chicken for a pleasant breakfast, luncheon, or supper dish.

2 eggs	dash of salt
1 cup milk	2 tablespoons melted butter or
1 cup flour	margarine

1 If desired, preheat oven to 425°.

2 Stir together the eggs, milk, flour, and salt, but do not beat. Batter should be slightly lumpy.

3 Coat 6 earthenware cups or popover pans very generously with melted butter. Divide batter among them.

4 Bake 30 to 45 minutes. It is important not to remove them immediately after they have "popped." If you wish to slow cooking time after they have "popped," last half of cooking may be done at 375°.

YIELD: 6 POPOVERS

VARIATION – Blueberry Popovers

Add $\frac{1}{3}$ cup of blueberries, lightly sugared, to the batter. Absolutely wonderful!

VARIATION – Cheese Popovers

Place a $\frac{3}{4}$-inch cube of Swiss cheese in each baking cup before pouring in batter.

Muffins

2 cups flour	1 egg, well beaten
3 teaspoons baking powder	1 cup milk
$\frac{1}{2}$ teaspoon salt	3 tablespoons melted butter
3 tablespoons granulated sugar	

1 Preheat oven to 425°.

2 Sift together dry ingredients. In separate bowl, combine egg, milk, and melted butter.

3 Stir egg mixture into the flour mixture, *quickly*. (This is the secret of light, tender muffins.)

4 Coat muffin tins with vegetable spray, or use paper muffin cups, and turn batter immediately into them, filling each cup two-thirds full.

5 Bake 20 to 30 minutes, depending on size of muffins.

YIELD: 12 MEDIUM-SIZE MUFFINS

VARIATION – Blueberry Muffins

Mix 1 cup blueberries with 2 tablespoons sugar and add to muffin dough. These are wonderful for breakfast, lunch, or supper in August—hot, juicy, and delicious.

VARIATION – Cherry Muffins

Unusual and good. Mix $3/4$ cup chopped, drained cherries with 2 tablespoons sugar and add to muffin dough. If cherries are very juicy, reduce milk by 2 tablespoons.

VARIATION – Cranberry Muffins

Mix $3/4$ cup chopped cranberries with 3 tablespoons sugar and add to sifted dry ingredients.

VARIATION – Nut Muffins

Add $1/2$ cup coarsely chopped nuts to sifted dry ingredients.

VARIATION – Bran Muffins

Using the recipe for Muffins, substitute 1 cup of bran for 1 cup of the flour, increase the baking powder quantity to $3^1/2$ teaspoons, and reduce the milk quantity to $2/3$ cup. Add the bran to the sifted dry ingredients. If you wish, use brown sugar instead of granulated sugar and add $1/2$ cup raisins to muffin dough.

VARIATION – Sour Cream Muffins

Using the recipe for Muffins, reduce the baking powder quantity to 1 teaspoon and add $1/2$ teaspoon baking soda. Use $1^1/4$ cups sour cream in place of the milk and melted butter. These muffins are also good with $1/2$ cup chopped dates added to the dough.

Cottage Cheese Poppy Seed Muffins

 Little fat or cholesterol in these and they taste wonderful! These freeze well.

³/₄ cup light cottage cheese	1 tablespoon baking powder
1 egg white, lightly beaten	¹/₂ teaspoon grated lemon rind
4 teaspoons granulated sugar	¹/₄ teaspoon salt
1¹/₄ cups old-fashioned oatmeal	1 cup skim milk
1¹/₄ cups all-purpose flour	¹/₂ teaspoon oil
³/₄ cup raisins	2 egg whites, lightly beaten
¹/₃ cup granulated sugar	
3 tablespoons poppy seeds	

1 Preheat oven to 375°. Coat 12 medium-size muffin cups with vegetable spray.

2 Combine first 3 ingredients. Set aside.

3 Combine next 8 ingredients and set aside. Combine the milk, oil, and 2 egg whites and add to dry ingredients, mixing until just moistened. Spoon 1 tablespoon of this batter into each muffin cup. Spoon 1 tablespoon of cheese filling into the center of each and cover with the remaining batter.

4 Bake for 22 to 25 minutes, until lightly browned.

YIELD: 12 MUFFINS

Baking Powder Biscuits

 Baking powder biscuits are quick to make and useful in many menus. They taste especially good served with fresh honey.

2 cups flour	4 tablespoons shortening or
1 teaspoon salt	margarine
4 teaspoons baking powder	³/₄ cup milk

1 Preheat oven to 450°.

2 Sift together the flour, salt, and baking powder and cut in shortening. Gradually add milk to make firm, soft dough.

3 Turn onto lightly floured board and knead just enough to shape into

smooth ball. Pat to $^1/_2$-inch thickness and cut out biscuits with a 1-inch-diameter floured biscuit cutter.

4 Place biscuits on ungreased baking sheet or pan—$^1/_2$ inch apart for crusty biscuits and close together for tall, soft biscuits.

5 Bake 12 to 15 minutes.

YIELD: 14 BISCUITS, EACH ABOUT 2 INCHES IN DIAMETER

Variations

All of these are good for buffets or cocktail parties. Nut Biscuits and Orange Tea Biscuits are nice for tea. (Cut out biscuits with a 1-inch-diameter cutter.)

VARIATION – Cheese Biscuits

Roll out the dough to $^1/_4$-inch thickness. Cut out biscuits. Place a small square of cheese—Cheddar, Roquefort, or any other that you like—on half of the biscuits. Use the remaining biscuits as tops. Press edges together.

VARIATION – Sausage Biscuits

Form $^1/_2$ teaspoon of sausage meat into tiny flat cakes and sandwich between biscuit rounds, as done with Cheese Biscuits.

VARIATION – Bacon Biscuits

Crumble crisp bacon into the biscuit dough before shaping.

VARIATION – Nut Biscuits

Add $^1/_2$ cup chopped black walnuts to biscuit dough.

VARIATION – Orange Tea Biscuits

Dip small lumps of sugar into orange juice and press one into each biscuit before baking. Then sprinkle biscuit dough with grated orange rind.

Ragamuffins

 This recipe comes from a dear old friend who ate these muffins as a child in Essex Junction, Vermont, and called them Ragamuffins because they are sort of ragged looking. Delicious with cold milk or with coffee.

1 recipe baking powder biscuit dough (p. 18)	**1 cup soft maple sugar**
1 cup butter or margarine, softened	**¹/₂ cup butternuts or walnuts, chopped (optional)**

1 Preheat oven to 425°.

2 Roll out dough very lightly on board until it is about ¹/₂ inch thick. Spread with butter, maple sugar, and nuts.

3 Roll up dough, jelly-roll fashion and slice. Place in flat pan or on baking sheet. (If you like more crust, bake in muffin tins.)

4 Bake about 8 minutes, or until light brown.

YIELD: 12 TO 14

GRIDDLECAKES AND WAFFLES

Long the breakfast standbys of New England, griddlecakes (or pancakes) and waffles give real warmth and substance to keep you through a cold winter day. They are usually served with butter and hot maple syrup or molasses, or with maple sugar, accompanied by sausages or bacon and fried apple slices.

The batter used for these breakfast cakes is very similar to the batter used for popovers. Griddlecakes can be baked on a heavy iron or aluminum griddle or pan, or on a soapstone griddle very lightly rubbed with grease. Waffles used to be made in a cast-iron waffle iron, but most people now use electric ones. After you have "seasoned" the waffle iron by giving it a preliminary rubdown with unsalted fat, you should not need to grease it again. The batter has enough fat in it to prevent sticking.

The iron or griddle is hot enough for baking when a drop of water dances rapidly on its surface. Waffles should be crisp and light, griddlecakes light, tender, and golden brown. You can fill thin pancakes with creamed cottage cheese and herbs and serve them as a luncheon or supper dish. You can top waffles with creamed chicken for lunch or with crushed fruit and sweetened whipped cream for dessert.

Griddlecakes

1 cup sifted flour
1 teaspoon baking powder
1/2 teaspoon salt
1 egg

3/4 cup milk
1 tablespoon melted butter or margarine

1 Sift together dry ingredients.

2 Combine egg and milk and add dry ingredients. Beat until smooth, then add melted butter.

3 Bake on lightly greased hot griddle, turning once.

YIELD: ABOUT 6 GRIDDLECAKES

VARIATION – Apple Pancakes

Add 1/2 cup finely chopped apple to the batter.

VARIATION – Blueberry Pancakes

Add 1/2 cup fresh blueberries to the batter. (In winter, you can use frozen berries, but first drain them carefully.)

 ## George Washington's Breakfast

This recipe was contributed by Stuyvie Wainwright, age 5, of New York. It is completely authentic, and we imagine that it was served with delicious smoked ham. Cherry jam would have tasted good with the hoe cakes, but knowing of the Father of Our Country's early encounter with that lovely fruit tree, one must assume that there was no cherry jam upon his breakfast table.

Hoe Cakes
cornmeal
salt
water

Mix ingredients to make a thin batter and cook on a hot griddle until brown on each side. Serve with butter and honey.

Rye Pancakes

Here's a recipe that dates back to the early 1700s, when great fields of rye waved in the wind all along the Taunton River Valley in Massachusetts. The molasses or sugar required for these pancakes was brought up the river in small sloops or brigs before the days of the Old Colony Railroad. This recipe is a cherished family tradition handed down from generation to generation.

1 1/2 pints rye meal
1/2 pint flour
1 gill sugar or molasses (1/2 cup)
1 teaspoon salt
1 teaspoon cream of tartar
1 egg
1 pint milk or water
1/2 teacup New England rum

Combine ingredients and fry pancakes in deep fat. Fill individual butter plates with sugar. Drop enough vinegar on the sugar to make it spreadable as butter. As you eat the pancakes, dab them with the mixture.

Waffles

Electric waffle irons do not need greasing, but pour in batter only after the iron reaches the correct temperature.

2 cups sifted flour
3 teaspoons baking powder
1/2 teaspoon salt
3 eggs, separated
1 1/4 cups milk
4 tablespoons melted butter or margarine

1 Sift together dry ingredients.

2 Beat egg yolks well and combine with milk. Add to sifted mixture and beat until smooth. Add melted butter, then fold in stiffly beaten egg whites.

3 To prevent overflow, pour into hot waffle iron only enough batter to partially fill each compartment. Close iron and bake until steam is no longer visible.

YIELD: 6 WAFFLES

DOUGHNUTS

Served with cold cider, milk, or quantities of hot coffee, doughnuts are another staple of the New England diet. They may be made in a number of shapes and in countless different ways. Rings, rounds, or twists, not to mention doughnut holes; plain, sugared, chocolate, spiced—every family has its own favorite variation.

The temperature of the fat is of prime importance in achieving a perfect doughnut. If it is not hot enough, the doughnuts will be greasy. If it is too hot, the doughnuts will not be cooked through. The cooking oil should be at 360° to 370°. The easiest way to determine temperature, of course, is with a thermometer, but our grandmothers knew that the fat was just right for frying doughnuts when a cube of bread would brown in it in 60 seconds.

Do not fry too many doughnuts at a time, or the fat will be cooled. As soon as the doughnuts rise to the top of the kettle, turn them once to brown the other side. Drain them on absorbent paper, place in a crock while warm, and leave the top ajar until they have cooled completely.

Auntie's Doughnuts

 From Mrs. Gertrude E. Olsen of Mansfield, Massachusetts, comes this recipe, along with her comments: "My mother was always known as 'Auntie,' or 'The Doughnut Lady' to the people of our community. Everyone loved her, and everyone loved her doughnuts. Each Saturday, she replenished our doughnut crock, and each Saturday the paper boy, the mailman, the milkman, and the grocer lingered to chat a bit and enjoy some hot doughnuts straight from the kettle on the old wood-burning range. We children could hardly wait for the first doughnut holes, which she would fry on the pretext of testing the fat, but really to see our delight in savoring their goodness to the accompaniment of ice-cold milk. This is the recipe as she wrote it out for me when I was married."

1 cup sugar	1 teaspoon soda
butter the size of a walnut	1 teaspoon cream of tartar
2 eggs	1 heaping teaspoon salt
2 cups (approximately) sour milk	1 heaping teaspoon ground nutmeg
4 cups flour	

Cream the sugar and the butter. Add the eggs, not beaten. Stir together and add sour milk. Sift together the dry ingredients and add the liquid mixture. Stir up well. If too thin to roll, add flour to handle. Roll, and fry in deep fat. Dip the doughnuts quickly in hot water immediately after cooking to remove the fat. Dip some in sugar, some in cinnamon and sugar, leave some plain. Place in the crock while warm, and leave top ajar until the doughnuts cool. (If you have no sour milk, add another teaspoon cream of tartar to sweet milk, but the doughnuts won't be as good.)

YIELD: ABOUT 3 DOZEN DOUGHNUTS

 ## Doughnuts in Rhyme

A poem-recipe.

1 cup of sugar, 1 cup of milk;
Two eggs, beaten fine as silk;
Salt and nutmeg (lemon will
   do);
Of baking powder teaspoons
   two.
Stir enough of flour in
To roll on pie board, not too
   thin;
Cut in diamonds, twists or
   rings,

Drop with care the doughy
   things
Into the fat that swiftly swells
Evenly the spongy cells.
Watch with care the time for
   turning,
Fry them brown, just short of
   burning.
Roll in sugar, serve when cool,
This is the never failing rule.

Spiced Doughnuts

 To be served with apple cider. Delicious with hot apple cider on a frosty fall day.

1 cup granulated sugar	4 teaspoons baking powder
1 cup milk	1/4 teaspoon ground cinnamon
5 tablespoons melted shortening or margarine	1/4 teaspoon ground nutmeg
	1/4 teaspoon ground cloves
2 eggs, beaten	1/4 teaspoon salt
4 cups flour	cooking oil for deep-fat frying

1 Add sugar, milk, and shortening to beaten eggs.

2 Sift flour before measuring, then resift with baking powder, spices, and salt.

3 Combine egg mixture with flour mixture and stir until blended.

4 Roll out dough to ¹/₄-inch thickness and cut with floured cutter.

5 Fry in hot oil at 360° to 370° about 3 minutes—first on one side, then the other.

6 Drain on paper towels. Sprinkle with confectioners' sugar.

YIELD: 30 DOUGHNUTS

Funnel Cakes

 A Pennsylvania Dutch favorite contributed by Lois Kenyon of Walpole, New Hampshire. To make this, you'll need a funnel that has a ³/₈- to ¹/₂-inch hole. It's intriguing to watch the cook make funnel cakes for breakfast or lunch. The batter forms rings around rings and the cakes may be made up to 6 inches across if you wish.

cooking oil for deep-fat frying	2 tablespoons granulated sugar
²/₃ cup milk	1 teaspoon baking powder
1 egg, well beaten	¹/₄ teaspoon salt
1¹/₄ cups flour	

1 Heat cooking oil to 370°, or until bread cube browns in it in 60 seconds.

2 Beat milk with egg.

3 Sift together dry ingredients and gradually add milk mixture, beating constantly until batter is smooth.

4 Put a finger over hole at bottom of funnel and fill funnel with batter. Hold funnel as close to fat surface as possible, then remove finger. Swirl funnel in circles, from center outward, to form spiral cake about 3 inches in diameter. Immediately replace finger on funnel hole, then repeat procedure to form additional cakes, as many as will float un-crowded.

5 Fry until cakes are puffy and golden brown, turning once. With slotted spoon, remove cakes to paper toweling to drain.

6 Sift confectioners' sugar lightly over cakes, or serve with molasses or maple syrup.

YIELD: 2 DOZEN CAKES

Sally Lunn

 This light cake originated in Bath, England.

2 cups flour

3 teaspoons baking powder

1/2 teaspoon salt

1/2 cup milk

2 eggs, separated

1/2 cup melted butter or
 margarine

1 Preheat oven to 350°.

2 Sift together dry ingredients.

3 Add milk to beaten egg yolks, then add to dry ingredients, stirring until just mixed. Stir in melted butter, then fold in stiffly beaten egg whites.

4 Coat 9-inch-square pan with vegetable spray. Pour batter into pan and bake about 30 minutes.

YIELD: 9 SQUARES

Apple Streusel Coffee Cake

 Quick and easy enough to make before breakfast.

1 tablespoon butter or
 margarine, softened

1/4 cup light brown sugar

1 teaspoon ground cinnamon

1 tablespoon flour

1/2 cup chopped nuts (walnuts
 or pecans)

1 1/2 cups sifted flour

2 teaspoons baking powder

1/2 teaspoon salt

3/4 cup granulated sugar

4 tablespoons butter or
 margarine

1 egg, unbeaten

1/2 cup milk

1/2 teaspoon vanilla extract

2 apples, peeled, cored, and
 thinly sliced

1 Prepare topping by mixing together softened butter, brown sugar, cinnamon, and 1 tablespoon flour. Stir in nuts and set aside.

2 Preheat oven to 350°. Coat 8-inch-square Teflon baking pan with vegetable spray.

3 Sift together 1 1/2 cups sifted flour, baking powder, salt, and granulated sugar. Add butter, egg, milk, and vanilla and beat about 2 minutes. Spread in prepared pan.

4 Distribute sliced apples over entire surface of batter. Sprinkle with topping. Dot with butter or margarine.

5 Bake 30 minutes, or until toothpick inserted into center comes out clean.

YIELD: 8 SERVINGS

Blueberry Breakfast Cake

 Quick and easy to prepare before breakfast.

1 1/4 cups blueberries

2 1/2 cups flour

1/4 cup butter or margarine, softened

1/4 cup granulated sugar

1 egg, well beaten

4 teaspoons baking powder

1/2 teaspoon salt

1 1/4 cups milk

2 tablespooons dark brown sugar

1 teaspoon butter or margarine, softened

1/4 cup dry cereal, oat or cornflakes

1 teaspoon ground cinnamon

1 Preheat oven to 400°. Coat an 8-inch-square pan with vegetable spray.

2 Rinse the blueberries and dredge in 1 cup of flour.

3 Cream together the butter and sugar.

4 Combine dry ingredients and sift.

5 Add egg, milk, and alternately the sifted dry ingredients to the butter and sugar. Fold in the berries. Stir together but do not beat. The dough should be lumpy. Pour into prepared pan.

6 Prepare topping by working together brown sugar, butter, dry cereal, and cinnamon with your fingertips. Sprinkle over the cake.

7 Bake 30 to 35 minutes, until a toothpick inserted into the center comes out clean.

YIELD: 1 8-INCH-SQUARE CAKE

Sour Cream Coffee Cake

½ cup brown sugar

½ cup chopped nuts

1 teaspoon ground cinnamon

½ cup butter or margarine, softened

1 cup granulated sugar

2 eggs, beaten

1 cup sour cream

2 cups flour (sift before measuring)

1 teaspoon baking powder

1 teaspoon baking soda

1 teaspoon vanilla extract

½ cup raisins

1 Prepare filling/topping by combining brown sugar, chopped nuts, and cinnamon. Mix well and set aside.

2 Preheat oven to 350°. Coat 2-quart Teflon tube pan with vegetable spray.

3 Cream together butter and sugar, then add eggs and sour cream. Sift together flour, baking powder, and baking soda and add to butter mixture. Stir in vanilla.

4 Pour half of batter into prepared tube pan. Sprinkle half of filling mixture, plus raisins, over batter. Pour in remaining batter and sprinkle with remaining topping.

5 Bake 35 minutes, or until done.

Pecan Coconut Cake

2 cups all-purpose flour

1½ cups brown sugar

¼ cup butter or margarine

½ cup pecans

⅔ cup sweetened shredded coconut

⅓ cup butter or margarine, softened

2 eggs, unbeaten

1½ teaspoons vanilla extract

1½ teaspoons baking powder

½ teaspoon salt

⅓ cup milk

1 Prepare topping by combining ½ cup flour, ½ cup brown sugar, ¼ cup cold butter, and ⅓ cup coconut. Mix well and set aside.

2 Preheat oven to 375°. Coat 8-inch-square Teflon baking pan with vegetable spray.

3 Combine softened butter with 1 cup brown sugar, eggs, vanilla, and ⅓ cup coconut. Blend well. Sift together 1½ cups flour, baking powder, and salt and add alternately with milk. Beat until smooth.

4 Pour into prepared pan and spread topping over batter.

5 Bake 30 minutes.

YIELD: 6 TO 8 SERVINGS

Old-Fashioned Corn Bread

1 cup cornmeal	1 egg, well beaten
1 cup sifted flour	1 cup milk
1/4 cup granulated sugar	1/4 cup melted shortening,
3 teaspoons baking powder	butter, margarine, or
1 teaspoon salt	chicken fat

1 Preheat oven to 425°. Coat 9-inch-square Teflon baking pan with vegetable spray.

2 Mix dry ingredients and wet ingredients separately. Combine. Stir lightly and pour into prepared pan.

3 Bake 20 to 25 minutes.

YIELD: 6 TO 8 SERVINGS

Sour Cream Corn Bread

  A corn bread with a light texture.

3/4 cup yellow cornmeal	1 cup sour cream
1 cup unsifted flour	1/2 cup milk
1/4 cup granulated sugar	1 egg, unbeaten
2 teaspoons baking powder	2 tablespoons melted
1/2 teaspoon baking soda	shortening, butter, or
3/4 teaspoon salt	margarine

1 Preheat oven to 375°. Coat 9-inch-square Teflon baking pan with vegetable spray. (If desired, substitute muffin tins.)

2 Place all ingredients in mixing bowl and mix with wire whisk. Pour batter into prepared pan.

3 Bake 25 minutes. (If using muffin tins, bake about 20 minutes.)

YIELD: 9 SERVINGS

VARIATION – Apple Corn Bread

Add 1 apple—peeled, cored, and finely diced—to either Old-Fashioned Corn Bread or Sour Cream Corn Bread.

Maple Corn Bread

1⅓ cups flour	⅓ cup maple syrup
⅔ cup cornmeal	½ cup melted shortening,
3 teaspoons baking powder	butter, or margarine
½ teaspoon salt	2 eggs, lightly beaten

1 Preheat oven to 425°. Coat 9-inch-square Teflon baking pan with vegetable spray.

2 Sift together dry ingredients, then add syrup, melted shortening, and eggs. Stir until mixed well, but do not beat.

3 Turn batter into prepared pan and bake 25 minutes.

YIELD: ABOUT 8 SERVINGS

Rhode Island Toads

 New Bedford (Massachusetts) tradition says these toads should be eaten with creamed codfish.

1 cup cornmeal	1 egg, unbeaten
1 cup flour	milk
2 teaspoons baking powder	1 cup cooking oil
1 teaspoon salt	

1 Combine cornmeal, flour, baking powder, and salt. Add egg. Add enough milk to make batter moist.

2 Heat oil to 360° and drop walnut-size portions of batter into oil. Fry to golden brown.

3 Drain on paper towels.

YIELD: ABOUT 20 CAKES

Scrambled Eggs

 In recent years a lot of attention has been focused on the perfect omelet, yet somehow scrambled eggs—just as delicate, just as versatile, and just as good, perhaps better—seem to have been forgotten. They are wonderful poured over a slice of hot toast or accompanied by toast points just buttered with sweet butter. You can mince parsley, watercress, chives, or tarragon into the eggs, or use the herbs to garnish them.

This simple procedure can be varied by adding 1 tablespoon of creamed cottage cheese and 1 teaspoon grated orange rind for each portion. For more important presentations, try them with smoked salmon. (Prince Charles sometimes scrambles his that way.) Other ingredients might be crabmeat, some excellent ham, creamed chicken, or asparagus tips. A dash of sour cream and caviar can be heavenly.

For a party, the eggs can be scrambled in a chafing dish at the table. It's very effective. Just remember to scramble the eggs as slowly and lightly as possible until barely firm and to serve them immediately. To make scrambled eggs an elegant dish, serve them on hot porcelain plates.

For each portion (up to six portions can be cooked together), mix 2 lightly beaten eggs with 1 tablespoon water. For each portion, allow 1/2 tablespoon sweet butter or margarine to melt slowly and coat the pan. Pour in the beaten eggs and cook as slowly as possible, stirring slightly until just set. Add a dash of coarse salt.

Highland Eggs

 These eggs are very light and tender due to a "secret ingredient" that cannot be detected—a little vinegar.

4 eggs
1 teaspoon white vinegar
salt to taste
freshly ground pepper to taste
butter the size of a walnut
    (1 tablespoon)

1/2 cup milk
grated orange rind, chopped
    parsley, or chopped chives
    (optional)

1 Break eggs into bowl and mix in vinegar, salt, and pepper.

2 Melt butter in skillet. Add milk, then the eggs, stir, and cook very gently, stirring with wooden spoon, until firm.

3 These eggs too are good with a little grated orange rind, chopped parsley, or chopped chives added when cooking.

YIELD: 2 SERVINGS

Scotch Eggs

7 eggs

¹/₂ cup flour

salt to taste

freshly ground pepper to taste

¹/₂ pound sausage meat

¹/₂ cup breadcrumbs

1 tablespoon cooking oil

1 Hard-boil 6 of the eggs. Drain and place in cold water to cool. Shell eggs.

2 Mix the flour, salt, and pepper on piece of waxed paper and roll shelled eggs in mixture.

3 Divide sausage meat into 6 equal portions and shape around each egg until each is covered evenly. Beat remaining egg and brush over sausage meat.

4 Spread breadcrumbs on piece of waxed paper and roll each egg in crumbs.

5 Heat oil to 390° and fry eggs until golden brown—about 3 minutes.

6 Drain eggs on paper toweling. Cut crosswise and serve with toast.

YIELD: 6 SERVINGS

Favorite Breakfast Sausages

Chicken sausages have no cholesterol and little fat, yet taste similar to old-fashioned pork sausage.

1 pound ground chicken

1 packet Butter Buds

2 tablespoons oat bran, pulverized

¹/₂ teaspoon salt

¹/₂ teaspoon basil

¹/₂ teaspoon thyme

¹/₂ teaspoon sage

¹/₄ teaspoon marjoram

¹/₄ teaspoon oregano

¹/₄ teaspoon black pepper

¹/₄ teaspoon cayenne pepper

¹/₈ teaspoon ground nutmeg

¹/₈ teaspoon ground ginger

¹/₈ teaspoon chili powder

1 small clove garlic, minced

¹/₂ cup oat bran

1 Mix together all ingredients except ½ cup oat bran. If possible, refrigerate to blend flavors.

2 Form sausage into small patties.

3 Pour ½ cup oat bran into small saucer. Coat patties with oat bran.

4 Coat heavy skillet with vegetable spray and fry sausage patties until golden brown. Drain patties on paper toweling.

YIELD: 6 TO 8 PATTIES

Toad-in-the-Hole

 This plain but excellent dish makes a perfect weekend breakfast or light supper. Good served with fried tomatoes.

1 pound small breakfast sausages	**1 recipe Yorkshire pudding batter (p. 324) made with sausage drippings**

1 Fry sausages until they are crisp and brown. Drain off most of fat, reserving 4 teaspoons.

2 Meanwhile, mix Yorkshire pudding batter, using some of sausage drippings.

3 Preheat oven to 450°. Put 3 tablespoons of sausage drippings in bottom of 1½-quart soufflé dish. Add sausages and cover with Yorkshire pudding batter.

4 Bake 10 minutes. Reduce heat to 350° and bake 15 minutes more, until batter has risen well and is golden brown. (Try not to open oven door while toad is cooking.)

YIELD: 4 TO 6 SERVINGS

Codfish Balls

 The real Bostonian Sunday Breakfast, of course, is codfish balls (or cakes, or creamed codfish), baked beans, and brown bread. The mixture is often made ahead on Saturday to use for Sunday breakfast. Small codfish balls are also good served on toothpicks with cocktails.

1¼ cups salt codfish
2½ cups potatoes, peeled and
   quartered
1 egg
1 tablespoon butter or
   margarine

1 tablespoon light cream
pepper to taste
cooking oil for deep-fat frying

1 Wash the codfish in several waters to remove the salt. Cut fish in pieces and cook with potatoes in water to cover until potatoes are done. Shake to dry thoroughly.

2 Purée fish and potatoes in blender or food processor with egg, butter, and cream until mixture is fluffy. Turn out into mixing bowl and season with pepper. When cool, place in refrigerator until ready to use.

3 When ready to serve, drop mixture by the tablespoonfuls into deep fat (375°) and fry until golden brown.

YIELD: 10 TO 16 BALLS

Codfish Cakes

 These are fluffier, fancier fare than Codfish Balls. Sliced hard-boiled eggs in a curried cream sauce make a good combination with these cakes.

2 cups salt codfish
2 cups potatoes
1 egg white, beaten until fluffy

1 tablespoon light cream
cooking oil

1 Soak codfish overnight, then pick apart into fine pieces.

2 Cut potatoes into small pieces and boil together with codfish. When potatoes are done, mash fish and potatoes together. Fold in beaten egg white and cream. Mixture should be light and fluffy. If potatoes are dry, add more cream.

3 Drop mixture by the tablespoonfuls into deep fat (375°) and fry until light brown. The cakes should be uneven and fluffy.

YIELD: 10 TO 12 CAKES

Eggs Bostonia

8 Codfish Cakes (see above)
1 cup Cream Sauce (p. 315)
white pepper to taste
cooking oil
8 eggs

$^3/_4$ teaspoon salt
1 tablespoon white vinegar
paprika to taste
chopped parsley to taste

1 Form fishcake mixture into 8 flattened patties, each about $^1/_2$ inch thick.

2 Prepare cream sauce and season highly with pepper.

3 Fry codfish cakes, 4 at a time, in oil heated to 385°. Fry 3 or 4 minutes, until cakes are golden brown. Drain on paper toweling and place in deep, heated platter.

4 Poach eggs in one large or two small skillets containing 1 inch water to which salt and vinegar have been added. (Small poaching rings for containing the eggs are helpful.)

5 When egg whites are firm, remove eggs with slotted spoon and place on codfish cakes. Cover generously with cream sauce and sprinkle with paprika. Garnish with chopped parsley.

YIELD: 4 SERVINGS

Provincetown Creamed Codfish

$^1/_2$ pound salt codfish
2 tablespoons butter or
    margarine
2 tablespoons flour

$^1/_4$ teaspoon white pepper
1 cup milk
dash of Tabasco sauce
1 egg, beaten

1 Cut the codfish into $^1/_4$-inch slices across the grain. Soak overnight in lukewarm water to draw out salt and soften fish.

2 In morning, drain fish and simmer in fresh water 10 minutes. Drain again and set aside.

3 Melt butter in saucepan, whisk in flour and pepper, and blend well. Add milk gradually, cooking until thickened. Add Tabasco sauce.

4 Pour small amount of cream sauce into beaten egg, stirring constantly. Then combine fish, egg, and cream sauce.

5 Serve on hot buttered toast.

YIELD: 4 SERVINGS

Finnan Haddie Delmonico

2 cups finnan haddie

4 hard-boiled eggs, sliced

1½ cups cream sauce (made without salt)

pinch of cayenne pepper

buttered toast points

chopped parsley

1 Soak the finnan haddie 30 minutes. Drain and flake the fish, removing any bones. Simmer 25 minutes in fresh water. Drain again.

2 Combine fish with sliced eggs and cream sauce. Mix eggs carefully into sauce so they don't get mushy. Season with cayenne.

3 Serve on hot buttered toast and sprinkle with chopped parsley.

YIELD: 6 SERVINGS

Connecticut Kedgeree

2 cups cooked rice

2 cups cooked, flaked fish

4 hard-boiled eggs, chopped

2 tablespoons minced parsley

½ cup milk

salt to taste

white pepper to taste

1 Place hot rice in top of double boiler and add remaining ingredients. Reheat and serve immediately.

YIELD: 6 SERVINGS

Casseroles, Brunch, and Luncheon Dishes

Here we have a potpourri of recipes—good for lunch or supper, for a buffet party, a first course, or sometimes just a snack. Included are egg and cheese dishes, our famous New England baked beans, casseroles, and other old favorites that "taste even better the next day."

Boston Baked Beans

 This dish, long New England's favorite Saturday night supper served with Boston brown bread, is apt to be eaten again with codfish balls for breakfast on Sunday morning. And I doubt if a church supper has ever been held here that didn't offer big pots of beans along with baked ham, chicken pie, and cole slaw.

32 ounces pea beans	1 teaspoon salt
½ pound salt pork	1 teaspoon baking soda
⅓ cup granulated sugar	½ teaspoon dry mustard
⅓ cup dark molasses	

1 Wash and sort the beans and soak overnight in cold water. In the morning, drain and cover with fresh water. Simmer about 1 hour, until the skins break.

2 Preheat oven to 250°.

3 Put beans in bean pot, filling it three-quarters full. Score pork and press on top of the beans. Add sugar, molasses, salt, baking soda, and mustard. Cover with boiling water.

4 Cover pot and bake, without stirring, 8 hours. Keep beans almost covered with water. Remove the cover for last 30 minutes of baking to allow the salt pork to brown.

YIELD: 8 SERVINGS

Sunrise one morning during the late 1600s revealed a weathered sloop riding at anchor in Boston Harbor. Shorefront observers saw that it rode low in the water, evidently carrying a heavy cargo. They had no way of knowing that this cargo was the first of its kind ever to reach New England and was to initiate changes in New England's eating and drinking habits, as well as play its part in bringing a country yet undreamed-of to civil war.

Down in the sloop's creaking hold, hogsheads of molasses crowded each other, lumbered aboard weeks before in the West Indies. Soon the sweet syrup would be on every Yankee table, poured over breakfast dishes and desserts, mixed into hasty pudding, and used as the sweetening ingredient in countless New England recipes. Shortly, men would be distilling it into rum, most of which would go to Africa to be traded for slaves, these to be traded in the South for sugar molasses, and money—to the completion of the triangle and the enrichment of the Yankee trader.

Not too long after the landing of that first cargo of molasses, Boston housewives and their cooks were experimenting with the new ingredient in cookies, cakes, and candies—not to mention Baked Beans!

Baked Beans II

 Here's another baked bean recipe for those who like their food more spicy.

32 ounces pea beans	3/4 cup black molasses
2 medium onions, chopped	1/2 cup brown sugar (optional)
3/4 pound salt pork, diced	1 teaspoon dry mustard
1 ham bone	1/2 teaspoon ground ginger
2 cloves garlic, chopped	2 tablespoons cider vinegar
salt to taste	

1 Wash and sort the beans and soak them overnight in cold water. In the morning, drain and add fresh water. Parboil until soft, along with onions, salt pork, ham bone, and garlic. Add salt to taste.

2 Preheat oven (if it is not already on) to 250°.

3 Put beans in bean pot. Add black molasses (and brown sugar if desired), mustard, ginger, and vinegar for piquancy.

4   Put beans in oven—along with anything else that is baking, except cake. Cover at first, then uncover during the last hour of cooking. The longer the beans bake, the better they are. "They are best the second day's baking"—or so the old housewives say. (Six to 8 hours should do it. Add more water if necessary.)

YIELD: 8 SERVINGS

Boston Brown Bread (Steamed)

1 cup yellow cornmeal	1 teaspoon baking soda
1 cup rye flour	3/4 cup molasses
1 cup graham flour	2 cups sour milk
1 teaspoon salt	1 cup raisins

1   Mix and sift cornmeal, flours, and salt.

2   Dissolve baking soda in small amount of water and stir into the molasses. Combine molasses with sour milk, then mix into dry ingredients.

3   Shake raisins in a paper bag with a little flour in it and add to batter. Mix thoroughly.

4   Coat 2 round molds with vegetable spray. (Old baking powder cans used to be the standard molds.) (Molds should have tight-fitting covers, and covers need to be greased or coated with vegetable spray before use.)

5   Fill the molds with batter, place covers on the molds, then tie covers down with string so that the bread will not force off cover as it rises.

6   Place molds on a rack in a kettle containing boiling water that comes halfway up around the molds. Cover the kettle and steam 3 hours, adding more boiling water if needed.

7   Unmold. The traditional way to slice brown bread is to use a length of taut string.

YIELD: 2 SMALL LOAVES

Baked Brown Bread

This recipe is similar to the preceding one but can be whipped up at an hour's notice.

2 cups buttermilk	1 cup raisins
3/4 cup dark molasses	1/4 cup melted shortening or
1 cup graham flour	butter
1 cup white flour	1 teaspoon baking soda
1 cup yellow cornmeal	1 teaspoon salt

1 Preheat oven to 350°. Coat loaf pan with vegetable spray.

2 Sift together dry ingredients. Combine with remaining ingredients and place in prepared loaf pan.

3 Bake 1 hour.

YIELD: 1 LOAF

Cassoulet

 A New England adaptation of an old French dish that comes down to us through Canadian settlers, this is a highly flavored version of baked beans that well deserves the praise it always gets. Cassoulet is even better when prepared a day or two in advance and reheated.

2 pounds dried white beans	1/2 pound salt pork or bacon
(yellow eye or soldier beans)	scraps
2 tablespoons salt	1/2 pound chicken livers
1 bay leaf	1/2 can tomato paste
1 sprig thyme or 1/2 teaspoon	1/2 pound garlic sausage
dried thyme	2 tomatoes, sliced
6 cloves garlic, crushed	1 cup breadcrumbs
2 onions, chopped	1/2 cup chopped parsley

1 Wash and sort the beans and soak overnight in water. (They will double in bulk.) In the morning, rinse beans and place in fresh water to cover.

2 Add the salt, bay leaf, thyme, garlic, onions, and salt pork and bring to a boil. Simmer very gently about 1 1/2 hours, or until just tender.

3 Discard bay leaf and thyme sprig. Remove salt pork or bacon and cut into cubes. Cut up chicken livers and brown in a skillet with cubes of salt pork. Add tomato paste. Cube garlic sausage.

4 Preheat oven to 250°.

5 Reserve cooking liquid from beans. Arrange layer of beans in 4-quart earthenware pot. Spread part of chicken livers, sausage cubes, pork cubes, and tomato slices over beans. Continue in layers until all ingre-

dients (except breadcrumbs and parsley) have been used. Pour bean cooking juices over dish and add (now or later) some drippings from ham or lamb if you are cooking either. Taste for seasoning.

6 Combine breadcrumbs and parsley and spread over cassoulet. Place in oven and bake 4 hours or longer. The finished dish should be liquid and succulent.

YIELD: 12 TO 14 SIDE-DISH SERVINGS; 8 TO 10 MAIN-DISH SERVINGS

CASSEROLES AND LUNCHEON DISHES

Chicken and Veal Pejarsky with Hazelnut Butter

 An interesting luncheon dish.

1/4 cup blanched hazelnuts, toasted	salt to taste
	white pepper to taste
1/2 cup plus 2 tablespoons sweet butter	ground nutmeg to taste
	1 1/4 cups very fine breadcrumbs
1/2 pound boneless chicken breast, ground	1/2 cup heavy cream
1/2 pound boneless veal, ground	

1 Chill a mixing bowl. Meanwhile, prepare the hazelnut butter. Pulverize nuts in food processor. Add 1/2 cup sweet butter and blend well. Chill until needed.

2 In a separate chilled mixing bowl, combine the chicken and veal. Season with salt, white pepper, and nutmeg. Gradually add half of the breadcrumbs and the cream. With wooden spatula, mix thoroughly and vigorously until mixture forms stiff, compact mass.

3 With a large spoon, form balls of desired size and roll in remaining breadcrumbs. Flatten balls to make patties, hamburger style.

4 Melt remaining butter in skillet and sauté patties over low flame.

5 Serve with chilled hazelnut butter.

YIELD: 4 SERVINGS

Chicken Livers with Mushrooms

1 pound chicken livers
3 tablespoons flour
salt to taste
pepper to taste
cooking oil
4 tablespoons butter or
   margarine

1 large onion, coarsely
   chopped
$^1/_2$ cup sliced mushrooms
$^1/_2$ cup sherry
4 slices hot buttered toast

1 Toss the chicken livers in the flour seasoned with salt and pepper.

2 Heat the oil in a skillet and fry livers, a few at a time, until nicely browned.

3 In a separate skillet, melt butter and sauté the onion until soft. Add mushrooms and sauté a few minutes more, stirring. Add livers and sherry and simmer together about 5 minutes.

4 Serve on hot buttered toast.

YIELD: 4 SERVINGS

Chicken Timbales

A longtime New England favorite, chicken timbales are attractive and digestible. Usually served with rice, they may be accompanied by Brown Mushroom Sauce (p. 314).

10 saltines or soda crackers,
   finely crumbled
2 tablespoons butter or
   margarine
$1^3/_4$ cups milk
2 eggs, lightly beaten

2 cups cooked chicken, finely
   diced
2 teaspoons onion juice
$^1/_2$ teaspoon paprika
1 teaspoon salt
$^1/_2$ teaspoon white pepper

1 Preheat oven to 325°.

2 Mix the cracker crumbs, butter, and milk in saucepan, stirring and heating until mixture is of a creamy consistency. Pour it over the beaten eggs and add chicken, onion juice, and seasonings.

3 Coat 4 individual molds (6 ounces each) with vegetable spray. Fill molds with chicken mixture and place in shallow pan of hot water.

4 Bake 30 minutes, or until silver fork inserted in timbales comes out clean.

YIELD: 4 SERVINGS

Chicken or Turkey Pâté

 This pâté makes a fine luncheon or supper dish but it is very handy also to have a loaf in the refrigerator ready for that unexpected hour when hunger strikes. It's good for you—with little fat or cholesterol. Serve the pâté warm or cold with Dijon mustard or Yogurt Mustard sauce.

2 pounds ground chicken or
    turkey meat
1/2 large sweet onion, about 1/2
    pound, chopped
1 egg, beaten
1 egg white
3/4 cup old-fashioned oatmeal
1/2 cup tomato juice
1/2 cup white wine
1 tablespoon white wine
    vinegar or lemon juice

4 sprigs fresh tarragon,
    chopped or 1 teaspoon dried
1/4 cup blanched almonds,
    pistachio nuts, or black
    walnuts
2 teaspoons salt
1/2 teaspoon freshly ground
    white pepper
1/2 teaspoon ground ginger
1/2 pound filleted chicken
    breasts

1 Pre-heat oven to 350°. Coat a 4″ x 8″ loaf pan with vegetable spray.

2 In a large bowl combine the ground chicken or turkey meat with the rest of the ingredients (except the chicken breasts) in the order given. Mix well. Press half of the mixture into the bottom of a 4″ x 8″ loaf pan, lay the fillets of chicken over the dish, and add the remaining mixture.

3 Bake for 1 1/4 to 1 1/2 hours until no pink juices ooze from the loaf. Drain if there is still some liquid in the dish.

4 To serve warm let stand for 5 minutes before slicing. To serve cold cover with plastic, weight with a brick or a heavy can of that approximate shape and chill.

YIELD: 6 TO 8 SERVINGS

Codfish Puff

1 pound fresh codfish,
parboiled, drained, and
flaked

2 tablespoons flour

3 eggs, separated

3 1/2 cups milk

salt to taste

freshly ground white pepper to
taste

1 Preheat oven to 375°. Coat 1 1/2-quart soufflé dish with vegetable spray.

2 Sprinkle the flour over the flaked codfish in a mixing bowl. Add 3 beaten egg yolks, milk, salt, and pepper. Fold in well-beaten egg whites. Place mixture in the prepared soufflé dish.

3 Bake 15 minutes, until top is golden.

YIELD: 4 SERVINGS

Creamed Chicken

Creamed chicken made with velouté sauce can be varied by adding a little sherry or other white wine, chopped fresh tarragon, mushrooms, almonds, or white grapes. A teaspoon of curry powder and a tablespoon of chutney give it another incarnation. Creamed chicken can be served over white rice or wild rice, in popovers, over baking powder biscuits, in artichokes or firm red tomatoes, or from a chafing dish for a supper party. It is very useful, very versatile.

1 chicken, quartered

1/2 onion, sliced

half a lemon, sliced

1 stalk celery, sliced

1 bay leaf

1 teaspoon salt

6 peppercorns

4 whole cloves

1 chicken bouillon cube

4 tablespoons butter or
margarine

4 tablespoons flour

1 1/2 cups chicken stock

1/2 cup light cream

salt to taste

freshly ground white pepper to
taste

pinch of ground nutmeg

1 Rinse the chicken and put (with the giblets and neck if whole bird is used) with next 8 ingredients in a saucepan just large enough to hold them. Cover, bring to boil, simmer 5 minutes, and cool in the broth.

2 Remove the chicken. Strain and refrigerate broth. Skin and bone chicken pieces and cut meat into bite-size pieces.

3 Skim chicken broth and use for preparing velouté sauce. In a skillet, melt butter over low heat and blend in flour. Gradually add chicken stock and cream and stir until thick and smooth. Season with salt, pepper, and nutmeg.

4 Mix together chicken and sauce.

YIELD: 6 SERVINGS

Creamed Dried Beef

¹/₂ pound dried beef
2 tablespoons butter or
   margarine

2 tablespoons flour
1 cup light cream
white pepper to taste

1 Separate the pieces of meat and soak in hot water 10 minutes to remove some salt. Drain.

2 Melt the butter in a skillet and blend in flour. Gradually, while stirring, add the cream. Season with pepper.

3 Add drained beef to cream sauce and serve over hot buttered toast or stuffed baked potatoes.

YIELD: 4 SERVINGS

Fried Salt Pork

Traditional Yankee fare, a New Hampshire recipe. Crisp salt pork is often served as an accompaniment to creamed dried beef over baked potatoes.

1 pound fat salt pork

1 Cut the salt pork in 12 thin slices (or have butcher do it). Fry the slices in skillet, turning frequently, until well browned.

    The pork may be served with a cream gravy made by adding a cup of thick cream to one tablespoon of pork fat left in the skillet. As soon as the cream is hot, pour it over the salt pork slices.

YIELD: 4 SERVINGS

Fettuccini with Fresh Tomato and Mushroom Sauce

1 tablespoon olive oil
1/4 cup finely chopped onion
1 clove garlic, minced
1 bay leaf
salt to taste
freshly ground pepper to taste

4 ripe tomatoes, peeled, seeded, and coarsely chopped
8 mushrooms, sliced
9 ounces fresh fettuccini
chopped fresh basil for garnish
grated Parmesan cheese

1 In skillet, heat oil, add the chopped onion, and sauté until wilted. Add garlic, bay leaf, salt, and pepper. Add tomatoes and mushrooms and sauté until just soft. Remove bay leaf.

2 Cook fettuccini according to package directions. Drain. Transfer to *very* hot plates and cover with tomato and mushroom sauce. Garnish with chopped basil and serve. Pass the Parmesan cheese.

YIELD: 4 SERVINGS

French-Fried Tomato Sandwich

1/2 cup mayonnaise
2/3 cup grated Swiss or Gruyère cheese
1 teaspoon snipped fresh dill
1 teaspoon snipped fresh chives
8 slices white bread

salt to taste
pepper to taste
2 tomatoes, peeled and thinly sliced
3 eggs, beaten
2 tablespoons butter or margarine

1 Mix together mayonnaise, grated cheese, dill, and chives. Spread on the bread slices. Sprinkle with salt and pepper.

2 Arrange tomato slices on 4 bread slices. Top with other 4 slices. Press sandwiches together firmly.

3 Dip each sandwich in beaten eggs.

4 Melt butter in skillet and, when hot, fry sandwiches, turning carefully to brown both sides lightly and melt cheese.

5 Slice and serve.

YIELD: 4 SANDWICHES

Ham Mousse

This dish, fine enough for any luncheon or buffet party, uses up the last bits of a baked ham. (Boiled ham bought for the purpose can also be used—in that case, add $1/2$ teaspoon ground cloves.) Serve with Cumberland Sauce (p. 316), baking powder biscuits, and a green salad.

$1/2$ pint heavy cream
1 cup water
$1 1/2$ envelopes unflavored
   gelatine

2 to 3 cups ham leftovers
   (meat, jelly, and cloves)
1 drop red food coloring
   (optional)

1 Whip the cream in a chilled bowl and set aside.

2 Gradually mix the water with the gelatine. Add half the mixed gelatine to the whipped cream and coat the inside of a 1-quart mold with this. Refrigerate mold.

3 In food processor or blender, purée ham. (If blender is used, mixture will fluff up considerably.) Mix ham with remaining cream and gelatine. Add 1 drop red food coloring if desired.

4 Remove the mold from refrigerator (be sure the gelatine coating has set) and pour in ham mixture. Chill again to set the ham mousse.

YIELD: 6 SERVINGS

Lasagne Bolognese

3 tablespoons butter or
   margarine
3 tablespoons flour
1 cup milk
1 cup light cream
salt to taste
freshly ground pepper to taste

ground nutmeg to taste
1 cup grated Parmesan cheese,
   plus more for the topping
$1/2$ pound lasagne noodles,
   green or white
4 cups Sauce Bolognese (recipe
   follows)

1 Preheat oven to 375°. Coat a large square or oblong baking dish (15″ x 10″ or 10 inches square) with vegetable spray.

2 Melt butter in a skillet and blend in the flour, milk, and cream. Stir over moderate heat until sauce bubbles and is thick and smooth. Add seasonings, stir in 1 cup grated Parmesan, and set aside.

3 Cook lasagne in the boiling salted water according to package directions. Drain, rinse, and spread in a single layer on a damp towel.

4 Spread a thin layer of meat sauce in the prepared baking dish, then build casserole with layers of lasagne, cheese sauce, and meat sauce. Sprinkle top with grated Parmesan.

5 Bake 35 to 40 minutes, until bubbling hot and glazed brown. Cool 5 minutes before serving.

YIELD: 6 TO 8 JUMBO SERVINGS

Sauce Bolognese

Ancient Bologna has for many centuries been the gastronomic capital of Italy. (This sauce can be used on all sorts of pasta—among them spaghetti, linguine, and green or white fettuccini.)

6 slices bacon, diced
2 onions, chopped
1 stalk celery, chopped
1 carrot, diced
2 cloves garlic, minced
3 tablespoons butter or
   margarine
1/4 pound chicken livers, diced
1 pound ground round steak

2 tablespoons white vinegar
1/4 cup tomato sauce
1/4 teaspoon ground nutmeg
1 teaspoon salt
freshly ground pepper to taste
1 1/2 cups beef bouillon
1 cup sliced mushrooms
1/2 cup dry white wine

1 Fry bacon in a heavy saucepan and drain off most of fat. Add the onions, celery, carrot, and garlic and sauté until soft. Add 2 table-spoons butter and chicken livers and brown lightly. Add beef and cook until well browned, 10 to 15 minutes. Add vinegar, tomato sauce, nutmeg, salt, pepper, and bouillon. Cover and simmer 30 minutes more.

2 In separate skillet, melt 1 tablespoon butter and sauté mushrooms. Add mushrooms and wine to sauce and simmer until well blended.

YIELD: 4 CUPS

Macaroni Ring

 A most versatile dish, this ring may be served with grilled ham and filled with a vegetable, such as peas, creamed mushrooms, or creamed carrots. Or fill the ring with creamed chicken or fish and surround with a vegetable.

1 cup macaroni

2 teaspoons onion juice

1½ tablespoons chopped fresh
  parsley

2 tablespoons chopped green
  pepper

1 teaspoon salt

1 cup grated cheese

1 cup light cream

1 cup soft breadcrumbs

¼ cup melted butter or
  margarine

3 eggs, well beaten

1 Preheat oven to 350°. Coat a 2-quart ring mold with vegetable spray.

2 Cook the macaroni al dente, according to package directions. Drain.

3 In a mixing bowl, combine macaroni with the remaining ingredients. Spoon into the prepared ring mold. (The mixture will rise during cooking because of the eggs.)

4 Bake 45 minutes, or until firm.

YIELD: 6 SERVINGS

Linguine with Kielbasa and Clams

 For a low-fat/low-cholesterol dish, leave out the kielbasa.

3 tablespoons olive oil

3 cloves garlic, crushed

¼ cup chopped onion

8 ounces kielbasa, cubed

1 cup chopped fresh plum
  tomatoes

½ cup dry white wine

36 littleneck clams or mussels,
  scrubbed

1 pound linguine

parsley for garnish

basil for garnish

1 Heat the oil in a heavy saucepan. Add the garlic, onion, and sausage and cook over low heat until onions are tender. Stir in the tomatoes, wine, and clams or mussels. Cover and cook over medium heat until clams or mussels have opened.

2 Cook the linguine al dente, according to package instructions. Drain.

3 Transfer the linguine to very hot plates and cover with sauce, placing open clams on top of sauce. Garnish with parsley and basil.

YIELD: 6 SERVINGS

Onion Sandwich

 This kind of hearty sandwich delighted Yankee President Calvin Coolidge. It is particularly tasty made with rye bread.

1 large Bermuda or Vidalia onion (about 1 pound)	salt to taste
3 hard-boiled eggs	pepper to taste
2 small gherkins	12 slices bread
mayonnaise	ripe tomato wedges
1/2 teaspoon dry mustard	ripe olives

1 Chop the onion, eggs, and pickles finely and add enough mayonnaise for a good spreading consistency. Add the mustard, salt, and pepper to taste.

2 Spread lavishly on bread and garnish with tomato wedges and olives.

YIELD: 6 SANDWICHES

Shrimp and Artichoke Casserole

 Serve this dish with rice or buttered noodles, mixed green salad, and garlic bread.

6 tablespoons butter or margarine	1 tablespoon Worcestershire sauce
1/4 pound mushrooms, sliced	1 package frozen artichoke hearts, cooked
4 tablespoons flour	1 1/2 pounds shrimp, shelled and cleaned
3/4 cup milk	
3/4 cup heavy cream	
salt to taste	1/4 cup grated Parmesan cheese
white pepper to taste	paprika
1/4 cup sherry	

1 Preheat oven to 375°. Coat baking dish with vegetable spray.

2 Melt the butter in a skillet and sauté the mushrooms 2 minutes. Stir in the flour and blend. Gradually add milk and cream, whisking constantly. When sauce is thick, add salt and pepper to taste. Then add sherry and Worcestershire sauce.

3 Arrange the artichoke hearts in prepared baking dish and layer shrimp

over them. Pour mushroom sauce over all and sprinkle with grated cheese and paprika.

4　Bake 20 to 30 minutes.

YIELD: 6 SERVINGS

Tasty Corn-Sausage Casserole

1 pound sausage meat
1 can (16 ounces) cream-style
　corn

2 eggs, lightly beaten
$1/4$ teaspoon salt
$1 1/2$ cups soft breadcrumbs

1　Preheat oven to 400°. Coat $1 1/2$-quart soufflé dish with vegetable spray.

2　Brown sausage in heavy skillet until crumbly. Remove from skillet with slotted spoon and drain on paper towels.

3　In a mixing bowl, combine the corn, eggs, and salt. Place half of the corn mixture in the prepared soufflé dish. Next spread a layer of sausage, then top with remaining corn mixture.

4　Pour off half of the fat in the skillet. Stir breadcrumbs into remaining fat and spread crumbs over casserole.

5　Bake until set and browned, 20 to 25 minutes.

YIELD: 4 SERVINGS

Yodeling Good Swiss Casserole

A fine veal casserole to accompany a fresh spinach salad.

$1 1/2$ pounds veal cutlets,
　pounded $1/4$ inch thick
$1/2$ pound Swiss cheese, sliced
3 tablespoons flour
$1 1/2$ teaspoons paprika
1 teaspoon salt

$1/4$ cup butter or margarine
$1 1/2$ cups beef gravy
$1/2$ cup light cream
2 cups wide noodles, cooked
2 teaspoons chopped fresh
　chives

1　Preheat oven to 375°. Coat 2-quart casserole with vegetable spray.

2　Cut the veal into serving pieces. Place 1 slice of cheese on half of the pieces and top with a second piece of veal. Press edges together.

3　Combine the flour, paprika, and salt on a sheet of waxed paper. Coat the veal with seasoned flour.

4 Melt the butter in a skillet, brown veal well, and remove. In same skillet, stir together gravy and cream and simmer 5 minutes.

5 Arrange alternate layers of noodles, sauce, and veal in prepared casserole. Sprinkle with chives and cover. Bake 1½ hours.

YIELD: 6 SERVINGS

Thai Spring Rolls

 This Asian specialty makes an inspired luncheon dish. Cut half size, the rolls are attractive for cocktail bites or as a first course. My son's Thai wife, El, makes them by the hundreds for the Yankees of Putney, Vermont, who gobble them up. Ground chicken or ground pork may be substituted for shrimp or crabmeat.

½ cup transparent vermicelli noodles	2 tablespoons oyster sauce
½ cup chopped carrots	1 tablespoons fish sauce (nampla)
½ cup chopped celery	1 cup large fresh bean sprouts
2 tablespoons chopped green onions	(shredded lettuce may be substituted)
salt to taste	2 tablespoons chopped ginger
1 tablespoon sesame oil	6 dried black mushrooms,
1 teaspoon minced garlic	chopped (fresh morels may
½ cup chopped shrimp	be substituted)
½ cup flaked crabmeat	2 cups vegetable oil
½ teaspoon white pepper	24 spring roll wrappers
2 tablespoons soy sauce	1 egg yolk

1 Soak the noodles in water to cover for 30 minutes; cut into ½-inch lengths.

2 Cook the carrots, celery and green onion in boiling water for 2 minutes and drain. When cool squeeze to get rid of excess water.

3 Heat sesame oil in a large skillet; cook garlic until golden. Combine shrimp, crabmeat, soy, oyster and fish sauce, sugar, pepper and salt and sauté in the skillet for 3 minutes, stirring. Add the noodles, cooked vegetables, bean sprouts and ginger and sauté for 4 minutes more, stirring. Cool.

4 Use the thinnest spring roll wrappers available. Place about 2 tablespoons of the mixture on a spring roll. Roll up envelope fashion and seal with egg yolk.

5 Fry in 1 inch of vegetable oil for 3 to 5 minutes until golden. Turn frequently so they do not burn. Drain on paper towels. Serve hot with peanut sauce.

YIELD: 24 PIECES

Peanut Sauce for Spring Rolls

3/4 cup water

1/2 teaspoon corn starch

1 cup sugar

1/2 cup vinegar

2 teaspoons salt

1 tablespoon catsup

1 teaspoon chopped garlic

1/2 cup coarsely chopped fresh
    unsalted peanuts

1 Mix cornstarch with 3 or 4 teaspoons of the water. Set aside.

2 In a small saucepan bring the rest of the water, the sugar, vinegar and salt to a boil. Add the catsup and garlic and stir. Add the cornstarch and stir until the sauce thickens. Cool and add the peanuts.

YIELD: ABOUT 1 CUP

Zucchini Wild Rice Casserole

 This dish is a tasty main dish for luncheon or supper. It also works well as a side dish with chicken, ham or turkey.

1/4 pound sausage meat

1 small clove garlic, minced

1/2 medium onion, sliced

1 large firm red tomato, about
    1/2 pound, cut in chunks

1 medium zucchini, cut in
    julienne strips (about 1
    pound)

1 cup wild rice, cooked

salt to taste

pepper to taste

2 tablespoons sherry

2 tablespoons soy sauce

fresh, chopped herbs to taste,
    thyme, basil, chives, parsley

1 Preheat oven to 350°. Coat an 8-inch casserole dish with vegetable spray.

2 Brown the sausage meat in a large iron skillet over low heat. Pour off the fat, leaving enough to coat the skillet. Add the vegetables. Cook until tender.

3 Wash the wild rice thoroughly. Cook in 2 cups of water until tender. Add to the skillet.

4 Season to taste with salt, pepper, sherry, soy sauce and freshly chopped herbs. Simmer for about 4 minutes. Remove to a casserole dish. Before serving heat in oven for 10 minutes.

YIELD: 4 SERVINGS

EGGS AND CHEESE

Omelets

An omelet can be made in less than two minutes and can be filled with all sorts of good things to make a wonderful light meal. Put in the warmed filling just before folding the omelet. A few sliced mushrooms cooked in butter, a little crumbled bacon, some sour cream, cottage cheese, grated Swiss or Parmesan cheese, together or alone. Chopped herbs—parsley, chives, and watercress—or whatever ones are available may be mixed with the egg before making the omelet. Small amounts of leftover delicacies—vegetables, meat, or fish—may be folded into the omelet.

Individual Omelet

Use an 8-inch omelet pan with sloping sides—one that is kept exclusively for making omelets will give the best results.

2 eggs, at room temperature	**pepper to taste**
2 teaspoons water	**1 tablespoon butter or**
salt to taste	**margarine**

1 Beat the eggs lightly with water, salt, and pepper until just blended.

2 Melt the butter in an omelet pan over rather high heat, tilting pan to coat entire surface. When butter sputters, pour in the egg mixture and scramble quickly once to cook most of the egg.

3 Lower heat and cook, shaking pan to keep omelet loosened from pan and rolling pan to let the uncooked egg slip to bottom.

4 When the surface has only filmy coating of liquid egg, fold outer edges toward center. Slide omelet to edge of pan and turn onto warm plate.

VARIATION – **Omelet**

Suggested fillings for lunchtime omelets are: cooked asparagus tips; purée of spinach with sour cream; diced chicken, chicken livers, or ham in cream sauce; creamed crabmeat, lobster, or fish.

An omelet filled with jam or jelly and dusted with confectioners' sugar makes a breakfast or supper dish that children love. Adults do, too. Omit the pepper and use only a pinch of salt. You can also fold sour or whipped cream into these sweet omelets.

Garnish a filled omelet with a hint of its contents—a sprig of watercress, a lobster claw, three slices of mushroom, as the case may be. Or cover it with a big spoonful of mushroom, cheese, or tomato sauce.

Lobster Omelet

1 tablespoon butter or
  margarine
1/2 cup cooked, sliced lobster
  meat
1/4 cup dry white wine

1/2 cup thick Cream Sauce
  (p. 315)
6 eggs, made into 1 large or 3
  small omelets

1 Melt butter in skillet and add lobster meat and wine. Simmer until wine is partly reduced. Blend in cream sauce.

2 Fold lobster meat and part of sauce into center of omelet or omelets.

3 Pour remaining sauce over the top of cooked omelet and serve.

YIELD: 3 SERVINGS

Bedspread for Two

A very ample bedspread—a chafing-dish recipe.

6 eggs
12 medium oysters
1 teaspoon anchovy paste
3 tablespoons butter or
  margarine
salt to taste

freshly ground white pepper to
  taste
2 slices toast
watercress or parsley, for
  garnish

1 Whisk eggs in a soup bowl. Cut up oysters moderately fine and place in second soup bowl.

2 Rub bottom of chafing dish with anchovy paste. Add butter.

3 Cook eggs gently to a creamy scramble. Just as they are setting, put in oysters and stir until well blended and cooked through. Season to taste.

4 Spread toast lightly with anchovy paste. Spoon eggs over toast. Garnish with watercress or parsley.

YIELD: 2 SERVINGS

Eggs Goldenrod

 This pretty and soothing dish fills in for many occasions and is particularly popular with small children.

12 hard-boiled eggs	**6 slices buttered toast**
2 cups Cream Sauce (p. 315)	**parsley for garnish**

1 Slice 10 eggs and spread on a warm platter. Cover with the cream sauce. Sieve remaining eggs over the top of the sauce. (Be sure ingredients and platter are warm.)

2 Surround with hot toast points and garnish with parsley.

YIELD: 6 SERVINGS

Eggs à la Hitchcock

 Another subtly flavored chafing-dish specialty.

1 pint light or heavy cream	**salt to taste**
1 tablespoon Worcestershire sauce	**pepper to taste**
¹/₂ tablespoon tomato catsup	**6 large eggs**
¹/₂ tablespoon walnut catsup	**6 buttered toast rounds**
3 or 4 dashes of Tabasco sauce	**parsley or watercress for garnish**

1 Heat cream in chafing dish. When hot, add seasonings.

2 Break eggs into hot sauce. When eggs are set, place over toast rounds on hot plates. Pour remaining sauce over eggs and garnish with parsley or watercress.

YIELD: 6 SERVINGS

Country-Style Onion Pie

 For a change, put crumbled crisp bacon or slivers of cheese into the pie.

Basic Pie Crust (p. 352)	**3 eggs**
3 pounds onions, peeled and sliced	**2 cups light cream**
	salt to taste
3 tablespoons butter or margarine	**white pepper to taste**

1 Preheat oven to 350°. Line a deep pie plate with pastry.

2 Melt butter in skillet and sauté onions until golden brown.

3 Beat together eggs and cream and season with salt and pepper. Add to onions in skillet.

4 Pour onion mixture into pastry shell and add top crust.

5 Bake 1 hour, until crust is golden brown.

YIELD: 6 SERVINGS

Spinach Quiche

 Evart Andros of Walpole, New Hampshire, contributed this excellent recipe.

Basic Pie Crust (¹/₂ recipe) (p. 352)	**3 eggs, lightly beaten**
2 pounds fresh spinach	**1¹/₂ cups heavy cream**
2 tablespoons chopped scallions	**¹/₂ teaspoon salt**
	¹/₂ teaspoon white pepper
3 tablespoons butter or margarine	**¹/₂ teaspoon ground nutmeg**
	¹/₄ cup grated Gruyère cheese

1 Line 9-inch pie pan or quiche dish with pastry and chill. Preheat oven to 375°.

2 Wash the spinach thoroughly and discard all thick stems. Plunge the spinach into boiling water for about 1 minute. Drain well, pat dry with paper towels, and chop finely.

3 Melt 2 tablespoons butter in a large skillet. Add the chopped spinach and scallions and cook several minutes, or until *all* liquid has evaporated.

4 In a mixing bowl, combine eggs with cream, salt, pepper, and nutmeg. Add the cooked spinach and stir to blend.

5 Pour the spinach mixture into chilled pastry shell. Sprinkle the top with grated cheese and dot with 1 tablespoon butter cut into bits.

6 Bake 25 to 30 minutes, until set. Serve hot.

YIELD: 6 SERVINGS

VARIATION – **Mushroom Quiche**

Use same recipe as for Spinach Quiche, but substitute 1 pound of mushrooms, sliced, for 2 pounds of spinach. Use Watercress Pie Crust (below).

Watercress Pie Crust

Adds zing to a meat or vegetable pie.

1 cup sifted flour	2 tablespoons lard, butter, or
1½ teaspoons baking powder	margarine
½ teaspoon salt	⅓ cup finely chopped
pinch of powdered thyme	watercress leaves, well dried
	½ cup cold milk

1 Sift the flour again with the baking powder, salt, and thyme.

2 With two knives or pastry blender, cut the lard and watercress leaves alternately into dry ingredients. Gradually add milk. Shape into a ball and chill.

3 Roll out the chilled dough on floured board.

YIELD: 1 CRUST

Spoon Bread

 A favorite dish. It's pretty, soothing, and digestible. I find it fits into many meals.

1½ cups white cornmeal	3 tablespoons butter or
1½ teaspoons salt	margarine
1½ tablespoons granulated	1½ cups water
sugar	3 cups buttermilk
	5 eggs, well beaten

1 Preheat oven to 325°. Coat 2½-quart soufflé dish with vegetable spray.

2 In a saucepan, combine the cornmeal, salt, sugar, butter, water, and 1½ cups buttermilk. Cook over medium heat, stirring constantly, until mixture thickens.

3 Cool to room temperature before adding remaining buttermilk and eggs.

4 Pour the batter into the prepared soufflé dish. Bake approximately 45 minutes. Serve immediately with plenty of butter on top.

YIELD: 8 TO 10 SERVINGS

Cheese Woodchuck

 This comfortable supper dish is a Maine "receipt" from a family whose ancestors were among the first settlers.

2 tablespoons butter or margarine	½ pound diced Cheddar cheese
1 small onion, minced	½ teaspoon savory (or Worcestershire sauce)
½ teaspoon salt	2 eggs, well beaten
⅔ cup milk	6 slices toast
1½ to 2 cups corn kernels, scraped from cob	

1 Sauté the onion in the butter. Add the salt, milk, and corn and cook slowly, stirring constantly, about 10 minutes.

2 Stir in the cheese and savory and cook until cheese is melted. Add eggs and cook very gently, stirring constantly, 2 to 3 minutes more.

3 Serve on toast slices, with pickle or relish as an accompaniment.

YIELD: 6 SERVINGS

Welsh Rabbit

 Use a tangy Vermont Cheddar for this zestful dish. It's a good one to remember for an impromptu snack, for if you keep a good piece of cheese on hand, the ingredients are always ready. There are a number of easy ways to vary this dish. For a more substantial meal, garnish the rabbit with crisp bacon or fried ham.

1 tablespoon butter or margarine	1 teaspoon dry mustard
6 cups grated Cheddar cheese (about 1½ pounds)	Worcestershire sauce to taste
	salt to taste
4 egg yolks	few dashes of Tabasco sauce
1 cup beer	6 slices hot buttered toast or crisp heated crackers

1 Melt the butter in top of a double boiler or chafing dish over simmering water. Stir in the cheese and cook until melted and smooth.

2 Whisk the egg yolks into beer and add very slowly to cheese, stirring. Add seasonings and continue to cook, stirring until mixture is thick. (Taste and add more seasoning if needed.)

3 Serve at once on hot buttered toast or crisp heated crackers.

YIELD: 6 SERVINGS

VARIATION – Tomato Rabbit

Before pouring rabbit sauce over toast, place broiled tomatoes or drained canned tomatoes on the toast.

VARIATION – Oyster Rabbit

Add half a pint of oysters with their liquor to the cheese rabbit.

VARIATION – Scotch Woodcock

Place a poached egg on the toast before pouring rabbit sauce over it.

Baked Vermont Cheese Fondue

 This dish is somewhere between a cheese soufflé and a rabbit, but it is much easier to serve than either and guaranteed to please everyone. By simple arithmetic, it can easily be adapted to serve two, four, or twelve.

¼ pound butter or margarine, softened	3 cups milk, scalded
	4 eggs, lightly beaten
12 slices white bread, crusts removed	salt to taste
	freshly ground white pepper to taste
1¾ pounds extra sharp Cheddar cheese, grated	few dashes of Tabasco sauce

1 The night before serving, coat 8″ x 12″ baking dish with vegetable

spray. Spread butter on bread slices and arrange 6 slices in baking dish. Sprinkle with half of grated cheese and arrange 6 more slices over that.

2 Melt the remaining cheese with scalded milk and add eggs and seasonings. Pour over the baking dish, cover, and refrigerate overnight.

3 Before serving, preheat the oven to 300° and remove the baking dish from the refrigerator.

4 Bake the fondue 25 minutes, until puffy and golden.

YIELD: 6 SERVINGS

Baked Tomato Fondue

1½ cups soft breadcrumbs   2 cups Cheddar cheese, diced
1½ cups canned tomatoes   4 egg yolks, lightly beaten
1 teaspoon salt   4 egg whites, beaten stiff
¼ teaspoon paprika

1 Preheat oven to 350°. Coat a 2-quart soufflé dish with vegetable spray.

2 Combine the breadcrumbs and tomatoes in skillet. Season with salt and paprika and place over low heat. Add the cheese and melt, stirring occasionally.

3 Remove from the heat and add egg yolks. Fold in egg whites.

4 Pour fondue into prepared soufflé dish and bake 40 to 45 minutes.

YIELD: 6 SERVINGS

Cheese Soufflé

A beautiful and useful dish for any day of the week, cheese soufflé can be counted on to fill an emergency easily and with style. For variety, try making a soufflé with Swiss cheese or with a combination of cottage cheese and Roquefort. Or put a surprise ingredient (crabmeat, sliced tomatoes, or artichoke hearts) in the bottom of the dish. The recipe given is for a 6-cup soufflé mold and serves three people amply. If it is to be the main dish for four or five people, make 1½ times the recipe (6 egg yolks and 7 or 8 whites) and use an 8-cup mold. For six servings, it is best to double the recipe and use two 6-cup molds.

3½ tablespoons butter or
   margarine

¼ cup grated Parmesan cheese

3 tablespoons flour

1 cup milk

½ teaspoon salt

good pinch of dry mustard or
   cayenne pepper or both

1 cup diced Cheddar cheese

4 egg yolks

5 egg whites, at room
   temperature

1 Set a rack in middle of the oven and preheat oven to 400°. Generously butter (using about 1 tablespoon butter) a straight-sided soufflé dish and shake the grated cheese around it.

2 Melt 2½ tablespoons butter in a skillet. Remove from the heat and stir in the flour and ½ cup milk. Return to a low heat and gradually add remaining milk, plus seasonings and diced Cheddar. Stir well until thick.

3 Stir the egg yolks one by one into melted cheese mixture. Beat egg whites to stiff peaks. Stir a large spoonful of egg white (or the white that clings to beater) into the sauce, then very quickly and lightly fold remaining beaten whites into sauce.

4 Spoon the mixture into the prepared soufflé dish and place in oven. Reduce heat immediately to 375°. In 25 to 30 minutes, soufflé will be well puffed but still creamy in the center. Allow to cook 5 minutes more before taking it immediately to the table.

YIELD: 3 TO 4 SERVINGS

Quick Cheese Soufflé

1 thin slice white bread

½ teaspoon dry mustard

¼ teaspoon salt

dash of cayenne pepper

3 tablespoons butter or
   margarine

1 cup warm milk

1 cup diced mild cheese

4 egg yolks

5 egg whites, at room
   temperature

1 Preheat oven to 350°.

2 Into food processor or blender put bread, mustard, salt, and pepper. Blend 5 seconds. Remove cover and add butter, milk, cheese, and egg yolks. Blend for 25 seconds.

3 In 1½-quart soufflé dish, beat egg whites until stiff. Pour in cheese mixture and fold together until lightly blended.

4 Bake 35 minutes.

Soufflé Sandwich with Crabmeat

 16 slices white bread, buttered
   crusts removed
8 slices Swiss cheese
4 eggs, 1 egg white
1/2 pound crabmeat, cleaned
   and flaked

4 eggs
3 cups milk
2 teaspoons salt
cayenne pepper
Parmesan cheese

1 Preheat oven to 350°

2 Coat a shallow baking dish with vegetable spray. In it place half the bread, the cheese slices and crabmeat. Lay the remaining slices of bread on top of the crabmeat.

3 Beat together the eggs, milk, salt and pepper and pour over all. Refrigerate overnight or for at least 8 hours.

4 Before serving bake for 1 hour.

YIELD: 6 SERVINGS

Spinach Terrine with Tomato Coulis

 Here is a recipe that is healthy and light—with the pleasant contrast of the speckled green terrine and the vivid tomato coulis.

1 pound fresh or frozen
   spinach, chopped
4 eggs, beaten until light
1/2 cup heavy cream
1/3 cup Cheddar cheese, grated
1 sprig basil, chopped
salt to taste

pepper to taste
1 pound tomatoes, peeled,
   seeded, and diced
1 small onion, sliced
2 tablespoons olive oil
vinaigrette dressing

1 Prepare the terrine a day ahead. Preheat oven to 425°. Coat individual 4- or 6-ounce soufflé dishes with vegetable spray. Set dishes in baking pan of water so water comes two-thirds of the way up sides of dishes.

2 Combine spinach, eggs, cream, Cheddar cheese, basil, and small amount of salt and pepper. Divide mixture among dishes and bake 30 minutes, or until set. Cool overnight. Refrigerate.

3 Next day, prepare the tomato sauce. Sauté onion slices in olive oil until

soft. Add tomatoes and simmer gently, 10 minutes. Pour into a serving dish and chill.

4 Just before serving, spread tomato coulis on individual serving plates and turn out molds onto the sauce. Serve with vinaigrette dressing.

YIELD: 4 MAIN-DISH SERVINGS, 6 APPETIZER SERVINGS

CROQUETTES AND FRITTERS

Chestnut Croquettes

2 cups hot mashed chestnuts
4 tablespoons butter or
  margarine
2 eggs, lightly beaten
salt to taste

pepper to taste
2 tablespoons minced onion
1/4 cup breadcrumbs
1 egg, beaten
cooking oil

1 Combine the chestnuts, butter, 2 eggs, seasonings, and onion. Shape into croquettes.

2 Spread breadcrumbs on waxed paper. Roll croquettes in crumbs, then in beaten egg, and again in crumbs.

3 Fry in deep fat at 375° to 390° until crumbs are brown—2 to 5 minutes.

YIELD: 6 SERVINGS

Hominy Croquettes

1 cup hominy grits
6 cups salted water
2 eggs, beaten

2 tablespoons butter or
  margarine
cooking oil
grated cheese

1 Boil grits in water 1 hour.

2 Mix 1 1/2 cups hominy with eggs and butter. Shape into balls.

3 Fry croquettes in deep fat at 375° until lightly browned. Serve with grated cheese.

Ham Fritters

2 cups sifted flour
2 cups boiling water
4 eggs

1½ cups ground cooked ham
¾ tablespoon curry powder
cooking oil

1 Stir the flour into rapidly boiling water and continue to cook, stirring vigorously, until batter leaves sides of pan. Lower heat and beat in eggs, one at a time.

2 Remove from the heat and stir in ham and curry powder.

3 Heat the oil to 390° and drop batter into it by teaspoonfuls. Fry until golden brown, then drain on paper toweling.

4 Serve with Cumberland Sauce (p. 316) or Brown Mushroom Sauce (p. 314).

Quahog Fritters

This dish takes the place of meat on your dinner menu. Delicious with tomato catsup.

1 pint quahogs, finely chopped
    (squeeze out and discard
    blacks)
1 small onion, finely chopped
2 tablespoons olive oil or
    melted shortening
1 small clove garlic, crushed

1 egg, lightly beaten
½ teaspoon baking powder
salt to taste
pepper to taste
½ cup flour
cooking oil

1 Mix all ingredients well, using enough flour to make batter with consistency of whipped cream. Thin if necessary with quahog liquor.

2 Drop batter by tablespoonfuls into piping hot fat in skillet. (Do not use deep fat.) Fry slowly after starting. Serve fritters hot.

YIELD: 2 TO 3 SERVINGS

There is a nice element of surprise in a meat pie that makes it an exciting party dish. Pies are a wonderful convenience, too, for they can be prepared well in advance, leaving you free to devote the hours before dinner to other things. They freeze well, and you can keep one or two on hand for unexpected occasions. Place frozen casserole in preheated oven (400°) and bake. It takes twelve to twenty-four hours to defrost a meat pie, depending on its size.

Since meat pies contain vegetables, sauce, and a fine crust—and, of course, meat—very little else is needed with them. You probably will want to serve a simple salad or a vegetable not used in the pie—green beans, say, or asparagus or tomatoes au gratin—and add a jar of chutney or Brandied Peaches (p. 324) or Tabasco Jelly (p. 324) to the sideboard. French or Italian bread and a suitable wine complete the picture. After this, only a light dessert is needed.

If you don't know exactly when to expect your guests for an informal supper, it's handy to have a Frugal Pie tucked in your oven waiting. For large, informal dinner parties, try two or three meat pies all alike or all different. For a special holiday party, try a Pheasant Pie, a Steak and Kidney Pie, and a Veal and Ham Pie.

Frugal Pie

 Adapted from an old cookbook, this pie is simply delicious.

1 medium onion, diced	freshly ground black pepper to
butter, bacon drippings, or	taste
margarine	Kitchen Bouquet to taste
1¼ pound ground beef	1 cup carrots, carved in olive
1 tablespoon flour	shapes
1 cup beef stock	1 tablespoon butter or
2 teaspoon crumbled dried	margarine
thyme	1 cup sliced mushrooms
1 bay leaf, crumbled	2 cups mashed potatoes
salt to taste	milk for glaze

1 Preheat oven to 400°.

2 In a saucepan or skillet, brown onion gently in fat. Remove the onion and brown meat in the same pan. Add flour, stock, herbs, and seasonings and stir to make a nice gravy.

3 Cook the carrots in salted water until just tender.

4 Melt butter in a skillet and sauté mushrooms.

5 In 1½-quart soufflé dish, combine sautéed onion, meat, carrots, mushrooms, and gravy. Stir together. Cover with mashed potatoes and glaze top by brushing with milk.

6 Place pie in oven and bake until browned and bubbling hot, 15 to 20 minutes.

YIELD: 4 SERVINGS

VARIATION – Shepherd's Pie

Shepherd's Pie is made the same way as Frugal Pie, except that ground lamb is used instead of ground beef. Instead of beef stock, use chicken stock; instead of thyme, use rosemary. Shepherd's Pie is delicious too!

Pheasant Pie

 Cook this pie in a shallow dish because everyone will want a chunky piece of the crust.

2 pheasants (4 pounds each)	4 tablespoons butter or
1 carrot, sliced	margarine
1 onion, sliced	1 pound mushrooms, sliced
1 stalk celery, sliced	about 1 tablespoon cornstarch
1 bay leaf	¼ cup sherry
salt to taste	Basic Pie Crust (p. 352)
6 peppercorns	1 egg
8 medium potatoes	1 tablespoon milk

1 Cut up the pheasants and place in a kettle with carrot, onion, celery, bay leaf, salt, and peppercorns. Add water to cover and parboil 30 minutes. Remove, reserving broth. Discard the skin and bones and cut meat into chunks.

2 Peel, clean, and quarter the potatoes and set aside. Melt the butter in a skillet and sauté mushrooms briefly. Set aside.

3 Preheat oven to 350°.

4 Strain the pheasant stock and reduce by half (to make about 2½ cups). Thicken with cornstarch to medium-thick consistency. Add sherry and season to taste.

5 Arrange the pheasant meat, uncooked potatoes, and mushrooms in a shallow gratin dish (about 8 inches round or 7" x 10" oblong). Pour the sauce over the dish.

6 Roll out crust to cover the pie. Slit crust, and trim it with pastry cutouts if desired. Combine egg and milk to make egg wash, and brush over the crust.

7 Bake pie 1 hour. (Potatoes will be cooked through, absorbing and thickening the sauce.) The tastes are simply delicious.

YIELD: 8 SERVINGS

New England Chicken and Oyster Pie

 A dish native to Boston that has much merit. It is a bit unusual and very, very good.

3 cups cooked chicken, cut into
   large chunks
2 cups oysters
2 tablespoons butter or
   margarine
1 teaspoon salt

white pepper to taste
2 cups Cream Sauce II (p. 315)
Basic Pie Crust (p. 352) or
   Watercress Pie Crust
   (p. 58)

1 Preheat oven to 400°. Butter or coat with vegetable spray a 1½-quart soufflé dish.

2 Combine the chicken and oysters in the prepared soufflé dish. Dot with butter, sprinkle with salt and pepper, and pour cream sauce over all.

3 Cover the dish with pie crust. Slit the crust to allow steam to escape.

4 Bake 35 minutes.

YIELD: 6 SERVINGS

Steak and Kidney Pie

1/2 pound mushrooms, coarsely
    sliced

4 tablespoons butter or
    margarine

2 1/2 pounds lean beef (top
    round or sirloin tip), cubed

1 pound veal kidneys, cut up

1/2 cup flour, seasoned with salt
    and pepper

8 ounces red wine

3/4 pound carrots, peeled and
    cut in large pieces

2 packages (10 ounces each)
    frozen small onions

salt to taste

pepper to taste

1 clove garlic, crushed

chopped fresh parsley or other
    fresh or dried herbs

Watercress Pie Crust (p. 58)

1 egg

1 tablespoon milk

1 Sauté mushrooms briefly in 1 tablespoon butter. Set aside.

2 Dredge the beef and kidneys in seasoned flour and brown in a skillet
with remaining butter. When meats are brown, add wine, cover skillet,
and cook over very low heat until tender, about 30 minutes.

3 While meat is cooking, boil carrots and onions (frozen onions are very
good and save time and tears) until barely tender. Reserve the cooking
water and add some to the skillet with meats. Stir to make smooth
sauce. Season with salt, pepper, garlic, and herbs.

4 Combine meat and vegetables in 1 1/2-quart casserole. Cover with pastry. Slit pastry. Combine egg and milk to make egg wash, and brush
over crust. Refrigerate pie if you are not ready to serve it.

5 One hour before serving pie, preheat oven to 350°. Bake pie 50 minutes.

YIELD: 8 SERVINGS

Tourtière

A Canadian recipe for pork pie. Tasty warmed over, too.

1 onion, chopped

1 tablespoon butter or
    margarine

1 pound ground pork

1/2 teaspoon ground cinnamon

1/2 teaspoon ground cloves

salt to taste

pepper to taste

3 medium potatoes, boiled and
    finely chopped

1/2 cup leftover gravy

Basic Pie Crust (p. 352)

1 Preheat oven to 425°.

2 Sauté onions in butter, then add meat and stir until browned. Add seasonings. Add potatoes and gravy.

3 Line 8-inch pie pan with crust. Spread meat mixture over crust. Top with second crust.

4 Bake until brown, about 20 minutes.

YIELD: 4 SERVINGS

Veal and Ham Pie

2 tablespoons flour

salt to taste

black pepper to taste

cayenne pepper to taste

2½ pounds lean veal, cubed

2 tablespoons butter or
   margarine

1 cup beef stock

1 leek, thoroughly cleaned and
   sliced

1½ pounds lean ham, cubed

12 artichoke hearts, canned or
   frozen

grated rind of 1 lemon

chopped fresh herbs, as
   available and to taste

1 sheet filo pastry

1 Mix flour and seasonings and dredge veal in mixture. In large skillet, brown veal in butter. Add beef stock and leeks, cover skillet, and cook over very low heat until meat and leeks are tender.

2 Fill a 2-quart casserole with veal and leeks alternately with ham and artichokes, mixing in grated lemon rind and herbs as you go. Cover with pastry and decorate crust with pastry cutouts. Slash crust well. Refrigerate pie if you are not ready to serve it.

3 One hour before you are ready to serve pie, preheat oven to 350° and bake pie 50 minutes.

YIELD: 10 SERVINGS

Veal and Sweetbread Pie

2 pair sweetbreads

3 pounds cubed veal (breast or leg)

2 tablespoons butter or margarine

2 tablespoons vegetable oil

1 pound mushrooms, cleaned and quartered

6 cups veal or chicken stock

1/2 cup dry vermouth

1 cup heavy cream

1 tablespoon arrowroot

3 tablespoons tarragon leaves

2 bunches baby carrots, peeled and parboiled

2 packages frozen pearl onions, defrosted

1 sheet puff pastry

1 egg, beaten

1 Soak sweetbreads overnight. Blanch and weight down for 12 hours. Remove membrane from sweetbreads and cut into 2-inch cubes.

2 Preheat oven to 375°.

3 Sauté cubed veal in butter until well browned, then quickly sauté sweetbreads. Sauté mushrooms in same pan.

4 Pour off fat and add stock and vermouth. Cook over high heat until reduced by one-third.

5 Mix heavy cream with arrowroot and add to reduced sauce. Boil over high heat 5 minutes more. Add tarragon.

6 Combine all ingredients, including carrots and onions, and place in shallow gratin dish (about 8 inches round or 7″ x 10″ oblong). Lay puff pastry on top. Decorate and brush with beaten egg.

7 Bake 25 to 30 minutes, until pastry is well browned and cooked through.

YIELD: 10 SERVINGS

PÂTÉS

Country Pâté

This recipe contains only lean ingredients. It makes an excellent luncheon dish when sliced thickly and served over lettuce leaves or other dressed greens. A small slice is pleasant as a first course. Serve with Dijon-style mustard and gherkins.

2 pounds ground veal

1/2 cup chopped sweet onion

1 clove garlic, minced

4 slices whole wheat bread, crumbled

4 large eggs

1/3 cup tomato juice

2 teaspoons salt

1/2 teaspoon cayenne pepper

1 teaspoon dried tarragon or fresh sprigs

1/2 teaspoon dried rosemary or fresh sprigs

1/2 teaspoon dried oregano or fresh sprigs

3/4 pound calves' liver, thinly sliced and cut into strips

1 Preheat oven to 350°.

2 In large bowl, combine all ingredients except calves' liver and mix well.

3 Place layer of veal mixture in loaf pan and arrange half of calves' liver evenly over it. Cover with another layer of veal mixture, then add remaining calves' liver and finish with layer of remaining veal mixture.

4 Put loaf pan in larger baking pan in 1 inch of water and bake about 1 hour.

5 Drain off any juices and chill.

YIELD: 1 LOAF (2 1/2 POUNDS)

Jellied Chicken Pâté

 Prepared ahead of time and chilled, this pâté makes an excellent luncheon or buffet dish when sliced thickly and served on lettuce leaves or other greens. A small slice is pleasant as a first course, or the pâté may be used in sandwiches. Serve it with Dijon-style mustard.

1 whole chicken breast

about 2 1/2 cups water

2 teaspoons salt

6 to 8 white peppercorns

1 bay leaf

1 slice onion

half a lemon, sliced

1 1/2 pounds ground veal

3/4 teaspoon fresh tarragon leaves

1/2 teaspoon ground coriander

1/2 cup almonds, slivered (or pistachio nuts)

2 eggs

2 slices white bread, crumbled

1 cup chicken stock

1 envelope unflavored gelatine

1 Place chicken breast in water with salt, peppercorns, bay leaf, onion, and lemon. Cook over low heat 20 to 30 minutes, or until done.

2 Cool chicken, then remove skin and bones, reserving stock. Separate chicken into several pieces.

3 Preheat oven to 350°.

4 In large bowl, combine veal, salt, tarragon, coriander, almonds, eggs, and bread. Mix well.

5 Place layer of pâté in a glass loaf pan and arrange chicken pieces evenly over it. Fill pan with remaining pâté mixture. Put loaf pan in larger baking pan in 1 inch of water.

6 Bake covered 15 minutes, then uncover and bake 25 to 35 minutes more, until done.

7 Remove from oven and cool with weight (a brick or smaller weighted pan) on top of loaf. Chill.

8 Remove loaf from pan. Scrape off any fat, wash loaf pan, and fill with 1 cup chicken stock mixed with gelatine. (If desired, arrange herbs in ornamental design in gelatine.) Return loaf to pan and refrigerate until gelatine has set.

9 Unmold and serve.

YIELD: 1 LOAF

Tête à Fromage

 This old recipe for head cheese makes an unbeatable spread for sandwiches or crackers.

4 pounds fresh pork (allow for bones and leave fat in meat)	1 tablespoon ground mace
4 large onions, chopped	1/2 teaspoon (no more) ground cloves
salt to taste	chopped fresh parsley
pepper to taste	

1 Boil pork, onions, salt, and pepper slowly 3 to 4 hours, until meat falls from bones. (Meat will cook more quickly if cut into small pieces. Be sure to cook bones with meat because they produce the jelly that solidifies mixture.)

2 Add mace, cloves, parsley, and more salt and pepper if needed.

3 Remove bones, skim pot, and cool.

4 Store head cheese in crocks in refrigerator.

YIELD: ABOUT 1 POUND

3

Afternoon Tea

The pleasant custom of tea breaks up a long afternoon and gives us a nudge toward the rest of the day. It's bracing as a winter day ends, soothing at the peak of a summer afternoon. The very aroma of tea is a joy, and so many delicate blends are available that it's good to keep four or five types on hand and vary them to suit the moment.

As I scan my cupboard, I can spot Oolong (whose taste faintly suggests peaches), Jasmine (light, and loved by the Chinese), Lapsang Soochong (haunting and smoky), Orange Pekoe (very well known indeed, but excellent), and the wonderful, bracing Earl Grey.

Good tea is not difficult to prepare. Bring fresh cold water to a rapid, rolling boil (the better the water, the better the tea; pure spring water is ideal). Rinse a porcelain or earthenware teapot with boiling water, then dry it thoroughly. Spoon in the tea leaves, five teaspoons per quart of water, and allow to steep for a few minutes, and pour. Place extra boiling water on the tea tray to refresh the pot when the tea becomes too strong.

A hot cup of tea alone at four is strengthening; tea for two has made history; and middling or large tea parties can be just as much fun as cocktail parties. Men love them. (In Boston, some hosts add a bit of rum to the tea.) It seems to me a time for restful, subtle flavors, with small bits of food that are rich but subdued. The foods you serve should always complement the beverage.

First choice for an accompaniment is thinly sliced bread—white, orange, nut, or oatmeal—the finest you can make or buy. Spread with fresh, sweet butter or cream cheese and sprinkle, if you like, with herbs.

A glorious teatime indulgence is hot buttered toast with a pot of special jam—perhaps blueberry, pale green kiwi, or apricot. Cinnamon toast is a natural with tea, and it is easy to make quickly if you keep on hand a jar of cinnamon-and-sugar (go heavy on the cinnamon and light on the sugar). Spread the toast with butter and sprinkle with the mixture. Serve meltingly hot.

Thin sandwiches are fast to make, neat to serve, and easy to eat. You can prepare them three or four hours ahead of time—no longer, or they may become tired. Use melba-thin bread and butter it carefully. The butter will harden when the sandwiches are chilled, acting as a coating to prevent the bread from becoming soggy. Fill the sandwiches generously and trim off the crusts with a sharp knife. Cover the sandwiches and store in the refrigerator until needed. Then cut them into small fingers, squares, or triangles and arrange them on plates, garnish and serve.

Here are some suggestions for fillings for tea sandwiches:

- Cucumber slices
- Chopped watercress
- Guava jelly and cream cheese
- Toasted almonds with a little cream cheese
- Smoked salmon with whipped cream cheese
- Orange or ginger marmalade with cream cheese

- Butter processed with walnuts, pecans, or filberts
- Sliced mushrooms with a little Dijon mustard
- Chicken salad
- Tomato slices
- Pâté de foie gras and lettuce

TEA BREADS

Lemon Bread

6 tablespoons butter or margarine
1 1/2 cups granulated sugar
2 eggs
1 1/4 cups pastry flour
1/2 teaspoon salt

1/2 cup milk
grated rind and juice of 1 lemon
1/2 cup chopped maraschino cherries
1/2 cup chopped walnuts

1 Preheat oven to 350°. Coat loaf pan with vegetable spray.

2 Cream together the butter and 1 cup of the sugar and beat in eggs. Set aside. Sift together the flour, baking powder, and salt. Set aside.

3 To butter/sugar mixture add sifted ingredients alternately with milk. Add grated lemon rind, cherries, and walnuts.

4 Bake approximately 1 hour, or until toothpick inserted in center comes out clean.

5 Combine lemon juice and remaining 1/2 cup sugar and pour over baked loaf. Let stand 10 minutes before serving.

Orange Nut Bread

 Pistachio nuts make a particularly attractive pretty slice. Serve with sweet butter or cream cheese.

2 cups flour

1 teaspoon baking soda

3/4 teaspoon salt

1/2 cup granulated sugar

1 egg, beaten

3/4 cup strained orange juice

2 tablespoons lemon juice

1 teaspoon grated orange rind

1/4 teaspoon grated lemon rind

1/2 cup melted butter

1/2 cup sliced pistachio nuts

1 Preheat oven to 350°. Coat loaf pan with vegetable spray.

2 Sift together the flour, baking soda, salt, and sugar. Add egg, then juices and rinds. Blend well. Add melted butter and nuts and mix well.

3 Pour into prepared pan and let stand on counter 20 minutes. Then bake 1 hour. Bread is done when toothpick inserted into center comes out clean.

Pumpkin Walnut Bread

 4 1/2 cups flour

2 tablespoons baking powder

1 teaspoon ground cinnamon

1/2 teaspoon mace

1/2 teaspoon salt

1 1/2 cups light brown sugar

1/2 cup melted butter

1 1/2 cups puréed pumpkin
   (fresh or canned)

3 eggs, lightly beaten

1 cup milk

2 cups chopped walnuts

1 Preheat oven to 350°. Coat 2 loaf pans with vegetable spray.

2 Sift together the flour, baking powder, cinnamon, mace, and salt.

3 Combine brown sugar and melted butter. Add pumpkin and beaten eggs. Add dry ingredients alternately with milk to pumpkin mixture, mixing well after each addition. Stir in walnuts.

4 Pour into the loaf pans and bake about 1 hour. Bread is done when toothpick inserted into center comes out clean.

This recipe was passed down through six generations to Dorothy Hale Wires of Rockport, Massachusetts, who wrote that during the War of 1812, "the little settlement of Sandy Bay, now Rockport, was in constant fear of attack from marauding British privateers then prowling Cape Ann waters. In the early days of the war, many families planned escape through the woods to the larger settlement in Gloucester, some five miles away, which provided better protection. My great aunt, Lucy Hale Knutsford, known to all as 'Aunt Lute,' used to tell me many stories that, in turn, had been told her by her mother, Betsy Tarr Hale, who, having been born in 1800, thus was twelve years old at the time of the war. During the anxious days when fears of raids were uppermost in the minds of Sandy Bay residents, Betsy's mother used to keep ever in readiness clothing and food so that her family could quickly leave their home to follow woodland paths to the Gloucester settlement. Every morning she baked a fresh gingerbread for food along the way, should it be necessary to go. Aunt Lute always cherished this recipe and our family has enjoyed it for six generations. This is it, just as given me by Aunt Lute.

Take $1/2$ cup sugar, $1/2$ cup molasses, $1/2$ cup melted shortening, 1 egg, $1/2$ teaspoon cinnamon, $1/2$ teaspoon ginger. To this add alternately 1 cup flour to which has been added 1 teaspoon soda and $1/2$ teaspoon salt, and 1 cup boiling water. More flour should be added, if necessary, to make a fairly stiff batter. Then lastly add $1/2$ teaspoon vinegar. Bake in moderate oven until a straw comes out clean, or until it doesn't sizzle on holding the pan to the ear (325° for about 35 minutes).

Victorian Gingerbread

2 eggs
1 cup sour milk
1 cup dark molasses
1 cup brown sugar
2 cups flour
2 teaspoons baking soda
2 teaspoons ginger

1 teaspoon ground cinnamon
$1/2$ teaspoon allspice
$1/2$ teaspoon salt
1 cup finely chopped candied ginger
$3/4$ cup melted butter or margarine

1 Preheat the oven to 350°. Coat 9″ x 12″ Teflon cake pan with vegetable spray.

2 Beat eggs well and add sour milk, molasses, and brown sugar.

3 Sift together the flour, baking soda, spices, and salt. Stir into molasses mixture. Stir in candied ginger. Add melted butter and beat until well blended.

4 Fill the cake pan three-fourths full and bake 20 to 25 minutes. Reduce heat to 300° and continue baking until a toothpick inserted into center of gingerbread comes out clean.

Winchester Nut Bread

 Wonderful on a winter day.

½ cup light brown sugar	2½ teaspoons baking powder
¾ cup water	1 teaspoon baking soda
½ cup dark molasses	2 cups whole-wheat or bran
¾ cup milk	flour
1 cup bread flour	¾ cup chopped nuts (walnuts,
1½ teaspoons salt	pecans, or hazelnuts)

1 Preheat oven to 275°. Coat loaf pan with vegetable spray.

2 Dissolve the brown sugar in water and add molasses and milk.

3 Sift together the bread flour, salt, baking powder, and baking soda. Add whole-wheat flour unsifted. Mix together well and stir in nuts.

4 Bake 2 hours.

YIELD: 1 LOAF

COOKIES

If you are in the habit of buying cookies or cakes, you will be pleasantly surprised by the enormous savings—as well as the fun and variety of choice—that result from baking at home. Children love to be included in the ritual, and it's a wonderful way for them to pass an afternoon.

For quick, happy cookie-making, buy three Teflon cookie sheets, which will have many other uses. Just for good measure, spray each sheet before starting a batch so cookies will slide off easily with a nonmetallic spatula. Wipe sheets with paper towels and rotate them so you don't use the same one all the time. (Teflon cake pans also are happily stick-proof.)

The yield of cookies from these recipes may vary according to the size of the cookie you bake.

Applesauce Cookies

1/2 cup butter or margarine
1 cup granulated sugar
1 egg
1/2 cup thick applesauce
1 3/4 cups sifted flour
1/4 teaspoon salt

1 teaspoon baking powder
1/2 teaspoon baking soda
1/2 cup raisins
1 tablespoon grated orange
  rind

1 Preheat oven to 350°. Coat 2 cookie sheets with vegetable spray.

2 Cream the butter and add sugar gradually, beating until light and fluffy. Add egg and beat. Stir in applesauce.

3 Sift together the flour, salt, baking powder, and baking soda. Add raisins and orange rind.

4 Combine creamed butter mixture and dry ingredients and blend well. Drop by teaspoonfuls, 2 inches apart, on 2 cookie sheets.

5 Bake 15 minutes.

YIELD: ABOUT 3 DOZEN COOKIES

Apricot Buttons

1/2 cup butter or margarine
1 egg yolk
1/3 cup granulated sugar
1 cup flour
1/2 teaspoon vanilla extract
1/4 teaspoon salt

1 egg white, beaten
1/2 cup chopped nuts
  (preferably pecans or
  pistachios)
1 jar (8 ounces) apricot jam

1 Preheat oven to 300°. Coat 2 Teflon cookie sheets with vegetable spray.

2 Combine the butter, egg yolk, sugar, flour, vanilla, and salt to form dough. Shape into 24 small balls.

3 Roll balls first in egg white, then in nuts. Make indentation in each ball

with forefinger. Fill with small amount (about $1/8$ teaspoon) apricot jam.

4 Bake 25 minutes.

YIELD: ABOUT 2 DOZEN COOKIES

Beacon Hill Cookies

 These crunchy chocolate meringues make delicious snacks with milk or tea.

$1/8$ teaspoon salt
2 egg whites
$1/2$ cup granulated sugar
$1/2$ teaspoon white vinegar
$1/2$ teaspoon vanilla extract

$1/2$ cup sweetened shredded coconut
$1/4$ cup chopped walnuts
6 ounces semisweet chocolate chips, melted

1 Preheat oven to 350°. Coat 2 cookie sheets with vegetable spray.

2 Add the salt to egg whites and beat until foamy. Add sugar very gradually, beating well after each addition. Continue beating until stiff peaks form.

3 Add the vinegar and vanilla and beat well. Fold in coconut, chopped nuts, and melted chips.

4 Drop by teaspoonfuls onto cookie sheets. Bake 10 minutes.

YIELD: ABOUT 3 DOZEN COOKIES

Bedford Cookies

 Wickedly rich and almost irresistible to those who like sweets.

$1/2$ pound butter or margarine
1 tablespoon confectioners' sugar
1 teaspoon vanilla extract

2 cups sifted flour
1 cup chopped nuts (preferably English or black walnuts, hazelnuts, pecans)

1 Preheat oven to 350°. Coat 3 cookie sheets with vegetable spray.

2 Cream the butter and gradually add 1 tablespoon confectioners' sugar, plus vanilla and flour. Add nuts and mix well.

3 Shape dough into balls the size of small walnuts. Place on cookie sheets. With fork, press each cookie flat. Bake 10 or 15 minutes.

4 Remove from oven. While cookies are still hot, shake them gently in bag filled with confectioners' sugar.

YIELD: ABOUT 3 DOZEN COOKIES

Brown Sugar Cookies

 This recipe comes from a descendant of Massachusetts Governor Simon Bradstreet. These cookies always come out plump and golden, regardless of the type of stove used.

1 cup shortening	$1/2$ teaspoon baking soda
1 cup firmly packed brown sugar	$1/2$ teaspoon salt
	2 teaspoons baking powder
1 egg, beaten	$1/2$ teaspoon ground nutmeg
$1/2$ cup seedless raisins	$1/2$ cup sour cream
2 cups sifted flour	$1/2$ cup chopped nuts

1 Preheat oven to 400°. Coat 2 cookie sheets with vegetable spray.

2 Cream together the shortening and brown sugar. Add beaten egg and raisins.

3 Mix and sift the remaining dry ingredients and add alternately with sour cream to brown sugar mixture. Add nuts and mix well.

4 Drop by teaspoonfuls onto cookie sheets. Bake 12 to 15 minutes.

YIELD: ABOUT 3 DOZEN COOKIES

Butter Cookies

1 cup butter	$1/4$ teaspoon almond extract
1 cup granulated sugar	2 cups flour
2 eggs, well beaten	$1/4$ teaspoon salt
1 teaspoon vanilla extract	

1 Preheat oven to 350°. Coat 2 cookie sheets with vegetable spray.

2 Cream butter until light and gradually add sugar. Beat in eggs and extracts. Add flour and salt, a little at a time, to make a stiff dough.

3 Chill for several hours. Roll dough to $1/8$-inch thickness and cut out cookies. (This dough is good for fancy-shaped cookie cutters.)

4 If you wish, decorate cookies with pieces of candied fruit or nuts.

5 Bake until lightly browned, about 10 minutes.

YIELD: ABOUT 3 DOZEN COOKIES

Butterscotch Cookies

1 cup butter or margarine
2 cups light brown sugar
2 eggs, lightly beaten
2 cups flour

1 teaspoon cream of tartar
1 teaspoon salt
1 cup chopped, pitted dates
1 cup chopped walnuts

1 Preheat oven to 350°. Coat 3 cookie sheets with vegetable spray.

2 Cream together the butter and brown sugar. Beat in eggs. Sift together the flour, cream of tartar, and salt and add to brown sugar mixture.

3 Drop by teaspoonfuls onto cookie sheets.

4 Bake 3 or 4 minutes. Do not let cookies get too brown.

YIELD: ABOUT 3 DOZEN COOKIES

Caraway (Also Filled or Jumble) Cookies

A basic cookie recipe. Rolled thin with generous amounts of caraway (or chopped nuts or finely shredded coconut), this dough makes a crisp delicacy with an old-fashioned flavor. When it is rolled less thinly, with chopped raisins or dates, the cookie is moister. When cut into rounds (with a doughnut-shaped round on top), the dough makes old-fashioned "jumbles," which are topped with tart jelly. The same dough also may be used for cookies filled with mincemeat or raisins.

1 cup granulated sugar
1/2 cup shortening
3/4 cup sour milk
1 teaspoon baking soda
2 cups all-purpose flour

1/2 teaspoon vanilla extract (use lemon extract for jumbles)
caraway seeds, raisins, nuts, to taste

1 Preheat oven to 350°. Coat 2 cookie sheets with vegetable spray.

2 Combine all ingredients and mix well. Roll out onto floured surface.

3 Cut out cookies as desired and place on cookie sheets. Bake 10 to 15 minutes, depending on thickness of cookies.

YIELD: ABOUT 3 DOZEN COOKIES

Chocolate Lace Cookies

 This recipe comes from the Women's Industrial Union in Boston—and it's tops as far as I'm concerned. The cookies are rich, lace-thin, and a bit chewy.

¹/₂ cup (1 stick) butter or margarine	¹/₂ cup flour
2 squares unsweetened chocolate	¹/₂ teaspoon baking powder
	¹/₄ teaspoon salt
1 egg, lightly beaten	1¹/₂ cups granulated sugar
	¹/₂ teaspoon vanilla extract

1 Preheat oven to 325°. Coat 3 Teflon cookie sheets with vegetable spray.

2 Melt the butter and chocolate in top of double boiler. Remove from heat and add egg.

3 Sift together dry ingredients and add to chocolate mixture. Mix thoroughly.

4 Drop by scant teaspoonfuls onto the cookie sheets. (Finished cookies will be 3 to 4 inches in diameter, so space them accordingly.)

5 Bake about 12 minutes, watching carefully. Allow to become nearly completely cool before removing with spatula.

YIELD: ABOUT 2 DOZEN COOKIES

Chocolate Mint Cookies

1 cup butter or margarine	¹/₂ teaspoon vanilla extract
2 cups granulated sugar	36 chocolate-covered thin mints
3 eggs, well beaten	
1 cup sifted flour	36 pecan halves
¹/₄ teaspoon baking soda dissolved in 3 tablespoons hot water	

1 Preheat oven to 425°. Coat 2 cookie sheets with vegetable spray.

2 Cream together the butter and sugar until fluffy. Blend in the beaten eggs and then flour, little by little. Add baking soda and vanilla and blend well.

3 Chill the dough in a covered bowl until firm. Add more sifted flour, but absolutely no more than necessary to obtain consistency that can be rolled out.

4 On floured surface, roll dough to about ⅛-inch thickness and cut into rounds about 3 inches across. In center of half the rounds, place a thin mint. Place another round on top of each and press edges together with fork. Press pecan half into top of each cookie.

5 Bake until lightly browned—about 12 minutes.

YIELD: ABOUT 3 DOZEN COOKIES

Filled Cookies

 Jane Goyer of West Boylston, Massachusetts, contributed this recipe handed down from her grandmother, Malina Goodney. She calls them "Old-Fashioned Honeymoon Cookies"; her grandmother called them "Big Surprises." No matter what the name, they have long been popular with New England's children—a moist, rich treat with a glass of cold milk.

Filling

½ pound round, plump fresh raisins

1 cup nut meats (black walnuts if possible)

1 large, juicy apple (a Baldwin is best)

1 tablespoon firmly packed dark brown sugar

1 tablespoon fresh lemon juice

1 teaspoon ground cinnamon

½ teaspoon ground nutmeg

Dough

¼ cup butter or margarine, softened

½ cup granulated sugar

1 large egg, beaten

2 cups all-purpose flour

2 teaspoons baking powder

pinch of salt

Icing

½ cup confectioners' sugar

1 tablespoon heavy cream

1 Prepare the filling first. Put raisins, nuts, and cored apple through food grinder. Add the brown sugar, lemon juice, and spices and mix well.

2 Preheat oven to 350°. Coat 2 cookie sheets with vegetable spray.

3 Next make the dough. Beat together the butter, granulated sugar, and egg until creamy. Add flour sifted with baking powder and salt.

4 Combine 2 mixtures and blend well. Divide dough in half. Roll out thinly on a floured surface, using additional flour if necessary to prevent sticking.

5 Using glass tumbler whose rim has been floured, cut dough into rounds. On each round, place 1 teaspoon filling.

6 Roll out remaining half of dough and cut into rounds. Place 1 round over each filling-topped cookie and press down firmly around edges. Seal edges with fork and prick top of each cookie.

7 Bake about 15 minutes, or until pale brown. Remove from oven and allow to cool before adding icing.

8 Prepare icing by blending confectioners' sugar and cream until thin and creamy. Brush mixture onto top of each cookie.

YIELD: ABOUT 3 DOZEN COOKIES

Gingersnaps

3/4 cup (1 1/2 sticks) butter or margarine	1 tablespoon ground ginger
1 cup granulated sugar	1 teaspoon ground cinnamon
1 egg	1/2 teaspoon salt
1/4 cup dark molasses	2 teaspoons baking soda
	2 1/2 cups flour

1 Preheat oven to 350°. Coat 3 Teflon cookie sheets with vegetable spray.

2 Cream butter and gradually add sugar. Beat until light. Beat in the egg and molasses.

3 Sift together dry ingredients and beat little by little into sugar mixture.

4 Shape into small balls, roll in more granulated sugar, and place about 2 inches apart on cookie sheets. Cover with a damp towel and flatten each cookie with the bottom of a jar or glass.

5 Bake 10 to 12 minutes.

YIELD: ABOUT 3 DOZEN COOKIES

Golden Breadcrumb Cookies

 Children love these.

1 egg, lightly beaten
1 cup granulated sugar
1/2 cup shortening
1 teaspoon vanilla extract
1 teaspoon salt
1 1/2 cups toasted breadcrumbs

1/4 cup milk
1/4 cup water
1 cup maraschino cherries,
   finely chopped
1 1/2 cups sifted flour

1 Preheat oven to 375°. Coat 2 cookie sheets with vegetable spray.

2 Mix together the egg, sugar, shortening, and vanilla. Add salt, bread-crumbs, milk, water, and cherries. Little by little, add the flour. Mix well.

3 Drop by teaspoonfuls onto cookie sheets.

4 Bake 12 to 15 minutes.

YIELD: ABOUT 3 DOZEN COOKIES

Health Cookies

 These are crisp, healthful snacks.

1 cup brown sugar
1/4 cup granulated sugar
1/4 cup honey
1 cup shortening
4 egg whites, lightly beaten
1 teaspoon vanilla extract
1/2 cup all-purpose flour

1 teaspoon baking soda
1 teaspoon salt
1/2 cup wheat germ
1 1/4 cups whole-wheat or bran
   flour
2 cups rolled oats

1 Preheat oven to 350°.

2 Cream together the sugars, honey, and shortening. Mix well. Add beaten egg whites and vanilla and mix until fluffy.

3 Sift together the white flour, baking soda, and salt. Add wheat germ and whole-wheat or bran flour. Add dry mixture to creamed mixture, blending well. With a table knife, stir rolled oats into dough.

4 Drop by teaspoonfuls onto 3 ungreased cookie sheets and bake 8 to 10 minutes.

YIELD: ABOUT 4 DOZEN COOKIES

Lacy Oatmeal Cookies

 A classic favorite.

2¼ cups old-fashioned oats

2¼ cups light brown sugar

3 tablespoons flour

½ teaspoon salt

1 egg, beaten

½ pound butter, melted

½ teaspoon vanilla extract

1 Preheat oven to 325°. Coat 3 Teflon cookie sheets with vegetable spray.

2 Combine the oats, brown sugar, flour, and salt. Stir. Beat in egg, then beat in melted butter and vanilla.

3 Drop by teaspoonfuls onto the cookie sheets. Space cookies well apart.

4 Bake 12 minutes. Use spatula to remove from cookie sheets.

YIELD: ABOUT 2 DOZEN COOKIES

Macaroons

 Subtle and delicate.

1 pound almond paste

2 cups confectioners' sugar

4 egg whites

2 teaspoons vanilla extract

1 Preheat oven to 350°. Coat 3 cookie sheets with vegetable spray.

2 Break the almond paste into small pieces and combine with remaining ingredients in a food processor or blender. Chill the mixture.

3 Drop small teaspoonfuls of dough onto cookie sheets. Bake about 20 minutes, until pale golden. Cool on wire rack and store in airtight tin.

YIELD: ABOUT 3 DOZEN COOKIES.

Old-Fashioned Sugar Cookies

½ cup butter or margarine

½ teaspoon salt

grated rind of 1 lemon

1 cup granulated sugar

2 eggs, well beaten

2 tablespoons milk

2 cups sifted flour

1 teaspoon baking powder

½ teaspoon baking soda

½ teaspoon ground nutmeg

1 Preheat oven to 375°. Coat 2 cookie sheets with vegetable spray.

2 Cream the butter. Add salt and lemon rind, then gradually add sugar. Beat in eggs and milk.

3 Sift together the flour, baking powder, baking soda, and nutmeg. Add, little by little, to creamed mixture.

4 Drop by teaspoonfuls onto cookie sheets. Sprinkle each cookie with granulated sugar and bake about 12 minutes.

YIELD: ABOUT 3 DOZEN COOKIES

Petticoat Tails

These "icebox cookies" may be kept in the refrigerator and baked a few at a time as needed.

1 cup butter or margarine,
  softened
1 cup confectioners' sugar
$^1/_4$ teaspoon salt

2$^1/_2$ cups flour
1 teaspoon vanilla extract
1 cup chopped almonds

1 Cream together the butter and confectioners' sugar. Add salt to flour and sift into creamed mixture. Stir and add vanilla and half of the almonds.

2 Shape into a roll about 2 inches in diameter, wrap in waxed paper, and chill.

3 When ready to bake, preheat oven to 400°. Coat 3 cookie sheets with vegetable spray.

4 Slice dough very thinly, cover each cookie with remaining almonds, and bake 8 to 10 minutes.

YIELD: ABOUT 4 DOZEN COOKIES

True Scotch Shortbread

A cookie with excellent keeping properties.

3 cups all-purpose flour
1 cup rice flour
6 tablespoons granulated sugar

$^1/_2$ pound butter or margarine,
  medium soft

1 Preheat oven to 400°. Coat 2 cookie sheets with vegetable spray.

2 Sift together flours and gradually add with sugar to butter. Knead to soft dough.

3 Shape into medium-thick, round cakes the size of a saucer and place on prepared cookie sheets. Prick each cake with a fork and flute edges. (For modern consumption, shortbread may be more useful if cut in cookie-size squares or diamonds or in fancy shapes.)

4 Bake 30 minutes.

YIELD: ABOUT 5 8-INCH ROUNDS

Sister Minnie's Molasses Cookies

 This recipe is from the Shaker Colony in Alfred, Maine, now but a memory. It closed in 1925.

$^1/_2$ cup shortening	$^1/_4$ teaspoon salt
$^1/_2$ cup granulated sugar	1 teaspoon ground ginger
1 egg	1 teaspoon ground cinnamon
$^1/_2$ cup dark molasses	raisins, as desired
$2^1/_4$ cups flour	$^1/_2$ cup warm (not hot) water
2 level teaspoons baking soda	granulated sugar

1 Preheat oven to 375°.

2 Cream together the shortening and sugar until light and fluffy. Add unbeaten egg and molasses and beat well.

3 Sift together the flour, baking soda, salt, and spices. Add a little at a time to creamed mixture, cutting in a few raisins (if desired) at the same time. Add water.

4 Drop by small teaspoonfuls onto 3 ungreased baking sheets. Sprinkle with sugar and place 1 raisin on each cookie.

5 Bake 15 to 20 minutes, or until browned.

YIELD: ABOUT 4 DOZEN COOKIES

Walnut Wafers

1 tablespoon butter or margarine	1 teaspoon vanilla extract
1 cup brown sugar	1/2 cup flour, sifted
2 eggs, well beaten	1 teaspoon baking powder
	1 cup chopped nuts

1 Preheat oven to 350°. Coat 2 cookie sheets with vegetable spray.

2 Cream together butter and brown sugar, then add eggs and vanilla. Sift together flour and baking powder and add to creamed mixture. Stir in nuts.

3 Drop dough by the teaspoonfuls onto cookie sheets at widely spaced intervals and bake 12 minutes.

YIELD: ABOUT 2 DOZEN COOKIES

BROWNIES, BARS, AND SQUARES

Butterscotch Squares

1 cup butter or margarine	2 cups coarsely chopped pecans
2 cups brown sugar	1 teaspoon vanilla extract
2 eggs, beaten	pinch of salt
1 1/2 cups all-purpose flour	
2 teaspoons baking powder	

1 Preheat oven to 350°. Coat a cookie sheet with vegetable spray.

2 In a small pan, heat butter and brown sugar until sugar is dissolved. Cool.

3 Add the eggs, blend well, and sift in combined flour and baking powder. Mix well and add remaining ingredients.

4 Spread dough on cookie sheet. Bake about 15 minutes. Cut in squares.

YIELD: ABOUT 2 DOZEN 2-INCH SQUARES

Date Bars

 This is my mother's recipe, and I still consider these date bars the most delicious small cakes for tea, for picnic boxes, or to serve with fruit or ice cream. (For a different bar, substitute chocolate chips for dates.)

3 eggs, separated	1 teaspoon vanilla extract
1 cup granulated sugar	1 cup flour
1 cup chopped nuts	1 teaspoon baking powder
1 package pitted dates, chopped	$1/2$ teaspoon salt
	confectioners' sugar
$1/4$ cup sour cream	

1 Preheat oven to 350°. Coat 9″ x 9″ Teflon pan with vegetable spray.

2 Combine the egg yolks and sugar. Add remaining ingredients, except egg whites, and beat well. Beat egg whites until stiff and fold into batter. Spread in prepared pan.

3 Bake 30 minutes. Cut while warm into bars and roll in confectioners' sugar.

YIELD: ABOUT 1 DOZEN BARS

Fudgy Brownies

4 squares unsweetened chocolate	2 eggs, beaten
6 ounces ($1^{1}/2$ sticks) butter or margarine	1 cup sifted flour
	$1/2$ cup coarsely chopped nuts
2 cups granulated sugar	1 teaspoon vanilla extract
	$1/2$ teaspoon salt

1 Preheat oven to 325°. Coat the bottom of a 9″ x 9″ Teflon pan with vegetable spray.

2 Melt the chocolate and butter together in top of double boiler. Cool slightly.

3 Gradually add the sugar to eggs, beating thoroughly. Stir in flour, then add nuts, vanilla, and salt. Spread in prepared pan.

4 Bake about 40 minutes. Cool in pan, then cut into squares.

YIELD: ABOUT 4 DOZEN BROWNIES

VARIATION – Chocolate Peppermint Brownies

Bake brownies as above, then arrange 9 to 16 chocolate peppermint patties over hot brownies. Place in oven about 3 minutes to soften. Remove from oven and spread chocolate to cover entire surface of brownies. Cool and cut.

Fruit Brownies

 These brownies are fudgy, gooey, and delicious.

3 tablespoons powdered cocoa	5 egg whites
1 tablespoon instant coffee crystals	1 teaspoon vanilla extract
	1 cup oat-bran flour
1 ripe banana	1/4 teaspoon salt
1 ripe pear or 1/2 ripe cantaloupe	1/2 cup chopped nuts
	1/2 cup golden raisins
2 cups granulated sugar, less if you prefer	

1 Preheat oven to 350°. Coat the bottom of a 9" x 9" Teflon pan with vegetable spray.

2 Combine the cocoa, coffee, and fruit and mix well in blender or by hand. Add sugar, egg whites, and vanilla and mix well. Beat in oat-bran flour and salt. Fold in nuts and raisins.

3 Pour into the prepared pan and bake 45 minutes. Cool and cut.

YIELD: ABOUT 3 DOZEN BROWNIES

Indians

1/2 cup butter or margarine	3 eggs, beaten
2 squares chocolate, melted	1 cup chopped walnuts
1/3 cup bread flour	1 teaspoon vanilla extract
1/2 teaspoon baking powder	1/2 cup chopped dates
1/2 teaspoon salt	(optional)
1 cup granulated sugar	

1 Preheat oven to 350°. Coat 8-inch-square pan with vegetable spray.

2 Add the butter to chocolate and melt in double boiler. Let cool.

3 Sift flour, baking powder, and salt. Slowly add sugar to beaten eggs. Then add flour mixture, chopped nuts, vanilla, and chocolate mixture. Add chopped dates if desired.

4 Spread in prepared pan and bake 25 to 30 minutes. Cut while warm.

YIELD: 16 SQUARES

Lemon Squares

 These are easy to make and extremely good.

1 stick butter or margarine, softened	1 teaspoon baking powder
	dash of salt
1/2 cup plus 2 tablespoons confectioners' sugar	2 eggs, beaten
	juice and rind of 2 lemons
1 cup plus 2 tablespoons flour	confectioners' sugar
1 cup granulated sugar	

1 Preheat oven to 350°. Coat a 9-inch-square Teflon pan with vegetable spray.

2 Cream together the butter and 1/2 cup confectioners' sugar. Knead in 1 cup flour.

3 Press dough into prepared pan and bake about 20 minutes. Remove from oven.

4 While dough is baking, sift together 2 tablespoons flour, granulated sugar, baking powder, and salt and add mixture to beaten eggs. Stir in the lemon juice and rind.

5 Spread lemon/flour mixture over baked dough in pan and bake another 20 minutes.

6 Remove the pan from the oven and sprinkle top with confectioners' sugar. Allow to cool until just warm. Cut into squares but do not remove from the pan until ready to serve.

YIELD: 16 LARGE OR 24 SMALL SQUARES

Anytime Cake

 A useful cake for breakfast, tea, or "anytime."

1/3 cup nuts, finely chopped	1 1/2 teaspoons vanilla extract
1 1/2 teaspoons ground cinnamon	2 1/2 cups sifted flour
1/3 cup plus 1 cup granulated sugar	1/2 teaspoon baking powder
	1 teaspoon baking soda
1 cup shortening	1/4 teaspoon salt
3 eggs, beaten	1 cup sour cream

1 Mix together chopped nuts, cinnamon, and 1/3 cup sugar and set aside.

2 Preheat oven to 350°. Coat a large tube cake pan with vegetable spray.

3 Cream the shortening and 1 cup sugar. Add eggs and beat until fluffy. Add vanilla.

4 Sift together the dry ingredients. Add the dry ingredients alternately with the sour cream to the sugar mixture.

5 Spoon one-third of batter into a tube pan and sprinkle one-third of the nut mixture over it. Spoon second third of batter into pan and sprinkle with a second third of the nuts. Spoon remaining batter into pan.

6 Using table knife, stir contents of pan with circular motion to distribute nut mixture. Sprinkle remaining nut mixture over top.

7 Bake 45 to 50 minutes. No other frosting is necessary or desirable.

Blue Heaven Cake

 The name of this cake comes from its pleasant bluish color.

1/2 cup poppy seeds	3 teaspoons baking powder
1 1/2 cups milk	1/4 teaspoon salt
3/4 cup shortening	1 teaspoon vanilla extract
1 1/2 cups granulated sugar	4 egg whites, beaten to stiff peaks
2 1/2 cups flour	

1 Soak poppy seeds overnight in $^3/_4$ cup milk.

2 Preheat oven to 375°. Coat a 9″ x 13″ pan with vegetable spray.

3 Cream together the shortening and sugar. Sift together the flour, baking powder, and salt.

4 Add $^3/_4$ cup more milk to poppy seeds. Add dry ingredients, vanilla, and milk mixture alternately to creamed mixture, beating well as you do so.

5 Fold the beaten egg whites into batter. Bake 25 minutes, or until a toothpick inserted into the center comes out clean.

Carrot Cake

 This is the best carrot cake I have ever tasted.

1$^1/_2$ cups vegetable oil	2 teaspoons ground cinnamon
2 cups granulated sugar	2 tablespoons baking powder
3 whole eggs and 1 egg white, well beaten	1 cup chopped pecans
2 cups flour	$^1/_2$ cup golden raisins
1 teaspoon salt	3 cups grated carrots

1 Preheat oven to 325°. Coat two 9-inch-square Teflon cake pans with vegetable spray.

2 In a large bowl, mix vegetable oil and sugar and beat well. Add the eggs and blend.

3 Sift together the dry ingredients and add to egg mixture. Add the nuts, raisins, and grated carrots, a small amount at a time, and blend thoroughly.

4 Pour the batter into prepared cake pans and bake 1 hour, or until toothpick inserted into center comes out clean.

5 Turn onto wire rack to cool. When cool, spread Cream-Cheese Frosting (below) between layers and on the top (but not on the sides) of the cake. Finish off with some fancy swirls.

YIELD: 16 OR MORE SERVINGS

Cream-Cheese Frosting

4 ounces (1 stick) butter or margarine	2 cups confectioners' sugar
8 ounces cream cheese	2 teaspoons vanilla extract (or substitute brandy if desired)

1 Allow the butter and cream cheese to reach room temperature. Then cream butter and cream cheese and gradually beat in confectioners' sugar and vanilla (or brandy).

2 Spread between layers and on top of carrot cake.

YIELD: ENOUGH FROSTING FOR TOP AND FILLING FOR 2-LAYER CAKE

Cheese-Filled Chocolate Cake

³/₄ cup shortening	1 cup cottage cheese
3 tablespoons powdered cocoa	1¹/₂ cups flour, sifted
1¹/₂ cups granulated sugar	¹/₂ teaspoon baking powder
3 eggs, well beaten	pinch of salt
1¹/₂ teaspoons vanilla extract	

1 Preheat oven to 350°. Coat an 8-inch-square cake pan with vegetable spray.

2 Cream the shortening and add the cocoa.

3 Add the sugar gradually to beaten eggs, then add chocolate mixture. Add vanilla and cottage cheese and beat 1 minute.

4 Sift together the dry ingredients and add to batter. Blend well.

5 Pour into prepared pan and bake 40 minutes. Cool.

6 Frost with Fluffy Chocolate Frosting (p. 108) or serve warm with lightly whipped cream.

Cherry Devil's-Food Cake

This light, moist cake is great for church suppers or when friends drop in for tea.

2 4-ounce bottles maraschino cherries, drained	3 cups flour
²/₃ cup shortening	1³/₄ teaspoons baking soda
2 cups granulated sugar	1 teaspoon salt
2 eggs, separated	cherry juice plus buttermilk to make 2 cups
4 squares chocolate, melted	

1 Drain cherries way ahead of when you plan to mix the cake. Cut cherries in quarters to speed draining.

2 Preheat oven to 350°. Coat 10" x 14" cake pan (or two 9-inch-diameter pans) with vegetable spray.

3 Cream together shortening and sugar. Add egg yolks and mix thoroughly. Stir in melted chocolate.

4 Sift together (twice) flour, baking soda, and salt and add to creamed mixture alternately with buttermilk mixture.

5 Fold in stiffly beaten egg whites and then add drained cherries.

6 Bake 50 minutes. When cool, frost with white frosting.

Double Chocolate Cake

 This is very good and very easy.

4 ounces unsweetened chocolate, broken into small pieces	2 tablespoons flour
	3 eggs, separated
	6 tablespoons plus 2 tablespoons granulated sugar
6 tablespoons butter or margarine	

1 Preheat oven to 350°. Coat a 9-inch round Teflon cake pan with vegetable spray.

2 Melt the chocolate and butter in 2-quart saucepan over low heat. Remove from heat and cool about 3 minutes. Add the flour, egg yolks, and 6 tablespoons sugar, stirring well after each addition.

3 Beat the egg whites until stiff, adding 2 tablespoons sugar during last minute of beating.

4 Beat half the egg whites into the chocolate mixture, then fold in remaining egg whites.

5 Bake 15 to 20 minutes, or until toothpick inserted in center comes out clean. Cool in pan 20 minutes, then turn onto wire rack.

6 If desired, cover with Chocolate Glaze (p. 98) and serve with whipped cream.

YIELD: 10 TO 12 SERVINGS

Chocolate Glaze

2 ounces unsweetened
    chocolate, broken into small
    pieces
1 ounce semisweet chocolate,
    broken into small pieces

2 tablespoons water
2 tablespoons granulated sugar
2 tablespoons butter or
    margarine

1 Place all the ingredients in 1-quart saucepan over low heat until melted. Stir continuously.

2 Spread evenly over cooled cake.

YIELD: ENOUGH GLAZE FOR 1 CAKE

Fasnacloich Jelly Cake

 This delicacy was a closely guarded secret for years, the recipe given out only to family members. The cake actually improves with age—a few days after it is baked, the flavor is enhanced and the sliver-thin layers become slightly chewy. Although it can be made in the regulation two or three layers, it is much the best when made in six very thin layers—spread evenly in the pans to a thickness of about one-quarter inch.

$^1/_4$ cup melted butter or
    margarine
1 cup granulated sugar
1 egg
1 cup (approximately) thick
    sour milk (add 2 teaspoons
    vinegar to sweet milk)
$^1/_2$ teaspoon baking soda

2 cups flour
1 teaspoon (some prefer 2)
    ground nutmeg
pinch of salt
1 teaspoon baking powder
1 jar (8 ounces) red currant
    jelly
confectioners' sugar

1 Preheat oven to 350°. Coat 3 to 6 8-inch round cake pans with vegetable spray.

2 Cream together butter and sugar. Break egg into cup measure and fill cup with sour milk. Add to creamed mixture.

3 Sift together baking soda, flour, nutmeg, and salt. Add sifted ingredients and baking powder to creamed mixture and beat well.

4 Pour batter into each cake pan in thin layer, using spatula to make sure batter is even.

5 Bake until edges are brown and pulled away from sides of pans. Remove from oven and cool.

6 While cake is baking, whisk currant jelly until it liquefies. When cake is cool, spread top of each layer with jelly. Dust top layer with confectioners' sugar.

Grandmother Summers' 1-2-3-4 Cake

This recipe makes a very large cake. For convenience, you can cut the ingredients in half.

1 cup butter or margarine	1 cup milk
2 cups granulated sugar	4 teaspoons baking powder
3 cups cake flour	grated nutmeg
4 eggs, separated	

1 Preheat oven to 375°. Coat 2 9-inch cake pans with vegetable spray.

2 Cream together butter and sugar until light, then add well-beaten egg yolks.

3 Sift together cake flour, baking powder, and nutmeg and add to creamed mixture alternately with milk.

4 Beat egg whites to stiff peaks and fold into batter.

5 Bake 25 to 35 minutes.

6 If you wish, you can cut the cake into triangle-shaped pieces and frost them on the tops and sides with Canadian Frosting (p. 107). Then roll the pieces in almonds that have been blanched, toasted, and crumbled.

YIELD: 2 CAKES

Lemon Curd Tarts

This recipe comes from Mrs. Kenneth Hulbert, Jr., who says, "My English aunt frequently served Lemon Curd Tarts with a cup of tea. Nothing can describe the flavor of these tangy treats."

3 eggs	1 cup granulated sugar
1/2 cup butter or margarine	1/2 cup lemon juice

1 Beat eggs until light. Melt butter in top of double boiler, allow it to cool slightly, then add sugar and eggs. Mix well and cook, stirring constantly, 5 minutes.

2 Add lemon juice and cook 3 minutes, until mixture is thick and smooth.

3 Remove from heat and chill. At tea time, fill tiny tarts with lemon-curd mixture.

YIELD: ENOUGH FILLING FOR 12 TO 18 LITTLE TARTS

Old English Fruitcake

 Sometime in November, prepare this sumptuous cake. Easy and interesting to assemble, it will perfume your house with a foretaste of the holidays. This five-pound cake is big enough to see a large, hospitable family through the entire Christmas season. There may even be some left for the new year. The total cost of the ingredients is surprisingly modest, and the cake is far, far better than any cake you can buy.

4 to 5 pounds fruit and nuts:
  1 pound dark raisins
  1 pound white raisins
  $1/2$ pound dried currants
  $1/2$ pound candied cherries
  $1/2$ pound candied pineapple
  $1/4$ pound candied citron
  2 ounces candied orange peel
  2 ounces candied lemon peel
  $1/4$ pound blanched whole almonds
  $1/4$ pound whole pecans
$1/2$ cup Madeira
$1/2$ cup dark rum

$1/2$ teaspoon ground cinnamon
$1/2$ teaspoon ground cloves
$1/2$ teaspoon mace
$1/2$ teaspoon allspice
1 teaspoon baking soda
2 cups flour
$1/2$ cup butter or margarine
1 cup firmly packed brown sugar
1 cup granulated sugar
5 eggs, lightly beaten
1 teaspoon almond extract
1 jar (8 ounces) maraschino cherries

1 Put the raisins and currants in large bowl, add Madeira and rum, and let stand, covered, overnight.

2 Preheat oven to 275°. Coat a 10-inch tube or springmold cake pan with vegetable spray.

3 Add candied fruits to raisins and currants and mix well.

4 Sift together the spices, soda, and $1^{1}/2$ cups flour. Combine remaining

¹/₂ cup flour with nuts and then add, along with sifted ingredients, to fruit mixture. Stir lightly.

5   In another bowl, beat butter until light and cream in the sugars until light and fluffy. Beat in eggs and almond extract. Add fruit and nut mixture and stir well.

6   Turn the batter into tube or springform cake pan and bake 3¹/₂ to 4 hours, or until cake tester inserted near center comes out dry. (You can also make two smaller cakes, cutting the cooking time in half.)

7   Let the cake stand in pan on wire rack 30 minutes, then run knife around edges. For a springform pan, loosen and gently remove cake onto heavy aluminum foil large enough to enclose it completely. Fold edges double to seal. Once or twice before the holidays, open the foil and pour some rum or Madeira over cake.

8   When ready to serve, decorate top of cake with wreath of pecans and maraschino cherries and slivers of candied fruit.

YIELD: 1 10-INCH CAKE OR 2 SMALLER CAKES

Mother's Sponge Cake

4 eggs, separated
1¹/₂ cups granulated sugar
¹/₂ cup cold water (or orange
    juice, or water flavored with
    1 tablespoon lemon juice)

1¹/₂ cups flour
1¹/₂ teaspoons baking powder
pinch of salt
1 teaspoon vanilla extract (if
    you do not use fruit juice)

1   Preheat oven to 350°. Coat tube cake pan with vegetable spray.

2   Beat egg whites to soft peaks, beating in ¹/₄ cup sugar a little at a time. Without washing beater, beat yolks in separate bowl with water (or fruit juice, flavored water, or vanilla) and remaining sugar, until yolks have a creamy lemon color.

3   Sift together flour, baking powder, and salt and add to yolks. Fold in egg whites.

4   Bake 50 to 60 minutes, or until cake springs back when pressed lightly with finger. Invert on wire cake rack to cool. Loosen with spatula and unmold.

Pear Walnut Cake

 This excellent, healthful cake keeps well, thanks to the moisture from the pears. Although it is good served plain, it makes a splendid dessert course when sliced and covered with a few raspberries and a bit of crème anglaise.

1 egg	2 teaspoons ground cinnamon
2 egg whites	pinch of salt
1/2 cup granulated sugar	1/2 cup chopped walnuts
1 teaspoon vanilla extract	2 cups peeled, cored, diced
1 cup flour	pears (about 2 pears)
2 teaspoons baking powder	

1 Preheat oven to 350°. Coat an 8-inch Teflon baking pan, or loaf pan, with vegetable spray.

2 Combine the egg, egg whites, sugar, and vanilla until smooth.

3 Sift together the flour, baking powder, cinnamon, and salt and fold into sugar/egg mixture. Stir in nuts and pears.

4 Spoon the batter into baking pan and bake 25 to 30 minutes. Turn out onto wire rack to cool.

Crème Anglaise

A light, healthful dessert sauce.

2 cups skim milk	1/2 cup granulated sugar
1 stick cinnamon	1/2 ounce pear or raspberry
2 egg whites	liqueur
1 whole egg	

1 Scald the milk with cinnamon stick. Remove from heat and allow to steep 30 minutes. Remove cinnamon.

2 Beat the egg whites and whole egg until frothy, then beat in sugar until mixture is creamy.

3 Beat 1/2 cup milk into egg mixture, then slowly beat in remaining milk. Return to the pot in which milk was scalded and cook, stirring, over low heat, until mixture coats spoon. Stir in liqueur. Cool by transferring to bowl set into larger bowl filled with ice cubes.

YIELD: ABOUT 10 SERVINGS

Prize Coconut Cake

1³/₄ cups sifted cake flour

2¹/₄ teaspoons baking powder

³/₄ teaspoon salt

¹/₂ cup butter or margarine

1 cup plus 2 tablespoons
   granulated sugar

2 eggs

²/₃ cup milk

1 teaspoon vanilla extract

²/₃ cup shredded coconut

1 Preheat oven to 350°. Coat 2 9-inch Teflon cake pans with vegetable spray.

2 Sift together sifted flour, baking powder, and salt. Set aside.

3 Cream butter and add sugar gradually, until mixture is light and fluffy. Add eggs one at a time, beating well after each addition. Add sifted ingredients alternately with milk, beating until smooth after each addition. Stir in vanilla and coconut.

4 Pour batter into prepared pans and bake 30 to 35 minutes. Cool 10 minutes in pans, then turn out onto wire racks and continue cooling.

5 Frost with Seven-Minute Frosting (p. 109). Cover top and sides with shredded coconut.

Queen Elizabeth's Cake

This is said to be the cake that the queen likes to go into the royal kitchen and bake herself. It's a lovely cake.

1 cup boiling water

1 cup chopped dates

1 teaspoon baking soda

1 cup granulated sugar

¹/₂ cup butter or margarine

1 egg, beaten

1¹/₂ cups flour

1 teaspoon baking powder

¹/₂ teaspoon salt

1 teaspoon vanilla extract

¹/₂ cup chopped walnuts

1 Preheat oven to 350°. Coat 9″ x 12″ Teflon cake pan with vegetable spray.

2 Combine boiling water, dates, and baking soda in bowl and let stand 20 minutes.

3 Cream together the butter and sugar. Add beaten egg. Sift together flour, baking powder, and salt and add to creamed mixture. Add vanilla and nuts and beat well.

4 Pour the batter into prepared pan and bake 35 minutes. Remove from oven and frost when cool.

Frosting for Queen Elizabeth's Cake

1 cup shredded coconut

2/3 cup brown sugar

4 tablespoons butter or margarine

1/3 cup light cream

1 Preheat oven to 350° (or use toaster oven). Toast coconut until golden.

2 Cream together brown sugar and butter. Gradually add cream and blend well.

3 Frost cake and sprinkle top and sides with toasted coconut.

YIELD: ENOUGH FROSTING FOR 1 SHEET CAKE

Roxbury Spice Cakes

2 eggs, separated

1/4 cup butter or margarine

1/2 cup granulated sugar

1 teaspoon baking soda

1/2 cup sour milk

1 teaspoon baking soda

1 1/2 cups flour

1 teaspoon ground cinnamon

1/2 teaspoon ground cloves

1/4 teaspoon ground nutmeg

1/2 cup seedless raisins

1/2 cup chopped walnuts

1 Preheat oven to 350°. Coat 1 muffin tin with vegetable spray (or use paper muffin cups).

2 Beat egg whites until stiff. In separate bowl, beat egg yolks.

3 Cream together the butter and sugar and add beaten egg yolks. Dissolve baking soda in sour milk.

4 Sift together the flour and spices and add alternately with sour milk to creamed mixture. Fold in egg whites, then add raisins and nuts.

5 Pour into muffin tins and bake about 30 minutes. When cool, frost with Seven-Minute Frosting (p. 109).

YIELD: ABOUT 1 DOZEN MUFFIN-SIZE CAKES

Silver Nut Cake

3/4 cup vegetable shortening
1 1/2 cups granulated sugar
2 3/4 cups flour
3 teaspoons baking powder
1/2 teaspoon salt
1 cup milk

1/2 teaspoon vanilla extract
1 teaspoon almond extract
1 cup chopped walnuts
    (preferably English walnuts)
4 egg whites, beaten stiff

1 Preheat oven to 350°. Coat 9-inch-square cake pan with vegetable spray. Dust lightly with flour.

2 Cream together shortening and sugar. Sift together flour, baking powder, and salt and add to creamed mixture alternately with milk. Add extracts and nuts and blend well. Carefully fold beaten egg whites into batter.

3 Pour into prepared cake pan and bake 1 hour. Remove from oven and turn out onto wire cake rack. When cool, frost with Mocha Frosting (p. 108) or Maple Cream Frosting (p. 108).

Spice Cake

No commercial mix can match this delicious traditional spice cake.

1/2 cup lard (scant) or
    shortening
1 cup seedless raisins
1 cup granulated sugar
1 egg, beaten
1 1/2 cups bread flour
1 teaspoon baking powder
1 teaspoon baking soda

1/2 teaspoon salt
1 rounded teaspoon ground
    cinnamon
1/2 teaspoon ground cloves
1 teaspoon ground nutmeg
1 cup sour cream or sour milk
1 teaspoon vanilla extract

1 Preheat oven to 350°. Coat 8-inch-square cake pan with vegetable spray.

2 Place raisins in saucepan with enough cold water to cover and simmer until water has evaporated. Remove from heat and cool.

3 Cream together the shortening and sugar. Add beaten egg.

4 Sift together the flour, baking powder, baking soda, salt, and spices and add to creamed mixture alternately with sour cream or sour milk. Add softened raisins and vanilla and mix well.

5 Pour into prepared cake pan and bake about 35 minutes. Remove from oven and cool on wire cake rack. When cool, frost with Seven-Minute Frosting (p. 109).

White Plum Cake

 The cake was often used as a wedding cake or for special occasions. It is nice to have on hand, as it is firm and keeps well.

2 cups (4 sticks) butter or margarine

8 eggs, separated

2 cups granulated sugar

4 cups all-purpose flour

2 teaspoons baking powder

pinch of salt

1 cup slivered almonds

4 ounces citron, thinly sliced

4 ounces candied lemon peel, chopped

1 cup sultana raisins

1/8 teaspoon mace

2 tablespoons milk

1/4 cup brandy

1 Preheat oven to 325°. Coat a tube cake pan with vegetable spray and line pan with greased paper.

2 Cream butter. Add the egg yolks to butter, beating thoroughly. Add remaining ingredients except egg whites. Beat egg whites until stiff and fold into batter.

3 Bake 1 hour, or until done.

Wellesley Fudge Cake

 An old favorite, rich and good.

4 squares unsweetened chocolate

1/2 cup hot water

1 3/4 cups granulated sugar

2 cups sifted cake flour

1 teaspoon baking soda

1 teaspoon salt

1/2 cup vegetable shortening*

3 eggs

3/4 cup milk*

1 teaspoon vanilla extract

1 Preheat oven to 350°. Line bottoms of two 9-inch cake pans with paper.

2 Melt the chocolate in water in a double boiler, stirring occasionally. Add 1/2 cup sugar. Heat and stir 2 minutes. Cool to lukewarm.

3 Sift together sifted flour, baking soda, and salt.

4 Cream the shortening, gradually adding remaining 1¼ cups sugar until light and fluffy. (*If you substitute butter or margarine for shortening, use only ⅔ cup milk.)

5 Add eggs, one at a time, beating thoroughly after each addition. Add sifted ingredients alternately with milk, beating after each addition until smooth. Blend vanilla and melted chocolate into batter.

6 Pour into prepared cake pans and bake 30 to 35 minutes, or until cake springs back when pressed lightly with finger. Cool on wire cake rack. When cool, frost with Fluffy Chocolate Frosting (p. 108), Seven-Minute Frosting (p. 109), or Fluffy Marshmallow, Coconut, or Peppermint Frosting (p. 109).

FROSTINGS

Canadian Frosting

½ cup butter

2 cups confectioners' sugar

1 tablespoon heavy cream

½ teaspoon vanilla extract

1 Cream butter and confectioners' sugar. Gradually add cream and vanilla and blend well.

Chocolate Frosting

4 tablespoons butter

2 cups confectioners' sugar

2 squares chocolate, melted

½ teaspoon vanilla extract

pinch of salt

2 or 3 tablespoons light cream

1 Cream butter until soft. Gradually stir in 1 cup confectioners' sugar, then melted chocolate and remaining ingredients, including remaining 1 cup sugar. Blend well.

Easy Chocolate Frosting

This frosting stays soft indefinitely.

½ cup butter or margarine

2 eggs

1 ounce semisweet chocolate, melted

1 teaspoon vanilla extract

1 Cream butter or margarine and add eggs one at a time, beating after each addition. Add vanilla.

2 Allow melted chocolate to cool slightly. Add to creamed mixture, beating well. Continue beating until frosting is thick and smooth.

Fluffy Chocolate Frosting

This is a very fluffy frosting that spreads like whipped cream.

4 tablespoons butter

1½ cups confectioners' sugar

1 teaspoon vanilla extract

3 squares chocolate, melted

¼ teaspoon salt

2 egg whites, beaten stiff

1 Cream together butter and ¾ cup confectioners' sugar until light. Add vanilla, melted chocolate, and salt and mix well.

2 Fold remaining sugar, 2 tablespoons at a time, into stiff egg whites. Add chocolate mixture, folding gently and thoroughly, but only enough to blend.

Maple Cream Frosting

1 pound soft maple sugar

1 cup light cream

1 Boil together sugar and cream, without stirring, until soft ball forms when teaspoonful of mixture is placed in cold water.

2 Cool until frosting is of spreading consistency, beat well, and spread on cake.

Mocha Frosting

4 tablespoons (½ stick) butter

1½ cups confectioners' sugar

1 egg yolk

1 tablespoon powdered cocoa

1 tablespoon instant coffee crystals

1 Cream butter. Gradually add confectioners' sugar, then add egg yolk and flavorings. Beat well.

Seven-Minute Frosting

2 egg whites
1½ cups granulated sugar
pinch of salt

⅓ cup water
2 teaspoons light corn syrup
1 teaspoon vanilla extract

1 Beat together egg whites, sugar, salt, water, and corn syrup in top of double boiler. Place over boiling water and continue beating with rotary beater—preferably electric—4 to 7 minutes, or until frosting thickens and holds its shape when dropped from beater.

2 Remove pan from heat, add vanilla, and continue beating until frosting is of spreading consistency.

YIELD: ENOUGH TO FROST 24 CUPCAKES OR TOPS AND SIDES OF TWO 9-INCH CAKE LAYERS

VARIATION — Fluffy Marshmallow Frosting

Beat 1 cup diced marshmallows into frosting before spreading on cake.

VARIATION — Coconut Frosting

Put layers together and cover cake with Seven-Minute Frosting. Sprinkle immediately with 1½ cups shredded coconut.

VARIATION — Peppermint Frosting

Instead of 1 teaspoon vanilla extract, substitute few drops of peppermint oil.

VARIATION — Orange or Lemon Frosting

Instead of vanilla, substitute 1 teaspoon orange or lemon extract.

4

Hors d'Oeuvres

It's very useful to keep a few tidbits on hand to make a small party of the occasion when a friend drops by unexpectedly. A tray with three little bowls does the trick neatly. They may contain black or green olives, hot pecans, hot almonds, or other nuts. I keep a pan of salted nuts and one of melba toast in the oven ready to switch on for five minutes, a couple of jars of some cocktail mixtures (below) in the refrigerator with some celery sticks.

For the planned-ahead cocktail party, I suggest a few hot hors d'oeuvres, small sandwiches (some of those in chapter 3 are suitable for cocktail fare, too), pâté, or cheeses. Sometimes you may want to include on the buffet a smoked ham or turkey as well—both of them if it's a big party. Garnish them with fanfare—lots of paper frills, parsley, and tomato roses. Then light the candles and turn on soft music.

At the end of this chapter are a number of dishes that can be used as hors d'oeuvres or first courses for leisurely lunches or dinners.

Here is a list of things to keep on your shelf if you want to *be prepared:*

- Salted nuts
- Cheese straws
- Pâté de foie gras
- Olives

- Crudités
- Cheeses
- Smoked oysters

Here are a few suggestions for a cocktail party large or small:

- Oysters or clams on the half-shell served with buttered brown bread
- Shrimp with Green Mayonnaise (p. 308)
- Bacon-filled cherry tomatoes
- Tiny sausages or cheese baked in croissant pastry (pigs-in-a-blanket)

- Fillet of beef carpaccio
- Small hot buttered baking-powder biscuits filled with cheese or Smithfield ham
- Assorted sandwiches: chopped nuts, watercress, tongue, cucumber, or smoked salmon with cream cheese
- Bacon strips sprinkled with brown sugar

- Eggs stuffed with mushrooms, chopped olives, watercress, or ham, and topped with a dollop of red or gray caviar

Anchovy Canapés

2 tins (2 ounces each) anchovy fillets

2 medium garlic cloves, finely chopped

1 teaspoon tomato paste

1 to 1½ tablespoons olive oil

2 teaspoons lemon juice or white wine vinegar

freshly ground black pepper to taste

12 small slices French or Italian bread

1 teaspoon finely chopped fresh parsley

1 Preheat oven to 500°.

2 Drain anchovies and place in heavy bowl with garlic and tomato paste. Mash the mixture to a smooth purée.

3 Add oil, a few drops at a time, stirring until mixture becomes thick and smooth. Stir in the lemon juice (or vinegar) and pepper.

4 Brown the bread lightly on one side. While bread is still warm, spread the untoasted side with anchovy mixture.

5 Arrange bread on baking sheet and bake 10 minutes. Sprinkle with parsley and serve at once.

Anchovy Puffs

3 ounces cream cheese, softened

½ cup butter or margarine, softened

1 cup flour, sifted

anchovy paste

1 Preheat oven to 400°.

2 Blend cheese and butter, then add flour and chill.

3 Roll out dough very thinly and cut with 2-inch cookie cutter. Spread the dough rather generously with anchovy paste, then fold up and crimp edges.

4 Bake 8 to 10 minutes. Serve at once.

YIELD: 48 PUFFS

Bacon Roll-Ups

Bacon roll-ups always disappear quickly and are easy, because you can get them ready ahead of time. One good combination is a piece of pineapple and half of a water chestnut rolled in a half strip of bacon. Secure it with a toothpick and bake 10 minutes or so in a hot (400°) oven or until bacon is crisp. Marinate with a little pineapple juice and serve.

The Woodstock Inn in Woodstock, Vermont, serves kumquats wrapped in bacon, and they are delicious—even better with an almond slipped inside the kumquat.

Basil Beans

These are crisp and wonderful to add to a salad or to nibble with cocktails. Keep a batch on hand all during the summer when beans are ripening. They will last in the refrigerator for a week or so.

Fill a crock, large or small, with a brine made with 12 measures of water to one of salt. Add a small dash of vinegar and a small piece of garlic. Put a good amount of basil into the brine, then prepare the beans. Pick them while still young, remove the stems, and parboil them for just 2 or 3 minutes, until a bit tender and bright in color. Submerge them in the brine. Cool, then chill.

VARIATION – Dill Beans

Dill beans are made the same way as Basil Beans—just use dill instead of basil.

Curried Cantaloupe Dip

1 cup sour cream	1 teaspoon lemon juice
2 tablespoons mayonnaise	pinch of salt
1/2 teaspoon curry powder	mint leaves for garnish
1/2 teaspoon catsup	1 medium cantaloupe

1 Combine sour cream with mayonnaise. Add remaining seasonings and blend well.

2 Garnish with mint leaves and serve as a dip for melon balls.

YIELD: 1 1/2 CUPS

Chutney/Cream-Cheese Puffs

4 ounces cream cheese,
   softened
1 egg yolk
white part of 1 scallion, finely
   minced

1 teaspoon chutney
pinch of salt
9 slices white bread

1 Preheat oven to 350°.

2 Mash cream cheese. Beat in the egg yolk, minced scallion, chutney, and salt.

3 Toast bread lightly and cut out 1-inch-diameter rounds.

4 Heap the cheese mixture on the bread rounds and bake 5 minutes, until puffy.

   If you don't use all of the mixture at once, you can store it in a tightly covered container in the refrigerator for several days.

YIELD: 3 DOZEN

Corn Cups

These little cups are ideal for a snack. They can be filled with any of the cocktail spreads or a little seafood, chicken salad, lettuce, and pâté—all sorts of things.

6 tablespoons butter or
   margarine, softened
2 ounces cream cheese,
   softened

1 cup flour
1/2 cup cornmeal
1/4 teaspoon salt
pinch of cayenne pepper

1 Preheat oven to 350°.

2 Cream together the butter and cream cheese.

3 In separate bowl, mix together dry ingredients. Thoroughly combine the two mixtures.

4 Shape dough into small balls and press into miniature muffin tins. Bake 15 minutes.

YIELD: 4 DOZEN

Crudités

 Crisp raw vegetables make the healthiest and safest of all snacks and can be served with a number of cocktail mixtures. Try to get a variety of colors and textures—radish roses, cauliflower florets, large slices of raw mushroom, endive leaves, celery, carrot curls. Keep them in a bowl of salted water until needed.

Salted Mixed Nuts

 Salted nuts, either mixed or any one kind, are superior when prepared at home and a perfect standby for before-dinner drinks or a cocktail party. This recipe uses a tasty combination of mixed nuts.

¹/₂ **pound blanched raw almonds**	2 **tablespoons butter or margarine**
¹/₂ **pound raw hazelnuts**	¹/₂ **pound large raw walnuts**
¹/₂ **pound large raw cashews**	¹/₂ **pound mammoth raw pecans**
¹/₂ **pound raw Brazil nuts**	
2 **tablespoons olive oil**	**rock salt**

1 Preheat oven to 350°.

2 Mix the almonds, hazelnuts, cashews, and Brazil nuts with olive oil and butter in large roasting pan and place on the center rack of oven. Roast, stirring occasionally, 30 minutes.

3 Add the walnuts and pecans. (These do not need as much cooking time as the other nuts.) Salt to taste.

4 Roast 30 minutes more, stirring occasionally, until crisp and lightly golden. (The nuts will darken a little after they are removed from the oven, so do not overcook them.)

5 Drain on paper towels, cool, and store in airtight jars.

6 Serve with sprinkling of rock salt. (The nuts are always better if re-heated briefly before serving.)

   Salted nuts of a single variety may be prepared this way, too, and they are equally tempting.

YIELD: 3 POUNDS

Sesame Roll-Ups

12 slices white bread, crusts removed	butter or margarine, softened sesame seeds

1 Preheat oven to 300°. Coat baking sheet with vegetable spray.

2 Flatten bread slices with rolling pin and spread butter on both sides of each slice.

3 Roll up and sprinkle with sesame seeds.

4 Place on cookie sheet and bake 20 minutes, until golden brown.

YIELD: 12

The Cheese Tray

A cheese tray fills many useful roles. Accompanied by a variety of crackers or by French bread, it is an attractive addition to a buffet table at a cocktail party, or it may accompany the salad if you want to make that the final course. Served with fresh fruit, it can take the place of dessert.

Try to find a large, flat wicker basket or a large platter of natural wood. Arrange four or five cheeses on it. In summer, place the cheeses on fresh grape leaves. Or you may want to use paper doilies, particularly if you serve a runny cheese. Cheddar cheese, Swiss, blue cheese, Edam, and one or two of the French cheeses make good choices. A cheese crock (p. 117) may be served with these others. It's an easy way to make your meal more interesting.

Cheese ''Pear'' for the Cheese Tray

Form 8 ounces of cream or Neufchâtel cheese into the shape of a pear. Combine fine breadcrumbs with nuts and nut crumbs and spread on breadboard. Roll cheese pear lightly over board. Sprinkle paprika on one side of the pear to give it a sun-kissed look, and ''plant'' a few bay leaves atop the pear to complete the picture.

Hot Pecan Spread

8 ounces cream cheese, softened

2 tablespoons sherry

1 jar (2½ ounces) sliced dried beef

¼ cup finely chopped green pepper

2 tablespoons dried onion flakes

½ teaspoon garlic salt

freshly ground pepper to taste

½ cup sour cream

½ cup coarsely chopped pecans

2 tablespoons butter or margarine, melted

½ teaspoon salt

1 Preheat oven to 350°.

2 Combine softened cream cheese and sherry and mix until well blended.

3 Stir in the dried beef (cut up if necessary), green pepper, onion flakes, garlic salt, and pepper and mix well. Fold in sour cream.

4 Spoon into a small, ovenproof baking dish.

5 Heat and crisp the pecans in melted butter and salt and sprinkle over cream cheese mixture.

6 Bake 20 minutes and serve hot with crackers.

YIELD: 1 CUP

Roquefort Biscuits

2 cups sifted flour

1 teaspoon salt

3 teaspoons baking powder

¼ cup Roquefort cheese, crumbled

¼ cup butter or margarine

⅔ cup milk

country ham

1 Preheat oven to 425°. Coat baking sheet with vegetable spray.

2 Sift together the flour, salt, and baking powder. Cut in Roquefort and butter with pastry blender or 2 knives until mixture has the consistency of coarse cornmeal. Add milk slowly.

3 Turn onto floured board, knead slightly, and roll out to ½-inch thickness.

4 Cut dough into small rounds with floured 1-inch cutter and bake 12 minutes, or until done.

5 Split biscuits. Place pat of butter and sliver of country ham in each biscuit and serve quickly.

YIELD: 2 TO 3 DOZEN

Cheese Bites

½ pound Mozzarella or Swiss cheese
¼ cup flour

1 egg, lightly beaten
¼ cup seasoned breadcrumbs
cooking oil

1 Cut cheese into ¾-inch cubes.

2 Roll cubes in flour and dip in egg, then in breadcrumbs. Dip cubes again in egg and again in breadcrumbs.

3 Fry cubes in hot oil until browned. Serve on toothpicks.

YIELD: 18 PIECES

Cheese Crock

16 ounces sharp Cheddar cheese
8 ounces cream cheese, softened
1 tablespoon olive oil

pinch of dry mustard
1 clove garlic, crushed
4 ounces liqueur or spirits, or to taste

1 Grate Cheddar and blend with cream cheese and olive oil. Add mustard, garlic, and liqueur.

2 Put mixture in small crock.

3 After it is well blended, keep crock in refrigerator, ready for crackers and an unexpected guest. Never use it all up. Keep adding to it.

YIELD: 24 OUNCES

Hot Cheese Appetizers

2 cups grated Cheddar cheese
8 ounces cream cheese
2 tablespoons butter or
  margarine, softened
1/2 teaspoon baking powder

1 egg, beaten
toast rounds or crackers
chopped fresh parsley
mustard seed

1 Preheat broiler.

2 Beat all ingredients until creamy and pile on small rounds of bread or crackers.

3 Broil until slightly brown and puffy.

4 Sprinkle with chopped parsley and mustard seed.

YIELD: 3 DOZEN

PARTY SPREADS

Anchovy/Black-Olive Spread

1 tin (2 ounces) anchovies,
  drained
1 clove garlic, minced
8 black olives, pitted and sliced
1 heaping tablespoon capers

1 ounce cream cheese
1 ounce Roquefort cheese
2 tablespoons minced fresh
  parsley
dash of brandy

1 Mash anchovies and mix well with remaining ingredients.

2 Serve at room temperature.

Avocado Spread

1 ripe avocado
1 tablespoon grated onion
1 tablespoon lemon or lime
  juice

Tabasco sauce to taste
4 strips crisp bacon, crumbled
salt to taste
pepper to taste

1 Mash avocado, add remaining ingredients, and serve while bacon is still crisp.

Cream Cheese, Smoked Salmon, and Red Caviar Spread

1 ounce smoked salmon
6 ounces whipped cream
   cheese

finely snipped dill
1 ounce red caviar
dill sprigs

1 Tear salmon into small bits and mix with cream cheese. Stir in dill.

2 Carefully fold in caviar. Chill.

3 Serve garnished with dill sprigs.

YIELD: 2 CUPS

Cucumber/Cream-Cheese Spread

½ cucumber
salt

8 ounces whipped cream
   cheese
finely minced fresh dill

1 In blender, grate cucumber, sprinkle with salt, and drain in colander about 1 hour.

2 Press cucumber firmly with paper toweling and place in bowl. Mix with cream cheese and dill.

3 Chill before serving.

YIELD: 2 CUPS

Mushroom Spread

Do not prepare this mixture earlier than a half hour before serving. If you do, the mushrooms will give off liquid and become limp.

¼ pound small mushrooms,
   sliced paper thin
1 scallion, sliced paper thin

2 tablespoons yogurt
salt to taste
freshly ground pepper to taste

1 Mix mushrooms and scallion with yogurt and season to taste. Chill.

Roquefort Dill Spread

 Pale green and very appetizing.

4 ounces cream cheese

4 ounces Roquefort cheese

2 tablespoons plain yogurt

10 sprigs dill, snipped fine

1/4 teaspoon salt

Beat together the cheeses and yogurt until light. Add the dill and salt.

YIELD: ABOUT 1 CUP

Sardine Spread

 Use as a spread or a dip or to stuff celery sticks.

8 ounces cream cheese,
    softened

3 tablespoons lime or lemon
    juice

1 tin sardines, mashed

1 large onion, finely minced

2 hard-boiled eggs, chopped

salt to taste

1 Blend cheese with juice. Add sardines, onion, chopped eggs, and salt
  and blend thoroughly.

YIELD: 3 CUPS

Tomato/Cream-Cheese Spread

 1 medium tomato

salt to taste

1 clove garlic

8 ounces cream cheese

1 Skin and quarter tomato and squeeze out seeds and juices.

2 Chop tomato pulp, sprinkle with salt, and drain in colander at least 1
  hour.

3 Rub small bowl with cut garlic clove. Put cream cheese in bowl. Pat
  tomato pulp dry with paper towel and add to cream cheese. Mix well.

4 Chill before serving.

YIELD: 1 1/2 CUPS

Watercress Spread

 Very zingy!

1 bunch watercress, stems removed
1 ounce fresh horseradish

1 scallion, sliced
8 ounces cream cheese

1 Wash watercress and dry thoroughly. Squeeze horseradish dry in sieve.

2 Place watercress, horseradish, and scallion in food processor or blender with cream cheese and process thoroughly. Chill.

YIELD: 2 CUPS

Yogurt Spread

 Mix plain low-fat yogurt with instant chicken or beef bouillon granules for a very piquant dip for crudités. Add a little curry powder if you like.

FIRST COURSES

Here are two interesting ways to serve avocados as a first course.

Avocados with Hot Sauce

 2 tablespoons catsup
2 tablespoons butter or margarine
2 tablespoons white rum
1 tablespoon brown sugar
2 tablespoons lime juice

few dashes of Tabasco sauce
freshly ground white pepper
1 very ripe, very cold avocado, halved and stoned
hot buttered Triscuits
watercress for garnish

1 Combine the first 7 ingredients for sauce in saucepan. Bring to a boil, stirring constantly. Take sauce to table bubbling hot, preferably in a metal ramekin.

2 Pour sauce into avocado halves and accompany with hot buttered Triscuits. Garnish with watercress.

The contrast of the hot with the cold, the piquant with the bland, and the soft with the crisp is very appetizing.

YIELD: 2 SERVINGS

Avocados with Red Caviar and Sour Cream Sauce

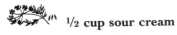

1/2 cup sour cream
1 egg yolk
1 teaspoon onion juice
1 very ripe, very cold avocado, halved and stoned

4 ounces red caviar
hot buttered Triscuits
lemon wedges

1 Combine the first 3 ingredients to make sauce. Spoon caviar into avocado halves and pour sauce over all.

2 Serve ice cold with hot buttered Triscuits and lemon wedges.

YIELD: 2 SERVINGS

Brie in Crust

When salad is the main course for luncheon or supper, this is a delicious accompaniment hot from the oven. Or, with plenty of paper napkins, it can be used for a cocktail or buffet party. This recipe is for two loaves—if you don't need both, wrap one in plastic and freeze it.

1 brie (about 2 pounds), cut in half to make 2 disks

2 round bread loaves, 3 inches larger than cheese

1 Preheat oven to 350°.

2 Cut bread loaves in half horizontally and place cheese disks between them. Fasten with toothpicks or tie securely with kitchen string.

3 Bake 10 minutes, until cheese has melted. Remove toothpicks or string. Cut in wedges at the table.

YIELD: 2 LOAVES

Celery Remoulade

If stored covered in the refrigerator, celery remoulade will keep for several days. It is very convenient to have on hand (and delicious). Serve it with cocktails, as a first course, or as a salad supplement. It is crisp and refreshing.

1 large celery root
about 1 cup Mayonnaise
  (p. 307)
lemon juice to taste
dry mustard to taste

finely cut fresh herbs (such as
  dill or parsley)
salt to taste
freshly ground white pepper to
  taste

1 Peel celery root, cut into pieces, and then into julienne strips. (Or run pieces through food processor using julienne blade.)

2 Blanch celery in rapidly boiling water for only 30 seconds. Drain thoroughly.

3 Combine celery with mayonnaise, lemon juice, dry mustard, herbs, salt, and pepper to taste.

YIELD: ABOUT 2 CUPS

Crabmeat Mayonnaise

A light but formal course that is convenient because it can be prepared ahead of time.

1 pound fresh or frozen
  crabmeat
hearts of 1 bunch celery
Mayonnaise (p. 307)

salt to taste
lemon juice to taste
6 young lettuce leaves
6 tablespoons capers

1 Pick over crabmeat to remove any membrane or shell pieces.

2 Mix with celery hearts and toss gently in mayonnaise, adding salt and lemon juice to taste.

3 Arrange crabmeat on lettuce leaves on individual plates and top each with 1 tablespoon mayonnaise and 1 tablespoon capers.

YIELD: 6 SERVINGS

Fillet of Beef Carpaccio

6 slices dark pumpernickel
  bread
sweet butter, softened
1/2 pound lean fillet of beef,
  sliced raw

2 tins (2 ounces each) flat
  anchovy fillets
capers
chopped fresh parsley

1 The day of the party, have the butcher cut the raw beef into thin slices and wrap them tightly.

2 Spread pumpernickel with sweet butter (remove crusts if you like). Cut each slice into 5 strips.

3 Cut 1 slice of beef to fit each bread strip. Arrange slices on bread strips and place 1/2 anchovy fillet on top of some (not everyone likes anchovies). Chill.

4 Serve sprinkled with capers and chopped fresh parsley.

YIELD: 30 PIECES

Firecrackers

Add plenty of Tabasco sauce to the filling. Firecrackers should be hot.

8 thin slices salami or prepared
  ham
1/2 Roquefort dill spread

Tabasco
chives

1 Spread the slices of meat with the cheese spread liberally sprinkled with Tabasco. Cut in two. Roll up tight with a chive sticking out from the end of each roll to form a wick.

YIELD: 16 PIECES

Gravlax

A delicious first course.

1 1/2 pounds salmon (from
  center of fish), thinly sliced
fresh dill sprigs to taste

salt to taste
granulated sugar to taste

1   Layer salmon with dill, salt, and sugar. Marinate between two heavy plates in refrigerator for 2 or 3 days, draining off liquid occasionally.

2   Serve on individual plates garnished with dill sprigs. If you like, serve with Fennel Sauce (below). Pass brown-bread sandwiches.

Fennel Sauce

3 or 4 shallots	**1 tablespoon water**
4 or 5 fennel	**1 cup yogurt or heavy cream**
dash of anisette	**salt to taste**
dash of dry vermouth	**white pepper to taste**

1   Chop white parts of shallots and fennel.

2   Steam with anisette, vermouth, and water in tightly covered pot until soft.

3   Purée in food processor or blender with yogurt, salt, and white pepper.

4   Serve hot with cooked fish or chilled with cold fish.

HORS D'OEUVRES VARIÉES

This is a very pleasant way to start a leisurely luncheon or dinner. Arrange a selection of the following (about six items) on individual plates and serve with herbed French or Italian bread.

- Shrimp
- Cucumber salad
- Tomato salad garnished with anchovies
- Raw mushrooms, sliced and served with mustard vinaigrette
- Celery Remoulade (p. 123)
- Slice of prosciutto
- Slice of salami
- Slice of goat cheese (chèvre) in garlic oil
- Greek olives

Oysters and Clams

 Have the fish market open the oysters or clams and place them on a bed of crushed ice. At serving time, place the ice on large serving plates, arrange the bivalves over the ice, and garnish with parsley sprigs and lemon wedges. Pass sandwiches of brown or black bread, sweet butter and herbs (chopped parsley, chives, and dill), and Mignonette Sauce (below) with this rare feast.

Mignonette Sauce

The ideal sauce for oysters and clams.

1 teaspoon red wine vinegar
1 teaspoon lemon juice
1/4 cup best olive oil
2 teaspoons chopped capers

1 teaspoon chopped shallots
salt to taste
freshly ground white pepper to
   taste

1 Slowly beat vinegar and lemon juice into olive oil.

2 Add remaining ingredients and blend well.

YIELD: 2 CUPS

Prosciutto, Roasted Peppers, and Goat Cheese

 4 green and red peppers
1 teaspoon olive oil
1/2 pound goat cheese (chèvre)
about 1/2 pound prosciutto,
   thinly sliced

salt to taste
freshly ground pepper to taste
capers
parsley sprigs
herbed French or Italian bread

1 Preheat oven to 300°.

2 Brush peppers with olive oil and roast them on a baking sheet until tender.

3 Quarter peppers and discard stem, pith, and seeds.

4 Slice goat cheese about 3/4 inch thick and sauté in olive oil.

5 Arrange prosciutto, sections of pepper, and 1 slice goat cheese on warm plates, season with salt and pepper, and garnish with capers and parsley. Serve with herbed French or Italian bread.

Smoked Salmon Rosettes with Cucumber and Dill

 A light, attractive first course served with melba toast.

½ English cucumber, unpeeled and thinly sliced	1 teaspoon granulated sugar
salt to taste	1 tablespoon white vinegar
freshly ground pepper to taste	8 slices smoked salmon
finely chopped fresh dill	capers
	watercress sprigs

1 Mix sliced cucumbers with salt, pepper, dill, sugar, and vinegar and marinate at least 30 minutes. Chill 4 plates.

2 When ready to serve, drain cucumbers and arrange a circle of cucumber slices on each plate. In center of each circle, shape 2 slices of smoked salmon to resemble a rose. Fill center of each "rose" with capers and garnish with 1 or 2 watercress sprigs.

YIELD: 4 SERVINGS

Shrimp

 Arrange cooked, chilled shrimp in small dishes on young lettuce leaves garnished with lemon wedges. Serve with Green Mayonnaise (p. 308) or Russian dressing.

5

Soups and Chowders

In all the branches of cookery, I don't think there is anything more *fun* than making soups. Because the flavor builds up gradually as the elements cook together and blend, it usually is a slow process, but one that leaves room for much experimentation and innovation. You must taste as you go along and probably will want to correct the seasoning with a touch or two of your own. An open cupboard with a large selection of herbs and spices ranged in full view is a wonderful source of inspiration in cooking. When making soup, it is often interesting to take the basic recipes given here and add any vegetables, herbs, or bones you may have on hand.

Among the soups that follow, there are many that, served with good bread, will make a complete lunch or supper. Soups are especially good suppers for small children, who often are too tired by the end of the day to manage anything more than a cup and a spoon.

On the other hand, the addition of a soup course can make a festive and leisurely occasion out of a family or party luncheon or dinner, well worth the extra effort. It enhances the flavor and texture of the repast and pleasantly prolongs the time at table. Conversation thrives, and appetites can be whetted or whittled, as you please, by your choice of soup. A soup tureen is a great help for keeping soup hot on the table.

The basis of most good soups (and of many other dishes as well) is soup stock—also called bouillon or broth. Some vegetable soups create their own uniquely flavored stock as the vegetables cook in water or cream, while others require meat, fish, or chicken stock. Chicken stock is commonly used as the base for delicate soups, while beef stock is needed for the more full-bodied soups. There are very good meat concentrates that may be used to make stock, and it helps to keep on hand commercial beef and chicken consommés or bouillon cubes. Nevertheless, homemade stock is easy to make, economical, and better. The yield of soup in these recipes varies according to the size of your soup pot and amount of liquid used. Figure on about 6 servings from a quart of soup unless it is being used as the main meal for adults who may request seconds.

Bouquet Garni

 An herb bag—bouquet garni—is useful in making soups and sauces and in cooking vegetables and meats or stews. Its ingredients lend their flavor to the dish and then may be removed easily. The combinations can vary according to individual taste, but this is a good all-purpose bouquet garni.

1 bay leaf   1 sprig thyme

6 peppercorns   1 sprig parsley

4 whole cloves

1 Place all ingredients in a small square of cheesecloth or nylon net and tie with a string, leaving a "tail" that allows easy removal of the bag.

SOUP STOCK AND BROTH

Beef Stock

 5 pounds beef bones with lots
    of meat and marrow
giblets from 1 chicken
2 small onions, sliced
1 carrot, sliced
1 small turnip, sliced
1 stalk celery (including
    leaves), sliced

3 fresh tomatoes (or 3 canned
    tomatoes and their juice)
mushroom stems (if available)
salt
peppercorns
bouquet garni—bay leaf,
    parsley, thyme, as available
Worcestershire or soy sauce

1 Place all the ingredients in a 4-quart kettle with cold water to cover. Simmer gently about 2 hours, skimming occasionally.

2 Strain out vegetables and meat and cool. The next day, skim off fat. Stock is ready for use.

YIELD: ABOUT 8 CUPS STOCK

Portable Soup

This recipe, included in *The Emigrant's Handbook*—published in 1845 as a "complete guide for the Farmer and the Emigrant"—tells how to make your own bouillon cubes.

To make Portable Soup.— Take a leg or a shin of beef, weighing about ten pounds; have it from a bullock recently killed; break the bones, and put it into your soup pot; just cover it with water, and set it on the fire to heat gradually, till it nearly boils. It should boil for nearly an hour. When scum rises, it should be carefully skimmed off, and a little cold water be poured in once or twice, which will cause more scum to rise on the surface, which must again be removed. When the scum has ceased rising, let it boil for eight or nine hours, and then strain through a hair-sieve into a stone jar, and place it where it will quickly cool.

The next day, after removing every particle of fat, pour it quite through a very fine sieve, or tamis, into a stew-pan, taking care that none of the settlings at the bottom go into the stewpan. After adding a quarter of an ounce of black peppercorns, let it boil briskly, the pan uncovered, until it begins to thicken and is reduced to about a quart. All scum that rises must be removed as in the preceding process, but without adding water to it. When it begins to thicken, withdraw it from the brisk fire, and place it where it can continue to boil gently, until it becomes a very thick syrup. Great care must be taken to prevent it burning, which would in one instant destroy the whole.

Pour out a little in a spoon to ascertain if it will jelly. If it does not, then boil it longer, and at length pour it into a little potting jar, about an inch and a half in depth and perfectly dry. These pots are recommended if the soup is intended for home consumption, and is sufficiently concentrated to keep for six months. If to be longer preserved, it may be put into bladders such as are used for German sausages; or it may be dried in the form of cakes, by pouring first into a dish until cooled. When cold enough to turn out, weigh the cake, and divide it into pieces of an ounce, or half an ounce each; place them in a warm room, and turn them twice a day for a week or ten days, by which time they will be thoroughly dried. If kept in a dry place, they may be preserved for years.

Chicken Stock

4 pounds chicken backs, necks, and giblets

1 onion

1 carrot

1 stalk celery

$^1\!/_2$ bay leaf

2 sprigs parsley

tarragon to taste

salt

few peppercorns

1 Rinse the chicken, cut up vegetables, and place in 3-quart kettle with cold water to cover. Simmer gently about 2 hours, skimming occasionally.

2 Strain out vegetables and meat, cool, and remove any fat.

YIELD: ABOUT 6 CUPS STOCK

Duck Soup

Duck makes an especially rich and flavorful soup.

1 duck carcass, with any leftover gravy, stuffing, and drippings

1 onion, sliced

1 carrot, sliced

1 small turnip, diced

1 or 2 stalks celery

1 bay leaf

salt

2 or 3 peppercorns

1 to 3 tablespoons mashed potato or potato flour

Worcestershire or soy sauce

5 or 6 mushrooms, sliced

chopped parsley

1 Place the duck carcass, gravy, drippings (after removing as much fat as possible), and stuffing in large kettle and cover with water. Add the onion, carrot, turnip, celery, bay leaf, salt, and peppercorns. Simmer 1 hour or more, until meat falls easily from bones.

2 Remove the carcass from pot, remove meat, and return the meat to soup. Cool soup and skim off fat.

3 Reheat soup and thicken with mashed potato or potato flour (amount used depends on thickness desired). Correct seasoning, adding Worcestershire or soy sauce if needed, as well as mushrooms and parsley.

Goose Soup

 When you are lucky enough to have a goose carcass, you can make a distinctive and wonderful soup using the method described for Turkey Bone Soup (below).

1 Remove any bits of goose meat and set aside to add to soup later.

2 Add a handful of lentils to cook with the soup (to absorb some of the goose's fat). Near end of cooking time, add sliced mushrooms—particularly good with goose.

Basic Turkey-Bone Soup

 You can use this soup as is or make a hearty concoction by adding some of the vegetables left over from the turkey dinner—mashed potatoes, creamed onions, celery, carrots, and/or mushrooms. If there is also leftover stuffing, you can purée it and add it to the soup. Either way, most New Englanders maintain that turkey soup is the very best part of the Thanksgiving dinner.

bones of 1 turkey and any leftover gravy	1 sprig parsley
	1 sprig thyme
1 onion, sliced	1 bay leaf
1 carrot, sliced	salt
1 stalk celery, sliced	2 or 3 peppercorns

1 Place all the ingredients in large kettle and cover with 3 or 4 quarts cold water. Simmer, covered, 2 hours, skimming as necessary.

2 Strain, cool, and remove the fat.

Almond Soup

This soup is delicate and unusually pleasant.

4 tablespoons butter or margarine	juice of half a lemon
4 tablespoons flour	salt
4 cups chicken stock	pepper
1 1/2 cups blanched, slivered almonds	1/2 cup cream
1 shallot or 1 scallion, minced	1 scant teaspoon almond extract
pinch of tarragon	whipped cream
	watercress sprigs

1 Melt the butter and stir in flour, half of the stock, and remaining ingredients except cream and almond extract.

2 Cook, stirring, about 10 minutes. Purée and return to stove, then add the remaining stock, cream, and almond extract.

3 Serve garnished with whipped cream and watercress.

YIELD: 6 SERVINGS

Apple Soup

This soup is a pleasant surprise on a hot summer day when served chilled, and it is equally intriguing when served piping hot in the winter.

1 large onion	2 cups chicken stock
4 stalks celery	1 teaspoon curry powder
2 tablespoons butter or margarine	1 teaspoon paprika
3 large green apples	juice of half a lemon
2 cups beef stock	1/2 cup heavy cream

1 Preheat oven to 325°.

2 Chop onion and celery and sauté gently in butter until golden brown. Peel, core, and slice apples and add to vegetables.

3 Place vegetable mixture in iron pan and bake, covered, 20 minutes. Remove from oven and add beef and chicken stocks, curry powder, paprika, and lemon juice. Season to taste and stir. Strain and bring to boil.

4 Remove from heat and add cream. Chill if soup is to be served cold.

YIELD: 6 SERVINGS

Avocado Soup

1 tablespoon minced onion

2 cups chicken stock

1 large, ripe avocado

1 small boiled potato

1 tablespoon lemon juice

2 tablespoons light rum

$1/2$ teaspoon salt

several dashes of Tabasco sauce

1 cup yogurt

sliced almonds, toasted

snipped dill or chervil

1 Cook the onion in some of the chicken stock until soft.

2 Combine first eight ingredients (including the remainder of the chicken stock) in a food processor or blender and purée until smooth.

3 Stir in the yogurt and chill. Serve garnished with almonds and dill or chervil.

YIELD: 4 SERVINGS

Bellevue Broth

5 cups chicken stock

3 cups clam broth

$1/2$ pint heavy cream

salt

pepper to taste

1 Combine and heat the stock and broth. Whip the cream and season lightly with salt.

2 Taste soup and season as needed. Ladle into heated bouillon cups and garnish with whipped cream.

YIELD: 8 SERVINGS

Boston Black Bean Soup

1 pound dried black beans

3 or 4 quarts water

2 tablespoons salt

1 ham bone

4 tablespoons butter or
   margarine

4 tablespoons flour

1 medium onion, minced

$1/4$ teaspoon black pepper

$1/4$ teaspoon dry mustard

2 cups light cream

1 Place the beans in a large kettle, with water to cover, and soak overnight.

2 In the morning, drain beans and return to kettle. Add 3 to 4 quarts water, salt, and ham bone. Cook about 2 hours, until beans are soft.

3 Remove ham bone and skim soup. Purée remaining mixture in blender or food processor.

4 Melt butter in saucepan and gradually whisk in flour, minced onion, pepper, mustard, and cream. Stir until slightly thickened, then add to purée and simmer a few minutes.

5 Ladle into soup bowls and garnish with thin slices of lemon and hard-boiled egg. Or cover with Boola-Boola Topping (below) and place under broiler until golden.

YIELD: 8 TO 10 SERVINGS

Boola-Boola Topping

This topping will transform a number of soups into a very special affair. It is good on split pea soup, or split pea soup mixed half and half with canned green turtle soup, Boston black bean soup, lentil soup, or tomato soup. Add a tablespoon of Madeira or sherry to the soup to make it even more festive.

1 egg yolk

3 tablespoons grated Parmesan
   cheese

1 cup whipped cream

1 Combine the egg yolk and cheese and mix to smooth paste. Fold in whipped cream.

2 Swirl topping onto soup in ovenproof bowls and brown quickly under broiler.

YIELD: ENOUGH TO GARNISH 6 BOWLS OF SOUP

Bright Red Soup

 A light, tangy soup from the autumn garden.

6 small beets, cooked and
   diced (canned beets may be
   used)
1/2 cup beet cooking water
2 large, ripe tomatoes, peeled,
   seeded, and diced
2 cups beef stock

2 teaspoons onion juice
juice of half a lemon
1 cup red wine—port or
   Bordeaux
salt to taste
3 whole cloves
6 peppercorns

1 Simmer all the ingredients together in large kettle until well blended.

2 Serve very hot, topped with cold sour cream and garnished with a
   green herb—preferably parsley or chives.

YIELD: 6 SERVINGS

Cauliflower Soup

 1 cauliflower
2 onions
1 tablespoon vegetable oil
2 tablespoons butter or
   margarine

1 small clove garlic, crushed
3 tablespoons flour
2 1/2 cups milk
1 bay leaf
1/2 cup light cream

1 Cut cauliflower and onions into pieces and sauté in oil, butter, and
   garlic 2 or 3 minutes. Then add enough water to cover vegetables and
   simmer until soft.

2 Over low heat, whisk in flour and slowly pour in milk. Stir until soup
   comes to boil, then add bay leaf. Simmer several minutes, then remove
   bay leaf.

3 Whip soup in blender or food processor until light. Return soup to
   stove and add cream. Heat briefly to warm through.

4 Ladle into soup bowls and garnish with finely chopped chives and
   croutons.

YIELD: 6 TO 8 SERVINGS

Cherry Soup I

This soup may be served hot or cold.

1/2 **pound red cherries, pitted**	1/4 **teaspoon salt**
1/2 **cup granulated sugar**	1/2 **cup orange juice**
2 **teaspoons cornstarch**	1 **cup red wine**
1/4 **teaspoon ground cinnamon**	

1 Chop cherries very fine and place in saucepan. Add sugar, cornstarch, cinnamon, and salt. Mix well. Stir in orange juice. Bring mixture to boil, stirring constantly.

2 Remove from heat and stir in wine.

YIELD: 6 SERVINGS

Cherry Soup II

If cherries are not in season when you feel like making cherry soup, here is a quick, good recipe that uses canned pie cherries.

1 **can cherry pie filling**	**ground cinnamon to taste**
1 **cup white wine**	**ground cloves to taste**
1/2 **cup orange juice**	**lemon juice to taste**
1/2 **cup beet juice**	**salt to taste**

1 Place the pie filling in blender or food processor. Add wine, orange juice, and beet juice and blend or process quickly. Taste and add seasonings as desired.

2 Serve cold, garnished with yogurt and fresh mint leaves; or serve hot, garnished with yogurt and grated orange rind.

YIELD: 6 SERVINGS

Cream of Chicken Soup

To make this soup, follow the recipe for Chicken Stock (p. 131) and include some chicken wings with the backs, necks, and giblets. When the broth is ready, cut the meat from the wings and reserve for this recipe.

3 tablespoons butter or chicken fat	4 or 5 mushrooms, sliced
3 tablespoons flour	1 egg yolk
6 cups chicken stock	1 cup light cream
1 carrot, finely chopped	meat from chicken wings
1 stalk celery, finely chopped	salt to taste
	pepper to taste

1   Melt butter or chicken fat. Add flour and 1 cup chicken stock, stirring or whisking to keep mixture smooth. Add vegetables and remaining stock. Simmer until vegetables are tender.

2   Beat egg yolk into cream and whisk slowly into soup. Add meat from chicken wings. Season to taste. (This soup may be puréed in blender or food processor, but it is more hearty with chunks of chicken and vegetables.)

3   Garnish with minced parsley, watercress sprigs, or toasted almonds.

YIELD: 6 SERVINGS

Chicken Soup Senégalaise

 This is a great taste teaser on a hot day.

1 apple, peeled, cored, and grated	curry powder to taste
1 onion, peeled and grated	ground ginger to taste
1 stalk celery, grated	4 cups chicken stock
2 tablespoons butter or margarine	1/2 cup light cream
1 tablespoon flour	1/2 cup white-meat chicken, finely diced

1   Sauté apple, onion, and celery in butter until soft. Add flour, curry powder, and ginger. Slowly stir in chicken stock. Simmer about 30 minutes.

2   Purée soup in batches in blender or food processor until perfectly smooth. Remove to mixing bowl, add cream and chicken, and chill.

3   Serve in chilled cups or soup bowls. Garnish as desired with grated orange rind, chopped chives, chopped green pepper, or garlic croutons.

YIELD: 6 SERVINGS

Cream of Fresh Asparagus Soup

 This soup tastes best if it is made a day ahead.

1 pound asparagus	1 medium potato, peeled and
4 tablespoons butter or	diced
margarine	3 cups chicken stock
1 medium onion, chopped	salt
1 leek, chopped	freshly ground white pepper
	1/2 cup heavy cream or yogurt

1 Cut off the tough ends of asparagus and peel stems. Remove the tips and reserve. Slice stems.

2 Melt the butter and sauté chopped onion and leek 2 minutes. Add asparagus stems, potatoes, and chicken stock and simmer, covered, until soft. Season to taste with salt and white pepper. Purée until very smooth in blender or food processor.

3 Cook reserved asparagus tips about 1 minute in boiling salted water. Drain. Add cooked tips and cream (or yogurt) to soup and stir carefully.

YIELD: 6 TO 8 SERVINGS

Cream of Young Carrot Soup

 A large bowlful of this creamy, golden soup makes a good main dish for lunch or supper.

4 tablespoons butter or	1 large potato, peeled and
margarine	sliced
white parts of 2 leeks, sliced,	1/2 clove garlic, crushed
or 1 bunch scallions	salt to taste
1/2 medium onion, sliced	white pepper to taste
1 stalk celery, sliced	pinch of granulated sugar
1 bunch (1 pound) young	bouquet garni (p. 129)
carrots (if older carrots are	1 tablespoon cornstarch
used, discard core and cut	2 cups milk
into narrow strips)	4 tablespoons light cream

1 Melt butter in heavy soup pot. Add sliced leeks (or scallions), onion, and celery and cook gently, covered, about 10 minutes.

2 Add carrots, potato, garlic, salt, pepper, sugar, and bouquet garni. Mix well, add enough water to cover, and simmer until vegetables are tender (about 40 minutes).

3 Mix cornstarch and milk in separate pan and simmer 3 minutes. Add to soup pot. Taste for seasoning. Just before serving, stir in cream.

4 Ladle into cups or soup bowls and garnish with finely chopped parsley or mint and tiny croutons sautéed in butter (and crushed garlic, if desired).

YIELD: 6 SERVINGS

Essence of Celery

6 large stalks celery   1 slice onion
8 cups well-seasoned chicken
   stock

1 Dice celery finely and simmer in chicken stock, uncovered, 30 minutes. Rub soup through fine-mesh strainer.

2 Serve hot or cold, garnished with thin slices of celery heart.

YIELD: 6 SERVINGS

Essence of Mushroom

1 pound mushrooms   1 cup water
4 cups chicken stock   sherry to taste

1 Clean mushrooms, chop finely, and simmer in stock and water 30 minutes.

2 Rub soup through fine-mesh sieve and stir in sherry to taste.

3 Serve garnished with thinly sliced mushroom caps.

YIELD: 6 SERVINGS

Cucumber Soup

3 cucumbers	1 egg yolk
4 scallions	1 cup light cream
3 cups chicken stock	salt to taste
1 tablespoon flour	pepper to taste

1 Peel, seed, and thinly slice cucumbers. Peel and thinly slice scallions. Simmer cucumbers and scallions in 1 cup stock until soft, about 15 minutes.

2 Stir in flour, cook briefly, then add remaining stock and simmer 10 minutes more.

3 Slowly stir in egg yolk and cream and heat, but do not allow to boil.

4 Serve hot or cold, garnished with finely chopped dill, watercress, parsley, or mint—or a combination of these.

YIELD: 6 SERVINGS

Cucumber Yogurt Soup

3 cucumbers	salt to taste
2 cloves garlic, crushed	pepper to taste
2 cups chicken stock	1/2 cup chopped walnuts
1 cup yogurt	finely chopped chives

1 Peel and quarter the cucumbers, remove seeds, and slice thinly. Mix with the remaining ingredients, except walnuts and chives, and chill several hours.

2 When ready to serve, stir in nuts and sprinkle soup with chives.

YIELD: 6 SERVINGS

Fresh Corn Chowder

6 ears fresh corn	1 tablespoon flour
1 small onion, chopped	3 cups light cream salt to taste
2 tablespoons butter or margarine	pepper to taste

1 Score each row of kernels with sharp knife and scrape kernels (and their milk) from cobs. Set aside.

2 Sauté onion in butter until soft but not brown. Add the flour and corn kernels and stir until mixture begins to thicken.

3 Transfer the mixture to double boiler and gradually add milk, stirring until warmed through. Season to taste with salt and pepper.

4 Serve hot, garnished with small additional pat of butter and lots of finely chopped parsley.

YIELD: 6 SERVINGS

French Onion Soup

 Wonderfully good, nutritious, and easy to prepare. On a busy day, you can put the casserole in the oven and a nice, hearty lunch or supper will be waiting for you.

2 tablespoons butter or margarine
1 very large Bermuda, Spanish, or Vidalia onion, very thinly sliced
1 chicken bouillon cube
2 cups dry white wine

4 cups chicken stock
1 cup beef stock
French bread
grated Gruyère, Emmenthaler, or Parmesan cheese
freshly grated black pepper

1 Preheat oven to 350°.

2 Put the butter in a 2-quart earthenware casserole, add onion slices and bouillon cube, and pour in wine. Cover and bake 1 hour, until onions are soft. Remove the casserole from oven and increase heat to 450°.

3 In saucepan, heat chicken and beef stock. Meanwhile, cut slices of French bread—enough to cover top of casserole.

4 Pour warmed stock into casserole, arrange slices of bread on top, and sprinkle generously with grated cheese. Return casserole to oven and bake until cheese is melted and bubbly. Season as desired with pepper. (If you have individual ovenproof serving casseroles, you can divide soup among them and top each with slice of bread and cheese. For easy handling, put them all on jelly-roll pan or sturdy cookie sheet.)

YIELD: 4 TO 6 SERVINGS

Onion Soup

This is one of Mrs. Anne Gibbons Gardiner's Receipts, from 1763.

Take half a pound of Butter, put it into a Stew pan & set it on the Fire, & let all the Butter melt, and boil until it is done making a Noise; then have ready ten or a Dozen middling sized Onions, peeled and cut small, which throw into the Butter, and let them fry for a Quarter of an hour; then shake a little Flour and stir them round; shake your Pan and let them do a few minutes longer; when you must pour in a Quart or three Pints of boiling water; stir them round, and throw in a good piece of the upper Crust of the stalest Bread you have. Season with Salt to your palate. Let it then stew or boil gently for ten Minutes observing to stir it often; after which take it off the Fire, and have ready the yolks of two Eggs beaten fine in a Spoonfull of Vinegar, and then stir it gently & by Degrees into your Soup, mixing it well. This is a delicious Dish.

[Indeed it is delicious, and substituting beef stock for half of the water gives this soup the fillip it needs today. Serve with grated Cheddar cheese.]

Fresh Tomato Soup

In August, September, and October, when your garden burgeons with fat, red tomatoes, consider this perfect homemade soup.

4 tablespoons butter or margarine	2 heaping tablespoons flour
5 or 6 large, ripe tomatoes	2 cups (or more) milk
1 clove garlic, crushed	fresh herbs as desired

1 Melt the butter in a soup pot. Rinse tomatoes and cut in pieces. Discard seeds that are easily removed without losing too much juice. Place tomatoes in the pot and simmer gently.

2 As tomatoes simmer, remove skins. Continuing simmering, adding garlic and flour. Gradually stir in enough milk to make moderately thick cream soup. Do not allow soup to boil.

3 Stir in whatever fresh herbs are available—especially basil, parsley, chervil, dill, chives, oregano. Serve hot or cold.

YIELD: 6 SERVINGS

Gazpacho

 1 cup peeled, seeded, and
chopped tomatoes

½ cup finely chopped celery

¼ cup finely chopped green
pepper

½ cup peeled, seeded, and
chopped cucumber

¼ cup finely chopped onion

2 teaspoons finely chopped
parsley

2 teaspoons finely chopped
chives

1 clove garlic, minced

3 tablespoons tarragon wine
vinegar

3 tablespoons olive oil

1 teaspoon salt

freshly ground black pepper

½ teaspoon Tabasco sauce

2 cups tomato juice

garlic croutons

1 Combine all ingredients in a large casserole. Chill 8 hours.

2 Serve in chilled bowls garnished with croutons.

YIELD: 6 SERVINGS

Greens Soup

 A tantalizing and elusively flavored soup from greens culled from the
garden—the fresh outside leaves of lettuce, green tops of scallions, celery tops, a little watercress or spinch, pot herbs.

4 cups chicken stock

salad greens as available

1 shallot or 1 clove garlic,
minced

2 tablespoons butter or
margarine

salt to taste

white pepper to taste

pinch of dry mustard

1 cup light cream

1 In a saucepan, cook together all ingredients except cream, until just
soft and still green. Whirl in blender or food processor.

2 Return to saucepan, add cream, and reheat, but do not boil.

3 Serve hot, garnished, if you wish, with whipped cream and chopped
chives.

YIELD: 6 SERVINGS

Lentil Soup

 A number of wonderful soups can be made with a leftover ham bone with a little meat on it. The spicy ham, dried legumes, and fresh vegetables make filling and tasty fare.

1 pound lentils	1 bay leaf
1 ham bone	1 sprig thyme
12 cups water	ground cloves to taste
2 carrots, sliced	salt to taste
2 onions, sliced	pepper to taste
1 stalk celery, sliced	

1 Soak lentils overnight in water to cover.

2 In the morning, place lentils in a kettle with 12 cups water, ham bone, vegetables, and seasonings. Cook 2 to 3 hours.

3 Remove ham bone, bay leaf, and thyme. Skim soup if necessary. Trim meat from bone and add to soup.

YIELD: 8 TO 10 SERVINGS

Minestrone

This soup makes a very satisfactory meal. I prefer not to soak the beans overnight, as is often recommended. This way, the beans are soft but not mushy, the soup is thick, and the vegetables are timed to remain bright and fresh.

1/2 pound dried white beans	1/2 cup uncooked macaroni or other pasta
1 large onion, diced	2 medium carrots, diced
1 large potato, peeled and diced	2 medium stalks celery, diced
2 large cloves garlic, crushed	1/2 cup fresh peas (or thawed frozen ones)
1 bay leaf	few sprigs parsley, finely minced
1 chicken bouillon cubes	grated Parmesan cheese
salt to taste	
white pepper to taste	

1 Rinse the beans several times, then put in a pot with water to cover. Simmer for about 2 hours.

2 Add the onion, potato, garlic, bay leaf, bouillon cubes and water to cover and simmer until soup begins to thicken, about 2 more hours.

3 Add macaroni and carrots and cook 10 minutes.

4 Add peas, celery, parsley and cook 5 more minutes. Salt and pepper to taste.

5 Ladle into soup bowls and serve with grated cheese.

YIELD: 4 TO 6 SERVINGS

Maine Potato Soup

4 medium potatoes

4 slices bacon

4 tablespoons bacon fat

1 onion, diced

2 tablespoons flour

1¹/₃ cups dried skim milk

³/₄ teaspoon salt

¹/₄ teaspoon pepper

¹/₄ teaspoon paprika

1 teaspoon dried chives

pinch of garlic salt

1 Wash and peel potatoes and boil in covered pot until cooked thoroughly. Drain off and reserve cooking water. When potatoes are cool, dice and set aside.

2 Fry bacon slices until crisp and set aside to drain.

3 Put bacon fat in heavy pot and sauté onion in it until soft. Stir in flour and cook until bubbly.

4 In separate bowl, mix potato cooking water with dried milk, adding enough extra tap water to make 1 quart (4 cups).

5 Stir milk mixture quickly into flour mixture, cooking until thickened. Add seasonings. Add potatoes and cook slowly 10 minutes.

6 Serve garnished with crumbled bacon.

YIELD: 6 SERVINGS

Mushroom and Scallion Soup

1 bunch scallions

1 clove garlic

4 tablespoons butter or chicken fat

4 tablespoons flour

salt to taste

pepper to taste

4 cups chicken stock

¹/₂ pound mushrooms, finely sliced

¹/₂ cup light cream

pinch of tarragon

juice of half a lemon

1 or 2 egg yolks

1 Slice scallions (green and white parts), crush garlic, and cook slowly in butter or chicken fat until soft but still green. Add flour, salt and pepper to taste, and half of the chicken stock. Cook until thick.

2 If desired, purée in blender or food processor. Return to stove and add mushrooms, remaining stock, cream, tarragon, and lemon juice. Cook a few minutes.

3 Stir about 3 tablespoons of soup into the egg yolks, then add to the remaining soup, being careful to stir quickly so egg will not curdle. Serve at once.

YIELD: 6 SERVINGS

New England Corn Chowder

 This hearty chowder can even be made in winter from canned corn. Served with corn bread and pickles or relish, this is a familiar New England supper.

½ cup diced salt pork
4 tablespoons chopped onion
¼ cup chopped celery
2 tablespoons chopped green
  pepper
1 raw potato, peeled and diced
½ teaspoon salt

2 cups water
2 tablespoons flour
2 cups warm milk
6 ears fresh corn or 1 16-ounce
  can creamed corn
chopped parsley

1 Sauté the salt pork, then add and sauté the onion, celery, and green pepper. Add the diced potato, salt, and water and simmer until potato is soft. Add the flour, milk, and corn and cook thoroughly.

2 Serve sprinkled with finely chopped parsley.

YIELD: 6 SERVINGS

Portuguese Gazpacho

 This is a white gazpacho—very tasty.

½ cup peeled, seeded, and
  chopped cucumber
½ cup finely chopped white
  radishes
¼ cup finely chopped leeks
½ cup finely chopped celery
¼ cup finely chopped green
  pepper
1 clove garlic, minced
3 tablespoons tarragon wine
  vinegar

3 tablespoons olive oil
1 teaspoon salt
freshly ground white pepper
½ teaspoon Tabasco sauce
2 cups yogurt
finely minced parsley
chives
jalapeño peppers
garlic croutons, heated

1 In large bowl or casserole, combine first 12 ingredients. Chill at least 8 hours.

2 Serve in chilled bowls garnished with parsley, chives, and peppers. Pass hot garlic croutons.

YIELD: 6 SERVINGS

Sorrel Soup

 Sorrel speaks of spring. Then and all summer long, it grows freely as a weed in most New England pastures and gardens. When picked young and fresh, it is ideal for cooking.

2 cups young sorrel leaves
2 tablespoons butter or
  margarine
2 teaspoons cornstarch
3 cups chicken stock

1 sprig parsley, minced
2 egg yolks
pinch of salt
1 cup light cream

1 Wash the sorrel leaves and sauté in butter until just wilted. Purée sorrel and add other ingredients, after dissolving the cornstarch in a little stock. Or purée wilted sorrel and remaining ingredients in blender or food processor.

2 Pour into saucepan and cook over low heat until slightly thickened.

3 Serve hot or chilled, garnished with sour cream and chives or with thin slices of lemon.

YIELD: 6 SERVINGS

Split Pea Soup

1 pound green split peas	2 or 3 peppercorns
12 cups water	1 bay leaf
1 meaty ham bone	1 carrot, sliced
2 medium onions, sliced	1 parsnip, sliced
1 clove garlic	1 stalk celery, sliced
1 sprig parsley	1 cup white wine
1 sprig thyme	mace
2 teaspoons salt	

1 Soak the split peas overnight in water to cover.

2 In morning, drain peas and place in a large pot with 12 cups water, ham bone, and all other ingredients except vegetables, wine, and mace. Simmer 2 hours or so, stirring occasionally.

3 Remove the bone from soup, scrape off meat, and add meat to soup. Add carrot, parsnip, celery, and wine and simmer 15 minutes, or until vegetables are tender.

4 Ladle into soup bowls and sprinkle each serving with pinch of mace. This soup is also splendid with Boola-Boola Topping (p. 135)

YIELD: 8 TO 10 SERVINGS

Vermont Cabbage Soup

3 cups cabbage, finely chopped	juice of half a lemon
1½ cups water	salt to taste
3 cups milk	freshly ground white pepper to
1 cup light cream	taste

1 Cook cabbage in water about 15 minutes, until soft but still green.

2 Add milk, cream, lemon juice, and seasonings to taste. Warm through but do not boil.

3 Ladle into cups or soup bowls and garnish with small pat of butter and finely chopped parsley.

YIELD: 6 SERVINGS

Esau's Pottage

From an old cookbook, here is the lineal descendant of the soup for which Esau reputedly sold his birthright.

1/2 **pound green split peas**
1/4 **pound red lentils**
2 **tablespoons pearl barley**
4 **tablespoons white beans**
1 **good soup bone**
1/2 **pound shin beef**
2 **carrots, diced**
2 **stalks celery, diced**
1 **onion, thinly sliced**
2 **quarts water**
salt and freshly ground
  pepper
1 **large sprig parsley**

Put the peas, lentils, barley, and beans into a large bowl, cover to twice their depth with cold water, and leave to swell overnight. Next day, rinse well. Put the bone and the meat (in one piece) with salt and water into a soup kettle. Bring slowly to the boil, skim, then add the other ingredients. Cover and simmer as slowly as possible for 2 or 3 hours, stirring occasionally. When the soup is ready, the legumes will have dissolved into a purée and sieving will be unnecessary. Before serving, taste for seasoning, remove the bone, and serve a little of the meat with each serving. Garnish with scissored parsley. Serves 6 to 8.

Vichyssoise

3 **medium potatoes, peeled and**
  grated
1 **bunch leeks, grated**
4 **cups chicken stock**
salt to taste

white pepper to taste
pinch of nutmeg
1 **pint light cream**
finely chopped chives

1 Simmer the potatoes and leeks in chicken stock 1 hour.

2 Purée in a blender or food processor until very smooth. Season with salt, white pepper, and nutmeg. Add cream and chill thoroughly.

3 Served in chilled bowls garnished with finely chopped chives.

YIELD: 6 SERVINGS

Watercress Soup

 This lovely, bright-green soup is as refreshing to look at as it is to taste.

1 small onion, sliced

1 potato, peeled and sliced

1 tablespoon butter or
   margarine

1 egg

1 cup heavy cream

1 bunch watercress, chopped

1 large sprig parsley, chopped

1 large sprig dill, chopped

2 cups chicken stock

1 Sauté onion and potato slowly in butter until softened but not brown. Add water to cover (about $1/2$ cup) and sauté until very soft.

2 Mix the egg with $1/2$ cup cream. Add egg mixture and sautéed mixture to chopped greens and stock. Purée in blender or food processor until light and frothy.

3 Serve hot or chilled, garnished with remaining cream, whipped and salted, and small sprig of watercress.

YIELD: 6 SERVINGS

Watercress and Spinach Soup

 This recipe makes a very piquant soup.

1 bunch watercress

1 cup fresh spinach

1 small potato, boiled or baked,
   and then peeled

2 small slices Bermuda onion

4 cups well-seasoned chicken
   stock

$1/2$ cup light cream

pinch of mace

1 Pick over watercress, discard yellow leaves, and trim stems. (If it is slightly wilted, it will still do.)

2 Put watercress, spinach, and potato into blender and purée, while adding stock, cream, and mace.

3 Return to stove and heat 5 minutes.

YIELD: 6 SERVINGS

White Turnip Soup

4 medium white turnips,
  peeled, sliced, and coarsely
  chopped
1 large onion, coarsely
  chopped
3 tablespoons butter or
  margarine
6 cups boiling water

salt to taste
pepper to taste
3 slices bread, oven-dried and
  crumbled
1 egg
$\frac{1}{2}$ cup light cream
finely minced parsley

1 Sauté turnips and onion in butter about 5 minutes. Add boiling water, salt and pepper to taste, and crumbled bread. Simmer 30 minutes.

2 Purée soup in blender or food processor and return to stove over low heat. Beat egg well with cream and stir into soup.

3 Serve at once, garnished with parsley.

YIELD: 6 SERVINGS

Zucchini Soup

There's always a surplus of zucchini by mid-August, and it takes only a few minutes to make this beautiful soup.

$\frac{1}{2}$ onion, finely chopped
1 potato, peeled and sliced
2 chicken bouillon cubes

3 medium zucchini, thinly
  sliced
curry powder to taste
1 cup yogurt

1 Simmer the onion, potato, and bouillon cubes in water to cover until vegetables are tender. Add zucchini and simmer about 1 minute, until zucchini is bright green.

2 Purée in batches in a blender or food processor until very smooth. Add curry powder to taste, then stir in yogurt.

3 Serve hot or chilled, garnished with thin slices of radish.

YIELD: 4 TO 6 SERVINGS

FISH AND SHELLFISH SOUPS AND CHOWDERS

Aunt Clara's Shrimp Gumbo

1 pound fresh shrimp
3 medium onions
4 cups water
2 tablespoons tarragon vinegar
1/4 cup uncooked rice
1/2 pound fresh okra
1 tablespoon butter or
  margarine
1 tablespoon flour

4 tomatoes, chopped (canned
  tomatoes may be used)
1 teaspoon Worcestershire
  sauce
1 teaspoon chopped parsley
2 bay leaves
pinch of salt
pinch of pepper
pinch of granulated sugar

1 Place shrimp and 1 onion (chopped) in kettle with water and vinegar. Boil 10 minutes. Remove shrimp and reserve water. Peel and clean shrimp.

2 In small saucepan, place rice, okra, and 1 inch water. Cook until water has evaporated.

3 In large skillet, sauté remaining onions, finely chopped, in butter over low heat until soft. Stir in flour, then add shrimp stock, okra, rice, shrimp, tomatoes, and seasonings. Simmer 20 minutes and serve piping hot.

YIELD: 6 SERVINGS

Lobster Chowder

1 2-pound lobster
1 1/2 cups diced, peeled potatoes
1 small onion, minced
3 tablespoons butter or
  margarine

2 tablespoons flour
4 cups milk, scalded
salt to taste
pepper to taste
6 common crackers

1 Boil lobster. Drain and cool. Remove meat from shell, reserving tomalley (liver), and cut meat in small pieces.

2 Scrub shells, then place in a kettle, cover with cold water, and simmer 15 minutes. Strain, add potatoes to stock, and cook until tender.

3 In saucepan, sauté onion in butter until delicately browned. Blend in lobster liver, then stir in flour. Add milk gradually, stirring constantly until thickened. Add lobster meat, potatoes with their stock, and seasoning. Simmer 5 minutes.

4 Split common crackers. Place in hot tureen and add chowder. Sprinkle with parsley.

YIELD: 6 SERVINGS

Billi-Bi

 A very pleasant cream of mussel soup with French origins. A great way to enjoy the mussels so prevalent along the New England coast. The mussels that are strained out of the soup can be removed from their shells and served on toothpicks for a cocktail snack.

3 pounds mussels, debearded
   and thoroughly scrubbed
1 onion, chopped
2 tablespoons butter or
   margarine

2 cups dry white wine
4 cups light cream
salt to taste
white pepper to taste
pinch of cayenne pepper

1 Place all the ingredients in a large pot and cook 10 minutes. Line colander with cheesecloth and strain. Serve soup very hot.

YIELD: 6 SERVINGS

Lobster Soup

 1 2½-pound lobster
2 cups water
½ teaspoon salt
2 or 3 white peppercorns
½ onion, sliced
½ carrot, sliced
1 large sprig parsley
½ teaspoon dried tarragon

1 small bay leaf
3 cups chicken stock
4 slices white bread, crusts
   removed
1 tablespoon butter or
   margarine
sherry or Madeira to taste

1 In a kettle containing about 2 cups water, put salt, peppercorns, onion, and carrot. Tie parsley, tarragon, and bay leaf into piece of cheesecloth

and add to pot. Bring ingredients to boil and add lobster. Simmer, covered, 15 minutes. Discard herb bag and set lobster aside to cool.

2 Strain the lobster stock and return to heat with chicken stock and bread. Stir until bread has dissolved.

3 Remove lobster meat from shell and cut up, reserving a few larger chunks for garnish.

4 Mash lobster liver (tomalley) with butter and add to soup, then add remaining lobster meat and cream. Add sherry or Madeira to taste. Serve hot.

YIELD: 6 SERVINGS

Mermaid Soup

½ pound scallops
½ pound halibut fillet
2 tablespoons butter or
    margarine
1 teaspoon onion juice
1 teaspoon lemon juice

salt to taste
cayenne pepper to taste
1 cup light cream or yogurt
finely chopped fresh chives,
    parsley, or dill

1 Sauté the scallops and halibut in butter with onion juice and lemon juice until just pink and white. Season to taste with salt and cayenne pepper.

2 Process in a blender or food processor until smooth. Stir in cream or yogurt and chill.

3 Serve in chilled bowls garnished with finely chopped herbs.

YIELD: 4 TO 5 SERVINGS

Nantucket Scallop Chowder

2 onions, sliced
4 tablespoons butter or
    margarine
1 pint scallops
1 cup potatoes, diced

2 cups boiling water
4 cups milk, scalded
salt to taste
pepper to taste
chopped fresh dill

1 Sauté the onions in butter and remove from skillet. Cut up scallops and sauté in skillet.

2 In saucepan, add sautéed onions and potatoes to boiling water and simmer 20 minutes. Add sautéed scallops and scalded milk and simmer 15 minutes more.

3 Add salt and pepper to taste and serve garnished with good quantity of chopped dill.

YIELD: 6 SERVINGS

Nauset/Eastham Fish Chowdy

 This chowder was a favorite of President John F. Kennedy's. The recipe, which comes from Albert E. Snow of Orleans, Massachusetts, is quick to prepare; the soup is nourishing and easy to digest.

1 4-pound haddock
3 cups cold water
1/4 pound fat salt pork, diced in
    1/4-inch cubes
6 onions, thinly sliced
2 tablespoons flour
2 cups peeled, diced potatoes
    (1/2-inch cubes)

4 cups milk, scalded
2 tablespoons butter or
    margarine
salt to taste
pepper to taste
3 sprigs parsley, minced

1 Skin the haddock, reserving head and tail. Cut out backbone and reserve. Cut fish into 2-inch pieces. Place head, tail, backbone, and any odd remnants into saucepan and add cold water. Bring slowly to boil, then simmer 30 minutes.

2 In a large skillet, place pork bits and fry until crisp and browned. Remove and set aside. Add onions to skillet and sauté slowly 5 to 10 minutes, till browned. Remove.

3 Stir flour into skillet, then slowly add broth drained from fish bones, stirring constantly to avoid lumping. Add diced potatoes, sautéed onions, and fish. Cover and simmer slowly 1 hour, until potatoes lose their stiffness.

4 Add the hot milk and butter, plus salt and pepper to taste.

5 Serve accompanied by warmed pilot biscuits, oysterettes, or common crackers.

YIELD: 8 SERVINGS

Clam Soup

Here is a unique contribution from Hildegarde Halliday of New York City.

Many a miss has yearned for a magic potion that would make the man of her dreams fall in love with her, and in Newport, Rhode Island, Miss Halliday's aunt had just such a romantic talisman before the turn of the century—a recipe for a very special clam soup. According to Miss Halliday, "Mr. G. F. Downing was already enamoured of my aunt, but upon feasting on this soup, he felt that a beautiful girl who was also such a beautiful cook should be his without further delay. This is one of the most delicious soups I have ever eaten."

W. A. Croffut—of whom nothing is known except that he favored this soup and was a gifted versifier—wrote the recipe.

First catch your clams along
   the ebbing edges
Of saline coves. You'll find
   the precious wedges
With backs up, lurking in the
   sandy bottom;
Pull in your iron rake, and lo!
   you've got 'em!

Take thirty large ones, put a
   basin under,
And cleave with knife their
   stony jaws asunder,

Add water (three quarts) to
   the native liquor,
Bring to a boil (and, by the
   way, the quicker

It boils the better, if you'd do
   it cutely),
Now add the clams, chopped
   up and minced minutely;
Allow a longer boil of just
   three minutes,
And while it bubbles, quickly
   stir within its

Tumultuous depths, where
   still the mollusks mutter,
Four tablespoons of flour
   and four of butter,
A pint of milk, some pepper
   to your notion,
And clams need salting,
   although born of ocean.

Remove from fire (if much
   boiled they will suffer;
You'll find that India rubber
   isn't tougher),
After 'tis off add three fresh
   eggs well beaten,
Stir once more and it's ready
   to be eaten.

Fruit of the wave: Oh, dainty
   and delicious!
Food for the Gods! Ambrosia
   for Apicius!
Worthy to thrill the soul of
   sea-born Venus
Or titillate the palate of
   Silenus!

New England Clam Chowder

¼ **pound salt pork**
1 onion, chopped
2 potatoes, peeled and diced
3 cups shucked
    clams—quahogs or
    littlenecks

salt to taste
pepper to taste
4 cups milk, scalded

1 Dice salt pork and fry in saucepan until crisp. Remove pork bits and set aside. Sauté onion in pork fat until soft. Add diced potatoes and just enough water to cover. Simmer until potatoes are tender.

2 Remove the black caps from clams. Strain clams, reserving their liquor, then chop clams. Add clams and liquor to potato mixture and cook 2 minutes more.

3 Add hot milk. Season to taste with salt and pepper. Return salt-pork bits to saucepan and stir. Serve immediately.

YIELD: 6 SERVINGS

 ## Oyster Soup

This delicious old-time recipe, which first appeared in an 1832 cookery book with a very long title—*A Boston Housekeeper, The Cook's Own Book, Being a Complete Culinary Encyclopaedia*—differs from the standard recipe used today only in the beneficial inclusion of flour and marjoram.

three pints of large fresh
    oysters
two tablespoonfuls of butter,
    rolled in flour
a bunch of sweet herbs

a quart of rich milk
pepper to your taste

Take the liquor of three pints of oysters. Strain it and set it on the fire. Put into it pepper to your taste, two tablespoonfuls of butter rolled in flour, and a bunch of sweet marjoram and other pot herbs. When it boils, add a quart of rich milk—and as soon as it boils again, take out the herbs and put in the oysters just before you send it to the table. Be sure to let the soup *simmer* for 3 minutes after adding the oysters.

Oyster Bisque

1 dozen oysters

2 cups chicken stock

3/4 cup soft breadcrumbs

1 onion, sliced

2 stalks celery

1 sprig parsley

1 bay leaf

1 tablespoon butter or
  margarine

1 tablespoon flour

2 cups milk

salt to taste

pepper to taste

whipped cream, lightly salted

chopped parsley or dill

1 Clean and pick over the oysters, reserving their liquor. Cut firm part of oysters from soft part, and chop separately.

2 Put chicken stock in a kettle and add breadcrumbs, onion, celery, parsley, bay leaf, and chopped firm part of oysters. Simmer 3 minutes. Remove bay leaf and purée.

3 Melt butter, stir in flour, then add puréed mixture and oyster liquor. Bring to boil. Add milk, chopped soft part of oysters, and salt and pepper to taste. Warm through. If desired, purée soup again.

4 Serve garnished with whipped cream and chopped parsley or dill.

YIELD: 4 SERVINGS

Purée of Oyster Soup

4 tablespoons butter or
  margarine

1/4 cup finely chopped onion

1 package frozen tiny peas,
  thawed

1 cup milk

1 pint fresh oysters with liquor

2 cups clam juice

1/2 cup dry white wine

salt to taste

freshly ground white pepper to
  taste

1 cup heavy cream

1 Melt 2 tablespoons butter in saucepan and sauté onions until soft but not brown. Add the peas and milk. Simmer until peas are just tender.

2 Add oysters, oyster liquor, and clam juice and simmer over low heat 10 minutes. Add wine, 2 tablespoons butter, plus salt and pepper to taste.

3 When the butter has melted, beat mixture well, or purée in blender or food processor until light. Return to saucepan.

4 When ready to serve, preheat broiler. Meanwhile, whip cream, seasoning lightly with salt.

5 Heat soup on top of stove almost to boiling, then spoon into hot, ovenproof bowls. Top each serving with generous dollop of whipped cream and place under broiler until cream is golden brown.

YIELD: 4 SERVINGS

6

Fish and Shellfish

The cod of Bay State fame was, along with corn, the mainstay of the diet of our earliest American ancestors, and a great liking for fish of all sorts is still prevalent in this part of the country. New Englanders enjoy a great variety of seafood, especially during the summer. But fish and shellfish once were more abundant than now, and ten-pound lobsters were taken with ease from the sea.

Fresh fish should not be kept for any length of time—one or two days at the most. It is best bought and used the same day. A whole fish, if fresh, has clear, firm eyes, tight scales, and is free of a slimy surface or strong fishy odor. Cut fish or fillets should be firm and fresh smelling. Always go to a reliable source for your fish. A fishmonger offers the greatest variety.

Since court bouillon and fish stock play a large part in the successful boiling or poaching of any fish (it is as important a part of fish cookery as meat and chicken bouillon are for soups), those recipes appear first. The general rule for poaching a large fish is to cook it in fish stock or water that simmers (not quite boiling) for ten minutes for each inch of the fish's thickness at its thickest part.

The term *mask,* as used in this chapter, means covering the surface of— frosting, if you will—the fish with the recommended sauce.

Often fish tastes best served simply with melted butter (sweet butter is best) and a dusting of finely minced parsley or other herbs (dill is especially good), accompanied by lemon wedges. Recipes for more elaborate preparations also are included in this chapter. Fish eaters on a low-fat, low-cholesterol diet might try the Cucumber Yogurt Sauce (p. 316) or Mustard Yogurt Sauce (p. 320).

Court Bouillon

3 tablespoons butter or
   margarine
1 onion, minced
1 stalk celery, minced
1 carrot, peeled and chopped
1/2 cup white vinegar

2 sprigs parsley, minced
4 cups boiling water
1 bay leaf
8 whole cloves
4 peppercorns

1 Melt butter in skillet, add onion, celery, and carrot and sauté 5 minutes. Add remaining ingredients and boil 20 minutes. Strain.

YIELD: 4 CUPS STOCK

Fish Stock

 Use for poaching fish or for making fish soups or chowders (see chapter 5). Ask your fish market for about 2 pounds of fish trimmings,
bones, and heads. Wash them thoroughly several times.

**2 tablespoons butter or
  margarine**
about 2 pounds fish trimmings
12 cups water
2 teaspoons salt

1 Bouquet Garni (p. 129)
1 onion, chopped
1 tomato, chopped
1 carrot, chopped
1 clove garlic, minced

1 Melt butter in large kettle. Add fish, water, and remaining ingredients.
2 Simmer 20 minutes. Cool, strain, and skim.

YIELD: ABOUT 12 CUPS STOCK

Baked Mackerel

 2 small mackerel
1 cup milk
salt to taste

pepper to taste
chopped chives
paprika

1 Preheat oven to 375°.
2 Split and bone mackerel. Coat 9″ x 12″ baking pan with vegetable
spray. Place fish skin side down in pan.
3 Season milk with salt and pepper and pour over mackerel.
4 Bake, uncovered, 25 minutes. Remove and sprinkle with chopped
chives and paprika. If desired, serve with melted butter or margarine.

YIELD: 4 SERVINGS

Baked Stuffed Shad

 Serve this, if desired, with Shad Roe (p. 172).

1 shad, split and backbone
  removed
salt to taste
pepper to taste

fresh lemon juice to taste
1/2 cup well-seasoned bread
  stuffing
2 strips bacon

1 Preheat oven to 250°.

2 Lay shad open and sprinkle interior generously with salt, pepper, and lemon juice. Fill with bread stuffing and close.

3 Place 2 strips bacon over fish, wrap tightly in foil, and bake 6 hours. (Bones will all be edible.)

YIELD: 6 TO 8 SERVINGS

Broiled Scrod

 Scrod is a young cod or haddock weighing about 2 pounds.

1 young scrod, split, boned,
  and cut into 4 sections
salt to taste
white pepper to taste
1/4 cup butter or margarine,
  melted

1/2 cup breadcrumbs
1 teaspoon chopped fresh
  parsley
paprika, a sprinkle

1 Preheat broiler.

2 Sprinkle fish pieces with salt and pepper. Dip in melted butter, then roll in mixture of fine breadcrumbs, chopped parsley, and paprika.

3 Place on ovenproof platter, about 3 inches from broiler flame, and broil until white and flaky (5 to 7 minutes). Baste with melted butter.

YIELD: 4 SERVINGS

Broiled Swordfish with Anchovy Butter

 2 pounds swordfish steaks, 1¼ inches thick

6 tablespoons butter or margarine, softened

1 teaspoon anchovy paste

freshly ground black pepper

chopped parsley

lemon wedges

1 Coat broiler rack with vegetable spray and heat in oven. Remove and place swordfish on rack.

2 Preheat broiler. Spread fish lightly with butter and broil 4 or 5 minutes. Remove from broiler and place on very hot platter.

3 In small saucepan, combine remaining butter with anchovy paste. Melt, blend, and pour over swordfish. Grind pepper over steaks and serve immediately, garnished with parsley and lemon wedges.

YIELD: 6 SERVINGS

Campfire Smelt

 3 pounds smelt, cleaned

2 teaspoons salt

freshly ground black pepper

⅓ cup chopped onion

⅓ cup chopped fresh parsley

3 strips bacon, cut in half

1 Prepare campfire.

2 Cut heavy-duty aluminum foil into six 12″ x 12″ pieces. Coat lightly with vegetable spray.

3 Place fish on foil and sprinkle with salt, pepper, onion, and parsley. Top with half strip bacon. Bring foil up and over fish and seal edges with double folds.

4 Place foil packets on grill about 4 inches above coals. Cook 10 to 15 minutes.

YIELD: 6 SERVINGS

Cold Salmon

 Cool and elegant hot-weather fare, low in calories and cholesterol. A good accompaniment is cold, cooked garden peas mixed with a little olive oil and sprinkled with chopped mint.

1 chunk of salmon	capers
court bouillon or fish stock to cover	chopped fresh parsley
	lemon wedges

1 Place salmon in baking dish, add court bouillon or fish stock, and poach.

2 Remove salmon carefully, place in casserole, and chill overnight.

3 Next day, carefully remove skin (and bones if desired). Mask fish with homemade mayonnaise or Green Sauce (p. 317). Surround fish with cucumber salad and serve garnished with capers, parsley, and lemon wedges. (For a low-calorie, low-cholesterol dish, serve with Mustard Yogurt Sauce (p. 320).)

Fillet of Sole in Sherry

 Easy to prepare and very impressive.

1½-pound fillet of sole	¼ pound baby shrimp
2 cups light cream	⅓ cup buttered breadcrumbs
½ cup sherry	1 cup white grapes
salt to taste	1 tablespoon butter or
freshly ground white pepper to taste	margarine

1 Preheat oven to 400°.

2 Place fillets in large skillet and cover with cream and sherry. Season with salt and pepper and cook about 5 minutes on top of stove.

3 Arrange fillets in shallow baking dish coated with vegetable spray. Sprinkle shrimp over top.

4 Bake until cream and sherry are thick, about 10 minutes. Meanwhile, preheat broiler. Remove from oven and top with breadcrumbs. Place under broiler until sauce bubbles and browns slightly.

5 Sauté grapes in butter and reserve.

6 Remove fish from oven and serve, garnished with sautéed grapes.

YIELD: 6 SERVINGS

Finnan Haddie with Oysters

Finnan haddie is haddock cured with the smoke of green wood. This dish is an old favorite for Sunday-night supper.

2 cups finnan haddie

1 pint oysters

1½ cups Cream Sauce (p. 315), made without salt

Tabasco sauce to taste

6 to 8 slices buttered toast

1 Soak finnan haddie in cold water 30 minutes. Drain and flake fish, removing any bones. Simmer 25 minutes in fresh water. Drain.

2 In saucepan, heat oysters in their liquor. When edges curl, add oysters to cream sauce.

3 Add finnan haddie and simmer gently about 5 minutes. Season with Tabasco sauce.

4 Serve on hot buttered toast points and sprinkle with paprika.

YIELD: 6 TO 8 SERVINGS

Fish en Papillote

A delightfully easy and foolproof way to prepare a perfect light meal. Low in calories and cholesterol. There are lots of possible combinations, and some are listed here. Use your imagination to invent others. Then follow the instructions below.

- **Fillet of Sole** with sliced almonds surrounded by sliced shiitake mushrooms and tomatoes. Season with a little butter, a tablespoon of white wine, salt, white pepper, and chopped dill.
- **Fillet of Flounder** with baby shrimp, thinly sliced mushrooms, and thinly sliced endive on the side. Garnish with capers and chopped parsley and season with salt, pepper, and butter.
- **Fillet of Scrod** with julienned carrots, baby green beans cut in half, paper-thin slices of radish. Season with butter, salt, white pepper, and chopped chives.
- **Halibut Steak** with spinach soufflé (thawed), quartered tomatoes, small mushroom caps, and seedless green grapes. Season with butter, salt, white pepper, and white wine.
- **Salmon Steak** with cucumber rings and green peas. Season with white wine, salt, and white pepper. Or try Salmon Steaks en Papillote (p. 171).

- **Swordfish Steak** with mozzarella cheese, anchovy fillets, and sliced tomatoes. Season with coarsely ground black pepper and finely minced parsley.

1 Preheat oven to 350°.

2 Cut one 12″ x 18″ piece of cooking parchment or aluminum foil for each serving. On each sheet, arrange fish fillet or steak, as desired.

3 Add vegetables, seasonings, and garnishes and fold, making tightly sealed packets.

4 Bake—about 12 minutes for fillets, about 15 minutes for steaks. (Bread and rolls may be put in the oven at the same time.)

5 Open packets and transfer carefully to individual heated plates.

Fisherman's Stew (Caldeirada a Pescadora)

 Another recipe low in calories and cholesterol.

¼ cup olive oil
4 large onions, sliced
2 cloves garlic, minced
freshly ground black pepper
1 teaspoon coriander seeds, or
    2 or 3 sprigs fresh coriander,
    chopped
2 pounds fish (such as
    haddock, flounder, or
    halibut)

6 potatoes, peeled and sliced
1 28-ounce can solid-pack
    tomatoes
1 bay leaf
salt to taste
1 cup white wine
½ bunch parsley, finely minced

1 In large casserole suitable for serving, heat olive oil. Add onions, garlic, pepper, and coriander and sauté until onions are golden.

2 In casserole, alternate layers of fish, then potatoes, then tomatoes, repeating until all are used. Add bay leaf, salt, and white wine.

3 Cover casserole tightly and simmer about 45 minutes, or until potatoes are done.

4 Remove bay leaf, stir in parsley, cover casserole, and take to table.

YIELD: 6 TO 8 SERVINGS

Fish 'n Meat Supreme

 1½ pounds haddock or cod
fillets

1 jar (8 ounces) chipped beef

butter or margarine

2 cups Cheese Sauce (p. 316)

paprika

1 Preheat oven to 325°.

2 Place fillets in baking dish with cold water to cover. Simmer until fillets flake.

3 Sauté chipped beef in butter until edges curl.

4 In casserole coated with vegetable spray, alternate layers of fish and chipped beef. Pour cheese sauce over dish, dot with butter, sprinkle with paprika, and bake 20 to 25 minutes.

YIELD: 6 TO 8 SERVINGS

Flounder Hyannis

 2 pounds flounder fillet

2 cups half-and-half

¼ cup sherry

salt to taste

freshly ground white pepper

1 pound baby shrimp, or meat
of 1 lobster, cut up

⅓ cup buttered breadcrumbs

parsley for garnish

lemon wedges

1 Preheat oven to 400°.

2 Lay fillets in large skillet and pour in cream. Add sherry, salt, and white pepper and simmer 4 or 5 minutes.

3 Remove to large, shallow baking dish, add shrimp or lobster, and bake until cream sauce is thick, about 15 minutes. Preheat broiler.

4 Sprinkle breadcrumbs over dish and place under broiler until bubbly and lightly browned.

5 Garnish with parsley and lemon wedges.

YIELD: 6 TO 8 SERVINGS

Fresh Tuna Steaks

 Low in cholesterol, low in calories, high in taste.

3 tablespoons dark soy sauce	1 tablespoon grated fresh
3 tablespoons lime juice	ginger
3 tablespoons olive oil	1 large clove garlic, mashed
1 tablespoon hot chili oil	4 fresh tuna steaks, about 1
	inch thick (about 2 pounds)

1 Combine first six ingredients and pour over tuna steaks in casserole or bowl. Marinate at least 4 or 5 hours, longer if possible.

2 Grill steaks outdoors over charcoal or indoors under broiler.

YIELD: 4 SERVINGS

Grilled Bluefish

1½ sticks (6 ounces) unsalted	1 teaspoon crushed red pepper
butter	flakes
¼ cup lemon juice	4 bluefish fillets, skinned
1 tablespoon dried thyme	chopped parsley
1 tablespoon dried basil	lemon wedges
coarsely ground black pepper	

1 In saucepan, melt butter and stir in lemon juice and seasonings. Simmer over very low heat 10 minutes. Pour into shallow dish.

2 Dip each fillet into butter mixture, coating thoroughly. Drain off excess and reserve.

3 Place fillets on plate, cover with plastic wrap, and refrigerate at least 1 hour.

4 Heat large, cast-iron skillet on top of stove until drop of water sizzles in pan. Remove fillets from refrigerator and arrange in single layer in skillet. Cook quickly at high temperature until done, about 3 to 4 minutes per side.

5 Remove fish to hot platter. Add remaining butter mixture to skillet and scrape loose any browned bits. Spoon sauce over fish. Serve garnished with parsley and lemon wedges.

YIELD: 4 SERVINGS

Halibut Mousse with Lobster Sauce

1 pint heavy cream
2½ cups soft breadcrumbs
1 tablespoon butter or
  margarine
1 teaspoon salt

1 teaspoon celery salt
1 pound halibut fillets
4 egg whites, beaten until stiff
parsley or watercress

1 Preheat oven to 350°.

2 Scald cream in double boiler, add breadcrumbs, and stir to make smooth paste. Add butter, salt, and celery salt and blend thoroughly.

3 Put halibut in blender or food processor and purée.

4 Add puréed halibut to mixture in double boiler. Allow to cool, then carefully fold in egg whites.

5 Coat mold with vegetable spray. Pour mixture into mold. Place mold into large pan containing about 1 inch of water.

6 Bake until set, about 1½ hours. Unmold and garnish with parsley or watercress. Serve with Lobster Sauce (below).

Lobster Sauce

3 tablespoons butter or
  margarine
3 tablespoons flour
1 cup Court Bouillon (p. 161)
2 egg yolks

½ cup heavy cream
½ cup diced lobster meat
dry sherry
salt to taste
paprika to taste

1 In saucepan, mix together butter and flour over low flame. Add court bouillon gradually, stirring and cooking until sauce thickens.

2 Beat egg yolks with cream and add to sauce, stirring constantly. Add remaining ingredients. Warm sauce through but do not allow to boil.

Monkfish Duglère

This classic French method of cooking fish adapts to many New England varieties—especially monkfish, halibut, bluefish, John Dory, and swordfish. If good, fresh tomatoes are available, they make the nicest sauce; otherwise, canned tomatoes can be used. (*Duglère* in the name indicates the recipe includes tomatoes.) Low in cholesterol and calories.

2 tablespoons butter or
  margarine
1 medium onion, chopped
2 pounds monkfish fillets cut in
  4 or 5 pieces
1 cup dry white wine
1 cup fish stock or court
  bouillon
1 cup chopped tomatoes

$1/2$ bay leaf, crumbled
$1/8$ teaspoon dried thyme
$1/8$ teaspoon dried dill
salt to taste
freshly ground white pepper to
  taste
4 small mushrooms, sliced
2 tablespoons chopped parsley

1 Heat butter in deep skillet, add onion, and simmer until tender. Place fish in skillet in single layer. Add remaining ingredients, except mushrooms and parsley, and simmer, covered, 15 to 20 minutes, until fish is flaky.

2 Remove fish to hot platter. Add mushrooms and parsley to sauce and boil until thick. Pour over fish and serve immediately.

YIELD: 4 OR 5 SERVINGS

Salmon Steaks en Papillote

This little meal is very easy and very stylish. You can prepare it ahead of time and pop it in the oven when needed. And you can multiply or divide it easily.

4 salmon steaks
salt to taste
freshly ground white pepper to
  taste

$1 1/2$ cups Cucumber Yogurt
  Sauce (p. 316)
8 fresh mushrooms, sliced
1 cup green peas, fresh or
  thawed

1 Cut four 12″ x 15″ pieces heavy aluminum foil or cooking parchment and place 1 salmon steak in center of each. Season with salt and pepper and spoon sauce over each steak. Arrange mushrooms and peas around sides of each steak. Bring up sides of foil or parchment and fold tightly to seal. Refrigerate until needed.

2 Preheat oven to 350°. Place foil-wrapped packages on baking sheet and bake 15 minutes. Remove to heated plates and serve.

YIELD: 4 SERVINGS

Shad Roe

 This tasty dish can be served with or without Baked Stuffed Shad (p. 163).

2 pair shad roe
½ cup water
salt to taste
white pepper to taste

2 tablespoons butter or
   margarine
8 strips crisp bacon
lemon wedges
parsley

1 With sharp knife, separate each pair of roe, being careful not to tear roe.

2 Place roe in skillet with water, salt, and pepper. Simmer, covered, until water has nearly evaporated.

3 Add butter to skillet and brown roe on both sides.

4 Serve garnished with crisp bacon, lemon wedges, and parsley.

YIELD: 4 SERVINGS

FRESHWATER FISH

Boiled Brook Trout

 2 brook trout, cleaned
salt to taste
pepper to taste
1 bay leaf
1 small onion, sliced

2 small carrots, sliced
butter or margarine
chopped parsley
2 lemon wedges

1 Place trout in deep skillet and add water to cover. Add salt and pepper, bay leaf, onion, and carrots and boil 6 to 8 minutes, or until fish turns blue and flakes easily when tested with fork.

2 Remove fish to hot platter. Remove vegetables, drain, and mix gently with butter. Arrange around sides of fish. Garnish with parsley and lemon wedges or serve with Mustard Yogurt Sauce (p. 320).

YIELD: 2 SERVINGS

Pan-Fried Fish

 Small freshwater fish—such as perch, smelts, trout, pike—freshly caught and cleaned are never more delicate than when simply sautéed in butter or margarine.

small fish (2 per person)	**chopped chives or parsley**
sweet butter or margarine	**lemon wedges**
(about 1 tablespoon per fish)	

1 Wash and clean fish, then remove scales with sharp knife and fins with small scissors.

2 Heat iron skillet to sizzling and add 1 walnut-size portion butter for each fish. Let butter brown slightly, then lower heat and add fish (only 2 or 3 at a time).

3 Fry about 2 or 3 minutes on each side, until flesh is flaky. Place fish on hot platter and repeat steps 2 and 3 as needed.

4 Return pan to stove and add 1 walnut-size portion butter per fish. Melt butter and stir in chopped chives or parsley. Scrape sauce from pan onto fish and serve garnished with lemon wedges.

Poached Salmon

 The traditional Fourth of July meal in New England is salmon with green peas, combining the best tastes of early summer (see menu, p. xiv).

1 chunk of salmon (about 3 pounds)	**court bouillon or fish stock to cover**
	lemon wedges

1 Poach salmon as recommended at beginning of chapter—10 minutes for each inch of thickness at center of fish.

2 Serve hot with egg sauce and capers. For low-calorie, low-cholesterol diets, serve with Mustard Yogurt Sauce (p. 320) and capers.

Flash-Grilled Salmon

 Salmon steaks can be prepared by this method on an outdoor grill, too. Be sure to brush the grill and the steaks well with oil so they don't stick.

3 tablespoons safflower or other mild-tasting oil

2 salmon steaks, 1 inch thick (about ½ pound each), at room temperature

salt to taste

1 In a large iron skillet, heat oil until it is smoking hot.

2 Broil steaks for 3 minutes on one side; turn and broil for 2 minutes on the other side.

3 Salt to taste and serve at once. The flesh will be juicy and coral pink inside its charred surfaces.

YIELD: 2 SERVINGS

Poached Striped Bass

 A low-cholesterol and low-calorie recipe.

1 5-pound striped bass
fish stock to cover

1 Poach bass as recommended at beginning of chapter—10 minutes for each inch of thickness at center of fish.

2 Serve hot with Hollandaise Sauce (p. 317). Or chill fish and mask with Green Mayonnaise (p. 308) and capers and surround with cucumber salad. For low-calorie, low-cholesterol diets, serve either hot or cold with Mustard Yogurt Sauce (p. 320) and capers, or with Cucumber Yogurt Sauce (p. 316).

YIELD: 8 SERVINGS

Trout in Oatmeal

 For this recipe, buy fish that have been cleaned but still have heads and tails.

1 1/2 cups Irish oatmeal	1/4 cup milk
1 tablespoon salt	4 3/4-pound trout
freshly ground Tellicherry pepper to taste	1/2 cup vegetable oil
	lemon wedges
2 eggs, lightly beaten	parsley

1 In food processor or blender, grind oatmeal to coarse consistency and blend in salt and pepper. Transfer to shallow dish.

2 In separate shallow dish, whisk together eggs and milk and set aside.

3 Pat trout dry with paper towels and sprinkle cavities with salt and pepper. Dip trout in egg mixture, then coat with oatmeal.

4 In large skillet, pour vegetable oil about 1/8 inch deep. Sauté trout until golden and flaky, about 7 minutes per side.

5 Transfer fish to hot serving platter and garnish with lemon wedges and parsley.

YIELD: 4 SERVINGS

Whitebait

 These tiny fish, whitebait, are one of the happy signs that spring is just around the corner.

1 bunch parsley, large stems removed	1/4 cup white cornmeal
	1/2 teaspoon salt
1 1/2-pound whitebait	4 cups safflower oil
1/4 cup flour	lemon wedges

1 In morning, wash and dry parsley so no dampness clings to it. Rinse whitebait, drain and pat dry with paper towels, and refrigerate until ready to prepare.

2 Mix together flour, cornmeal, and salt in largish plastic or paper bag.

3 Just before dinnertime, heat oil to 350° in deep fryer.

4 Gently shake whitebait in bag with flour mixture to coat thoroughly. Remove, place in sieve, and shake off excess flour.

5 Place fish in frying basket and submerge in hot oil. Cooking time will be less than 2 minutes. Remove to hot serving platter and garnish with lemon wedges.

YIELD: 4 SERVINGS

Bouillabaisse

 Bouillabaisse is best prepared ahead of time and allowed to sit for a while. Served with hot French garlic bread, it makes a famous meal.

1 stalk celery, coarsely chopped	1/4 cup olive oil
1 medium onion, coarsely chopped	1 cup fish stock
	1 cup white wine
1 leek, coarsely chopped	1 pound cod, halibut, or other white fish, cut up
1 carrot, coarsely chopped	2 large tomatoes, peeled and chopped
1 small stalk fennel, coarsely chopped	1 1-pound lobster
1 clove garlic, minced	1 dozen shrimp
1 bay leaf, crumbled	1 dozen clams or mussels
sprig of thyme or pinch of dried thyme	1/2 pound scallops
	1/4 pound squid
1/2 teaspoon Spanish saffron	chopped parsley
salt to taste	juice of 1 lemon
pepper to taste	

1 In large soup kettle, combine celery, onion, leek, carrot, fennel, garlic, bay leaf, thyme, saffron, salt and pepper, and olive oil. Simmer, tightly covered, 10 minutes.

2 Add fish stock, white wine, fish, and tomatoes to kettle and simmer 10 minutes more.

3 Boil lobster separately (p. 181), scrub it, split it, and remove dark vein. Cut into sections. Peel and devein shrimp. Scrub clams or mussels.

4 Add shrimp, clams or mussels, scallops, and squid to kettle and cook until clams or mussels open.

5 Just before serving, add lobster pieces, sprinkle with parsley and lemon juice, and heat through.

YIELD: 6 SERVINGS

Clam Casserole

3 pints clams, in shells
2 cups boiling water
2 medium potatoes, peeled and
   cubed
1 small onion, chopped
3 tablespoons butter or
   margarine, softened

3 tablespoons flour
1 cup milk
salt to taste
white pepper to taste
4 to 6 common crackers
paprika

1 Preheat oven to 425°.

2 Wash clams thoroughly several times. Steam in boiling water in covered kettle just until shells open. Remove clams, reserving broth, then snip off and discard tips of necks. Cut up clams and set aside.

3 Add potatoes and onion to clam broth and cook just until potatoes are tender.

4 Blend butter, flour, and milk and salt and pepper to taste until smooth. Add to vegetables in broth and simmer until thickened. Add chopped clams.

5 Coat casserole with vegetable spray and pour in clam mixture. Crumble crackers over dish, dot with butter or margarine, and sprinkle with paprika. Bake 25 to 30 minutes.

YIELD: 4 SERVINGS

Escalloped Clams

1 quart fresh clams, shucked
1/2 cup butter or margarine
4 cups common cracker
   crumbs

1/2 pint heavy cream
paprika

1 Preheat oven to 350°.

2 Chop raw clams finely but do not grind them. Set aside.

3 Melt butter, add cracker crumbs, and set aside.

4 Coat casserole with vegetable spray. Alternate layer of crumbs, then layer of clams and juices until all are used up. Finish with crumb layer.

5 Pour cream over dish, sprinkle with paprika, and bake 45 minutes.

YIELD: 6 SERVINGS

The ultimate in "garbage can" clambakes, for those with a Paul Bunyan appetite, is lobster, sweet and/or Irish potatoes, hot dogs, eggs, corn on the cob and clams. In the bottom of the can put a limited amount of water depending on the amount of food and seaweed to be above, usually 2 to 3 inches. To this add a cup of vinegar and several tablespoons of salt. Next place a two-inch cake rack in the can, covered well with seaweed. This keeps the lobsters out of water. Place the can over a robust fire and bring the water to a boil. Put the lobsters in back side up, then alternate thin layers of seaweed with potatoes, hot dogs, eggs, corn, and lastly clams. Cover tightly. The potatoes, hot dogs, eggs and corn can be put in cheese cloth, loosely. This makes them easier to remove after cooking. We use a wire basket made for the clams which gives them freedom to open; also you can more readily see when they are open, which is the hour glass indicating the bake is done.

Cooking time varies depending on the amount of food and seaweed from 1 and 1/2 to 2 hours or until the clams open. Never pack the can so tightly with food and seaweed as to prevent the steam from permeating up through all layers, and maintain a healthy fire. As seaweed is not too easy to come by, the bake can be done with only the bottom layer.

You will note we omitted chicken in the above. We used to include it wrapped in cheese cloth with an onion and 2 or 3 links of sausage, but now like it better done separately over charcoal. For Clambake Sauce, see p. 315.

For those fortunate enough to live right on the coast, a bake may be done right on the shore. Here you start with a large sheet of iron placed over an open fire of driftwood. Cover the plate well with seaweed, then your food and cover all with a large piece of canvas well soaked in water. Keep canvas well well throughout to hold in the steam and also to prevent it from burning. Cooking time is greatly reduced due to broader base of the fire and the food being spread out more.

Of course nothing compares with the old-fashioned way of doing a bake. Here you started with a pit filled with large round stones to the level of the ground. On this was built a big bonfire of 4-foot cord wood for several hours. The coals were raked off, a good layer of seaweed added covering all the coals, the bakes put on, then covered with wet canvas as above, with the sides sealed to the ground with dirt and stones to hold in the steam. The bakes were contained in wire baskets, one complete bake per person, or, if the baskets would hold it, two bakes serving two people. With our urban life today, this technique is out for most people.

Clams Portuguese Style

2 quarts hard-shell quahogs
2 onions, coarsely chopped
1/4 pound linguiça sausage, cut
   in bite-size pieces

1/4 pound melted butter or 4
   ounces oil blended with 1
   tablespoon white vinegar

1 Scrub clams and wash several times. Place in deep kettle with onions and sausage. Cover and steam until clams open.

2 Serve with melted butter or oil and vinegar and clam broth.

YIELD: 4 SERVINGS

Crab Cakes

2 eggs
3 slices white bread, crusts
   removed
1 pound fresh lump crabmeat,
   free of membrane
salt to taste

freshly ground white pepper to
   taste
2 tablespoons butter or
   margarine
lemon wedges

1 In mixing bowl, beat eggs lightly with fork. Crumble bread into bowl. Add crabmeat, salt, and pepper and toss lightly with fork. Shape into 6 cakes.

2 Melt butter in skillet, add crab cakes, and sauté until crisp. Serve garnished with lemon wedges.

YIELD: 6 SERVINGS

Crab Stew

4 tablespoons butter or
   margarine
5 tablespoons flour
2 cups milk
1/2 cup light cream
1 teaspoon celery salt
few dashes of cayenne pepper

2 tablespoons Worcestershire
   sauce
juice of half a lemon
4 cups fresh crabmeat, free of
   membrane
2 ounces sherry

1 Cream butter and flour until smooth. In double boiler, cook creamed mixture, gradually adding milk while stirring. Stir in cream, celery salt, cayenne pepper, Worcestershire sauce, and lemon juice. Stir in crabmeat and heat through. At last moment, add sherry.

2 Serve on fluffy white or brown rice.

YIELD: 6 TO 8 SERVINGS

Crab with Sherry in Shells

2 cups fresh crabmeat, free of
   membrane
2 hard-boiled eggs, chopped
1 cup mayonnaise
1 teaspoon grated onion
2 teaspoons chopped parsley

1 cup buttered breadcrumbs
1 tablespoon lemon juice
1 teaspoon Worcestershire
   sauce
1 teaspoon dry mustard
2 ounces sherry

1 Preheat oven to 400°.

2 Combine all ingredients, reserving 1/2 cup buttered crumbs, and spoon into scallop shells (or ovenproof ramekins). Top with reserved crumbs.

3 Bake 15 minutes.

YIELD: 6 SERVINGS

Soft-Shell Crabs

Soft-shell crabs are at their tender best in March and April, when they are no larger than a half dollar.

12 soft-shell crabs
flour
salt to taste
freshly ground pepper to taste
8 tablespoons (1 stick) butter
   or margarine

1 teaspoon Worcestershire
   sauce
2 teaspoons minced parsley
1/2 cup sliced almonds
parsley
lemon wedges

1 Rinse crabs well and cut off tails. Lift shells and scrape out spongy area between shell and flesh. Pat crabs dry with paper towels.

2 Season flour with salt and pepper. Dip crabs in flour and shake off excess.

3 Melt butter in skillet and sauté crabs quickly on each side until golden brown. Arrange on hot plates.

4 Add Worcestershire sauce, parsley, and almonds to butter and sauté until almonds are browned. Pour over crabs. Serve garnished with parsley and lemon wedges.

YIELD: 6 SERVINGS

 Boiled or Steamed Live Lobsters

A lobster feast is, of necessity, informal. No one can do real justice to a lobster and remain very dignified.

Buy live lobsters—dark green, active, and aggressive—on the day they are to be served. Then store them in the refrigerator until the kettle is boiling. Plunge the lobsters head first into the boiling water. A 1½- or 2-pound lobster makes a generous serving and should be boiled or steamed for 15 minutes; smaller lobsters take a bit less time, 3-pound lobsters take 20 minutes. The lobsters will be a clear, bright red when done.

Set each place at the table with a small bowl of melted butter, a finger bowl, a lobster pick, a lobster cracker, and a large napkin. (The best napkin is a crisp, neatly folded kitchen towel.) Place on the table a large bowl for discarded shells.

Steam the lobsters in two or three inches of salted water or boil them in water to cover for the required time. Remove them from the pot with tongs. Then lay them on their backs on a heavy breadboard. With a heavy knife, split them through the abdomen. Discard the dark vein, the spongy tissue, and the sac near the head. The green tomalley (the liver) and the coral (roe) of the female are edible and delicious. The coral may be used to make tastey Lobster Coral Sauce. With a large mallet or hammer, break the claws so that none of the meat will be wasted. (Watch out for water in the shells. Do this procedure near a sink or outdoors if possible.)

Serve these impressive creatures on the largest platter you own, garnished with lemon wedges and lots of parsley. Typical accompaniments are Rhine wine, sparkling wine or beer, plus a loaf of hot, garlicky French bread, corn on the cob, and a salad of cucumbers and dill.

Lobster in Cream Sauce

1 2½- to 3-pound lobster
2 tablespoons butter or
   margarine
2 ounces sherry
2 tablespoons flour

1 cup light cream
snipped fresh tarragon
salt to taste
cayenne pepper to taste

1 Boil or steam lobster (p. 181) and allow to cool. Split in two and remove claws. Save body shells and dice all meat, including claw meat.

2 Preheat broiler.

3 Melt butter in skillet, then whisk in sherry, flour, cream, and tarragon.
   Add salt and cayenne pepper to taste. Add diced lobster meat and
   simmer 10 minutes.

4 Fill shells with creamed mixture and broil until lightly golden.

   YIELD: 2 SERVINGS

Mussels Marinière

Mussels are abundant along the New England coastline—a great treat
and inexpensive, too. This makes an extremely pretty dish—with blue-
purple mussel shells, apricot-hued mussels, and the dish flecked with
green herbs.

3 pounds mussels in their shells
2 shallots, minced
2 cups medium-dry white wine

salt to taste
freshly ground pepper to taste
finely minced dill and parsley

1 Scrub mussels under running cold water with brush. If necessary,
   scrub several times to get shells thoroughly clean.

2 Put mussels in large kettle and add shallots, wine, and seasonings.
   Simmer, covered, 5 minutes, until shells open wide. (Mussels yield their
   own broth.)

3 Serve in large soup plates, accompanied by oyster forks for extracting
   mussels and soup spoons for broth.

   YIELD: 4 TO 6 SERVINGS

Scalloped Oysters

1 cup soft breadcrumbs

1 cup dry cracker crumbs

³/₄ cup melted butter or
  margarine

1 teaspoon salt

pinch of ground mace

1 teaspoon lemon juice

1 quart oysters, with liquor

¹/₄ cup milk

1 Preheat oven to 400°.

2 In mixing bowl, combine breadcrumbs, cracker crumbs, melted butter, salt, mace, and lemon juice. Spread half of mixture in large, shallow baking dish (such as a quiche dish). Arrange oysters in two layers over crumbs, add remaining ingredients, and top with additional crumbs.

3 Bake 30 minutes.

YIELD: 4 TO 6 SERVINGS

Oyster Spinach Casserole

Made with frozen spinach soufflé, this dish is quick and good.

2 packages frozen spinach
  soufflé

1 medium onion, sliced

2 tablespoons butter or
  margarine

1 pint oysters, cut up, with
  liquor reserved

1 can cream of celery soup

¹/₄ cup seasoned breadcrumbs

freshly ground white pepper to
  taste

paprika

1 Coat casserole with vegetable spray. Thaw spinach soufflé and place in bottom of casserole.

2 Preheat oven to 350°.

3 Sauté onion in butter until softened and distribute rings over spinach. Arrange oysters on top of onion. Blend oyster liquor with celery soup and pour over casserole. Cover with thick topping of seasoned breadcrumbs, sprinkle with pepper and paprika, and dot with butter.

4 Bake 30 to 35 minutes.

YIELD: 4 TO 6 SERVINGS

Sautéed Scallops

1½ pounds scallops
2 tablespoons butter or
   margarine
salt to taste
freshly ground white pepper to
   taste

¼ cup breadcrumbs, sautéed in
   butter
finely chopped parsley
lemon wedges

1 Rinse scallops and pat dry with paper towels.

2 Melt butter in large skillet. When it sizzles, sauté scallops very quickly, less than 1 minute.

3 Arrange scallops on warm plates and sprinkle with sautéed breadcrumbs and parsley. Garnish with lemon wedges.

YIELD: 4 OR 5 SERVINGS

VARIATION – Sautéed Scallops and Baby Shrimp

In separate skillet, sauté ½ pound baby shrimp peeled and deveined in small amount of butter or margarine. Mix shrimp and scallops before adding breadcrumbs and parsley.

Scallops

The delicate white sea scallops or the bay scallops from Cape Cod Bay or Long Island Sound are equally tender. The bay scallops, even sweeter in flavor, are not always available. It depends on the catch. One pound of scallops should serve three or four people, depending on how hungry they are for scallops.

1 pound bay or sea scallops
¼ pound fresh mushrooms
salt to taste
cayenne pepper to taste

1 cup Cream Sauce (p. 315)
1 cup breadcrumbs
¼ cup grated Parmesan cheese
paprika

1 Preheat oven to 375°.

2 In 1-quart baking dish, alternate layers of scallops and mushrooms. Sprinkle with salt and cayenne pepper and add cream sauce. Mix breadcrumbs with cheese and sprinkle over top.

3 Bake 30 minutes.

YIELD: 4 SERVINGS

Seviche

 These subtle morsels are "cooked" by marinating them in lemon and
lime juices, and they retain all the zest and vigor of the sea. This recipe
serves four for a luncheon salad, but it works equally well as a first
course or tasty hors d'oeuvres.

juice of 1 lemon

juice of 1 lime

1 tablespoon onion juice

few sprigs dill

salt to taste

freshly ground white pepper to
   taste

1 pound scallops

8 spinach leaves

olive oil

balsamic vinegar

lemon wedges

1   Starting a day ahead, combine lemon and lime juices, onion juice, dill,
salt, and pepper. Add scallops and stir to coat well. Cover and refrigerate. Remove occasionally to stir.

2   At serving time, toss spinach leaves in oil and vinegar and arrange on
salad plates. Drain scallops and place over greens. Top scallops with
warm bacon-garlic croutons and garnish with lemon wedges.

YIELD: 4 SERVINGS

Shrimp Curry

 This is a great production to prepare and dramatic to serve. It is easy,
but it does take time. A great way to enjoy New England's plentiful
shrimp catch.

3 onions, chopped

3 apples, peeled, cored, and
   chopped

1/2 cup raisins, halfed

2 tablespoons butter or
   margarine

4 tablespoons mango chutney
   (preferably Major Grey's)

2 cloves garlic, mashed

several tablespoons curry
   powder, to taste

4 cups chicken stock

flour (optional)

3 pounds shrimp

1   Sauté onion, apples and raisins in butter until soft. Blend in chutney,
garlic, and curry powder. Gradually add chicken stock, stirring to
blend. Simmer sauce, covered, 1 hour or more, stirring occasionally.

2 While sauce is simmering, peel and devein raw shrimp and wash three times. Pat dry thoroughly with paper towels.

3 If sauce is too thin, add flour a tablespoon at a time (mixed with 2 tablespoons sauce) and cook a bit longer to remove taste of flour. (Sauce should be rather thin—real Indian curry uses no flour.)

4 Add shrimp to sauce and simmer 5 minutes.

YIELD: 6 SERVINGS

Braumeister Shrimp

 Here's an unusual recipe from a group of Bostonians devoted to good food who used to meet in Louisburg Square for "Beacon Hill Wednesday Night Buffet."

3 pounds jumbo shrimp	³/₄ cup butter or margarine, softened
1 Bouquet Garni (p. 129)	
3 stalks celery	1 tablespoon anchovy paste
1 onion, sliced	1 cup heavy cream, scalded
3 cloves garlic, slivered	1 to 2 loaves French bread, warmed
1 teaspoon dried tarragon	
1¹/₂ tablespoons salt	1 pound bacon, fried crisp
beer to cover (1 8-ounce bottle)	finely chopped parsley

1 Wash shrimp three times, then put in large kettle. Add bouquet garni, celery, onion, garlic, tarragon, salt, and enough beer to cover. Bring to boil and cook only until shrimp turn pink. Allow to cool, then shell and devein shrimp. (This can be done a day ahead.)

2 Cream butter with anchovy paste and put in large skillet. Add cooked shrimp and sauté gently until warmed through. Add cream and stir to heat through. Do not allow to boil.

3 Serve on thick slices of French bread garnished with crumbled bacon and chopped parsley.

YIELD: 6 TO 8 SERVINGS

Grilled Jumbo Shrimp

 This is a treat!

jumbo shrimp, 4 or 5 per person	Shrimp Sauce (below)
salt	lemon wedges

1 Preheat broiler.

2 Arrange shrimp on bed of salt on baking sheet. Broil 2 minutes on each side.

3 Serve with shrimp sauce and garnish with lemon wedges. Provide bowl for shells and finger bowl at each place.

Shrimp Sauce

1 clove garlic, minced	salt to taste
1/2 cup tomato paste	freshly ground Tellicherry
1/3 cup olive oil	pepper to taste
2 tablespoons balsamic vinegar	

1 In small mixing bowl, blend garlic and tomato paste. Whisking continuously, dribble in olive oil and vinegar. (Sauce will separate if liquids are added too quickly.) Whisk in salt and pepper to taste.

YIELD: 1 CUP SAUCE

Dublin Bay Prawns

 Our own Atlantic shrimp pinch hit very nicely for the prawns.

2 pounds medium shrimp, thoroughly rinsed	juice of 1 lemon
4 tablespoons butter	salt to taste

1 Steam the shrimp over boiling water for 5 minutes, then cool. Shell, devein and rinse.

2 Melt butter in a heavy skillet and add the shrimp. Sprinkle lightly with salt and lemon juice. The butter will become a faint coral pink and enhance the delicate flavor of the shellfish.

7

Poultry and Wildfowl

From earliest memory, birds have been used for "best" occasions. A fine roast chicken on Sunday, stuffed, trussed, and garnished with style, silky creamed chicken for children's birthday parties, chicken salad with homemade mayonnaise for church suppers, turkey for Thanksgiving, goose for Christmas (if you are lucky), and ducks and pheasants and squabs for other special feasts. These attitudes have hardly changed by the passage of time, but it is a happy fact that due to the skill of the poultry industry the old promise of a chicken in every pot has very nearly become a reality.

CHICKEN

Roast Chicken

 There is no more delicate dish than a perfectly roasted plump chicken, and fortunately this is rather easy to achieve. The bird may be stuffed or not, as you choose. I like a stuffed bird myself. Stuffing lends a delicious flavor and captures the chicken's cooking juices—a good complementary arrangement. And the variety of stuffings is limited only by the imagination. Try chicken stuffed with sage and sausage, with watercress and saffron, or with black walnuts added to bread stuffing. Delicious! A chicken can also be roasted with just a cut-up lemon inside to flavor it, or an apple, or perhaps a lemon and some cloves of garlic, or the chicken's giblets. Suit your taste. Below is a good basic recipe.

1 roasting chicken, 5 to 6 pounds	paprika to taste
salt to taste	stuffing, as desired
pepper to taste	1 cup dry white wine

1 Preheat oven to 375°.

2 Remove giblets, then rinse out and dry the cavity. Cut away large piece of fat at the opening of the cavity and rub bird well all over with this fat. Season inside and out with salt and pepper, then rub paprika into breast to add nice color.

3 Stuff chicken, if desired, and close opening with skewer. Tie legs together with kitchen string. Place in roasting pan, breast side down, then add wine to pan. Cover chicken loosely with a tent of aluminum foil.

4 Roast 30 minutes. Remove from oven, turn bird over, and baste well. Return to oven and roast, breast side up, about 1 hour, basting every 15 minutes. When leg yields to gentle pressure, bird is done. During last 15 minutes of roasting, remove the foil tent to allow breast to brown.

5 Remove the chicken to a hot platter and allow to rest 5 minutes in a warm place while you make gravy (below).

YIELD: ABOUT 6 SERVINGS

Pan Gravy for Chicken, Turkey, and Other Poultry

In making gravy, always use 2 tablespoons of flour to 3 tablespoons of fat.

neck and giblets of bird	3 tablespoons flour
½ onion, sliced	½ cup red or white wine
salt to taste	Worcestershire sauce to taste
pepper to taste	(optional)

1 While bird is roasting, rinse giblets and simmer in water briefly with onion, salt, and pepper.

2 After the bird is removed from the roasting pan, pour off all but 3 tablespoons fat. On top of stove, over low flame, add some of giblet cooking broth and scrape to deglaze roasting pan. Whisk in flour, 1 tablespoon at a time, then more broth. Add wine, stirring to make thick gravy. Season to taste with salt and pepper and add chopped liver and heart. If desired, add Worcestershire sauce.

Baked Chicken Tarragon

 Wild rice is good with this.

3 chicken breasts, halved
flour
salt to taste
pepper to taste
minced fresh or dried tarragon

6 tablespoons butter or
    margarine
1/2 cup dry white wine
6 thin lemon slices

1 Preheat oven to 400°.

2 Clean and dry the chicken pieces. Dredge them in flour seasoned with salt and pepper. Arrange pieces in baking dish (such as Pyrex pie plate) and sprinkle with tarragon. Place 1 tablespoon butter on each piece and bake until lightly browned—about 30 minutes.

3 Remove from the oven and pour wine over the chicken. Baste well with pan juices and place 1 thin lemon slice on each piece.

4 Reduce oven temperature to 300° and bake 10 minutes more.

YIELD: 6 SERVINGS

VARIATION – Baked Chicken with Peaches

Follow directions for Baked Chicken Tarragon but place 1 clingstone peach half on each chicken piece instead of the lemon slice. Add a little peach juice.

VARIATION – Chicken Breasts with Mushrooms and Ham

Follow directions for Baked Chicken Tarragon and add a large, buttered mushroom cap to each chicken piece for last 10 minutes of baking. At same time, place small slice of cooked ham beneath each portion.

Broilers with Oyster Stuffing

2 broiling chickens
salt to taste
pepper to taste
4 tablespoons butter or
  margarine
1 medium onion, minced
1 cup breadcrumbs

1 tablespoon chopped parsley
1/4 teaspoon fresh or dried
  tarragon
1/2 teaspoon lemon juice
1/2 pint oysters, including
  liquor
6 tablespoons melted butter

1 Preheat oven to 400°.

2 Wash and dry chickens and season with salt and pepper. Rub skin well with 2 tablespoons butter or margarine.

3 Melt 2 tablespoons butter in skillet and sauté minced onion briefly. Add breadcrumbs and remaining ingredients, except oysters.

4 Halve oysters and add, with their liquor, to breadcrumb mixture.

5 Spread stuffing on inner side of each chicken piece. Place pieces on rack in center of oven. Put a large pan in the bottom of the oven to catch drippings and keep stove clean.

6 Bake chicken 10 minutes, then reduce temperature to 350° and bake 20 minutes more. Brush chicken with melted butter and serve.

YIELD: 4 SERVINGS

Chicken Breasts Prosciutto

A contemporary dish that can be prepared ahead of time.

3 chicken breasts, skinned,
  boned, and halved
2 tablespoons flour
salt to taste
freshly ground white pepper to
  taste
2 eggs, lightly beaten

1/2 cup seasoned breadcrumbs
6 thin slices prosciutto ham
1 cup grated Swiss cheese
1 tablespoon light cream
4 tablespoons sweet butter or
  margarine

1 Place boned breasts, skinned side down, on a wooden board. Cover with plastic wrap and flatten with a wooden mallet.

2 Dip the chicken in flour to coat and shake off excess. Dip in beaten egg and then in breadcrumbs. Lay pieces flat. Top each piece with pro-

sciutto, then grated Swiss cheese, and moisten with small amount of cream.

3 Fold corners of each chicken piece to center, envelope fashion, and secure by pressing firmly. You should have neat square packages. Cover "packages" with plastic wrap and refrigerate until ready to use.

4 When ready to cook, remove chicken from refrigerator and bring to room temperature.

5 Melt butter in skillet and sauté chicken until cooked through and golden brown on all sides.

YIELD: 6 SERVINGS

Charcoal-Broiled Chicken with Garlic and Herbs

 This barbecue specialty can be prepared equally well indoors using the broiler and the oven.

2 broilers (2½ to 3½ pounds each), quartered

juice of 2 lemons

2 teaspoons salt

1 teaspoon coarsely ground black pepper

1 teaspoon chopped fresh tarragon, or ½ teaspoon dried tarragon

1 teaspoon chopped fresh parsley, or ½ teaspoon dried parsley

5 cloves garlic, mashed

1½ cups olive or vegetable oil

1 loaf French or Italian bread

½ cup butter or margarine, softened

1 tablespoon mixed fresh herbs, preferably basil and parsley

1 Wash and dry chicken pieces and place close together in shallow pan.

2 Combine lemon juice, salt, pepper, tarragon, parsley, and 4 cloves of mashed garlic. Slowly add oil, stirring constantly to make thick sauce. Spoon marinade over chicken pieces and refrigerate 30 minutes, basting occasionally, until ready to grill.

3 Grill the chicken over a charcoal fire, basting frequently with marinade.

4 While chicken grills, slice bread diagonally (to make long slices). Com-

bine butter, remaining mashed garlic clove, and mixed herbs and spread on slices. Heat bread at edge of grill until partly toasted.

5 When chicken is ready, serve on top of bread to preserve cooking juices.

YIELD: 8 SERVINGS

Chicken Fricassee

 It is hard to improve upon this old New England favorite, most flavorful if cooked the day before using and left to blend overnight. Correct the sauce the next day if necessary, adding Worcestershire sauce, herbs, or lemon juice at your discretion. Serve the fricassee on a hot platter over baking-powder biscuits or surrounded with fluffy white rice or dumplings. A simple vegetable—carrots or green peas cooked with small onions—and some currant jelly are, I think the most appropriate accompaniments.

2 plump chickens, cut for
    fricassee (8 pieces each)
water to cover (about 4 cups)
2 tablespoons salt
16 white peppercorns
1 teaspoon dried tarragon
1 bay leaf
1 lemon, sliced
2 stalks celery, sliced
1 onion, sliced

1 carrot, sliced
1/2 cup butter or margarine
1/3 cup flour
3 cups chicken stock
1 pound mushrooms (optional),
    sliced and sautéed in 2
    tablespoons butter
2 egg yolks
1/2 cup heavy cream

1 Simmer chicken about 35 minutes in water with salt, peppercorns, tarragon, bay leaf, lemon, celery, onion, and carrot. Remove chicken from stock and allow to cool. (When cool, remove skin if desired.) Strain stock.

2 Prepare sauce. Melt butter in skillet and stir in flour. Add chicken stock and whisk continuously until thick. Simmer very gently and stir until thick and reduced by about one-half, approximately 45 minutes. Add sautéed mushrooms if desired.

3 Beat together egg yolks and cream and whisk into sauce. Pour sauce over chicken and serve.

YIELD: 8 TO 10 SERVINGS

Chicken in Oyster and Champagne Sauce

4 whole chicken breasts,
   halved
1³/₄ cups water
2 teaspoons salt
8 white peppercorns

¹/₂ teaspoon dried tarragon
¹/₂ bay leaf
half a lemon, sliced
1 stalk celery, cut up
4 cups fluffy white rice

1 Put chicken breasts in kettle and add remaining ingredients, except rice. Bring to boil and simmer 2 or 3 minutes. Remove from heat and allow chicken to cool, covered tightly, in broth. The chicken will be cooked through.

2 When chicken is cool, skin and bone the breasts. Strain the stock. Make Oyster and Champagne Sauce (below).

3 To serve, heat chicken pieces and arrange on hot platter. Surround with rice and pour the sauce over chicken.

YIELD: 8 SERVINGS

Oyster and Champagne Sauce

¹/₂ cup plus 2 tablespoons
   butter or margarine
¹/₃ cup flour
1¹/₂ cups chicken stock
1 half-bottle champagne

1 pound mushroom caps, sliced
1 pint oysters, picked over
2 egg yolks
1 tablespoon vegetable oil
¹/₂ cup heavy cream

1 Melt ¹/₂ cup butter and stir in flour. Add chicken stock gradually and whisk until thick. Add champagne and blend. Simmer very gently until thick and reduced by about one-half—approximately 30 minutes.

2 Sauté mushrooms in 2 tablespoons butter and add to sauce. Add oysters and cook 5 minutes.

3 Beat together egg yolks, vegetable oil, and cream and add to sauce.

YIELD: ABOUT 2 CUPS SAUCE

Chicken Piquant

3/4 cup rosé wine

1/4 cup soy sauce

1/4 cup vegetable oil

1 clove garlic, sliced

1 tablespoon chopped candied
ginger

1/4 teaspoon oregano

1 tablespoon brown sugar

3 chicken breasts, halved

1 Preheat oven to 375°.

2 Combine wine with soy sauce, oil, garlic, candied ginger, oregano, and
brown sugar.

3 Arrange chicken pieces in baking dish and add wine mixture.

4 Bake, covered, about 45 minutes, or until tender. Serve over rice.

YIELD: 4 TO 6 SERVINGS

Honey-Juiced Chicken

1 cup pancake mix

1 teaspoon salt

1/2 teaspoon pepper

1 broiler/fryer, cut in serving
pieces

1/4 cup shortening or vegetable
oil

1/2 cup honey

3/4 cup orange juice

1 orange, peeled and sliced
parsley

1 Combine pancake mix, salt, and pepper in shallow bowl. Dip chicken
pieces in mixture and coat well, shaking off excess.

2 Melt shortening in deep skillet and brown chicken—about 20 to 30
minutes.

3 Blend together honey and orange juice and pour over chicken in skillet. Cook, covered, over low heat, about 45 minutes.

4 Garnish with warmed orange slices and parsley.

Chicken Pinafore

This recipe, which comes from Mrs. Catherine T. Smith of Brunswick, Maine, was handed down, she notes, through the family of General Joshua L. Chamberlain, the hero of Little Round Top at Gettysburg and one of Maine's great men. He was with General Grant when General Lee offered his sword at Appomattox and later served as governor of Maine and president of Bowdoin College. As becomes a true Brunswick man, he sailed his own yacht, *Pinafore,* which gave her name to this recipe. This is the original version. (Mrs. Smith adds that in the early part of the century, shredded wheat was used in many ways: "It was coarser then, and more tasty.")

Simmer a large, meaty fowl for 2 to 2½ hours or until done, in a large kettle, the bird covered with water. Put in 1 large onion or several small ones, 2 bay leaves, a handful of celery leaves, and 1 tablespoon salt. Cook steadily until a little less than ½ the water remains. Remove carefully from kettle and place on platter, surrounded by 6 or 8 large cakes of shredded wheat, previously heated in a hot oven for a few minutes. Thicken the broth to a medium consistency and serve at table to be carved by the man of the house. Serves 6.

Maine Chicken Stew

 Prepare this ahead of time and reheat for serving.

2 chickens, 3½ to 4 pounds each, cut for stewing

6 potatoes, peeled and sliced

3 onions, sliced

cold water to cover

2 tablespoons butter or margarine

1 cup light cream or milk

salt to taste

pepper to taste

minced parsley

6 to 8 common crackers

½ cup cold milk

1 In iron kettle, alternate layers of chicken, potatoes, and onion. Cover with cold water and simmer gently, until chicken is tender, 45 to 60 minutes.

2 Add butter in small bits, then stir in cream. Season with salt, pepper, and parsley.

3 Split common crackers, moisten with cold milk, add to stew, and heat. Serve in deep bowls.

YIELD: 8 SERVINGS

Northern Fried Chicken

 This recipe produces a very crisp fried chicken that can be reheated successfully.

2 frying chickens, cut up (use a cleaver)
2 cups flour
salt to taste
pepper to taste

2 cloves garlic, minced, or pinch of tarragon
1 teaspoon paprika
$^1/_2$ teaspoon cayenne pepper
2 eggs
2 cups cooking oil

1 Preheat oven to 250°. Wash and dry chicken pieces.

2 Put flour in paper bag and season with salt, pepper, garlic (or tarragon), paprika, and cayenne pepper.

3 Beat eggs in shallow bowl and set aside.

4 Shake chicken pieces, one at a time, in paper bag, then dip into egg, then shake again in bag. (Replenish egg and flour mixtures if necessary.)

5 Heat oil (about 4 inches deep) in heavy kettle or Dutch oven. When oil is hot enough to brown a bread cube instantly (350 to 370°), add chicken pieces a few at a time. Fry until golden brown on all sides (8 to 10 minutes), turning once.

6 As chicken is browned, place each piece on toweling, not touching other pieces. When all pieces are browned, place on baking sheet, put in oven, and bake $1^1/_2$ hours, or until done.

YIELD: 8 SERVINGS

Orange-Almond Chicken

 1 frying chicken, about $3^1/_2$ pounds, cut up
1 teaspoon salt
$^1/_4$ teaspoon pepper
1 teaspoon paprika

$^1/_3$ cup butter or margarine
1 cup orange juice
$^2/_3$ cup slivered almonds, toasted

1 Wash chicken and pat dry. Combine salt, pepper, and paprika and rub into chicken until coated thoroughly.

2 Melt butter in large skillet and sauté chicken pieces until golden brown on both sides. Cover skillet, reduce heat, and cook 25 to 30 minutes, until chicken is tender. Remove chicken to platter and place in warm oven.

3 Deglaze skillet with orange juice, scraping up browned particles. Boil until liquid is reduced by about one-half. Pour sauce over chicken, sprinkle with slivered almonds, and serve at once.

If you prefer thicker sauce, blend 1 teaspoon cornstarch with 1 teaspoon water, stir into reduced orange juice, and cook until thickened.

YIELD: 4 SERVINGS

Sour-Cream Chicken

 An easy way to cook moist, perfect chicken.

2 broilers or fryers, quartered   **pepper to taste**
salt to taste   **1 cup sour cream**

1 Preheat oven to 350°.

2 Put chicken in baking pan, skin side up. Season with salt and pepper and cover with sour cream. Bake 1 hour.

YIELD: 8 SERVINGS

Steamed Chicken with Cream

1 whole chicken, 3 to 4 pounds	**1 cup light cream**
half a lemon	**2 eggs, lightly beaten**
salt to taste	**1 teaspoon capers, drained**
pepper to taste	**toast triangles, sautéed in**
2 whole cloves	**butter or margarine**
1 stalk celery, chopped	**4 chicken livers, sautéed in**
½ cup water	**butter or margarine**
½ cup dry white wine	**watercress**

1 Skin chicken, reserving skin. Rub chicken with lemon, salt, and pepper and place in Dutch oven with chicken skin, cloves, celery, water,

and wine. Cook until done, adding more water if needed. This should take about 1 hour over moderate heat (or in 350° oven).

2 Remove chicken to hot platter and strain stock. (There should be at least 1/2 cup.) Pour stock into saucepan and whisk in cream. Heat briefly, then remove from heat and stir in the eggs. Stir until thick, adding capers.

3 Pour sauce over chicken and arrange toast triangles on sides of platter. Place 1 sautéed chicken liver on each triangle. Garnish with watercress.

YIELD: 4 SERVINGS

Veal-Stuffed Chicken Breasts

1/2 pound ground veal
1/4 pound mushrooms, sliced
4 tablespoons butter or
   margarine
2 eggs, beaten separately
1/2 clove garlic, crushed
1 tablespoon chopped parsley
salt to taste

pepper to taste
4 chicken breasts, skinned,
   boned, and halved
1/2 cup flour seasoned with salt
   and pepper
1/2 cup breadcrumbs
1 cup chicken stock

1 Sauté the ground veal and mushrooms in 2 tablespoons butter. Place mixture in bowl and add 1 beaten egg, plus garlic, parsley, salt, and pepper. Blend well.

2 Place chicken breasts on wooden board between 2 sheets of plastic wrap and pound with mallet until very thin.

3 Put some of veal mixture on each flattened breast. Fold or roll up securely and fasten with toothpicks.

4 Place remaining beaten egg in shallow dish, put seasoned flour in second dish, and breadcrumbs in third dish. Dip each rolled breast first in flour, then in egg, then in breadcrumbs.

5 Refrigerate breaded breasts at least 1 hour to allow breading to adhere.

6 Heat remaining 2 tablespoons butter in skillet and sauté breasts over medium heat until thoroughly browned. Cover skillet and cook several minutes longer.

7 Remove sautéed breasts to hot platter and remove toothpicks. Deglaze

skillet with chicken stock, scraping to loosen browned particles, and pour sauce over chicken.

YIELD: 4 SERVINGS

Yankee Chicken Hash

 3 cups coarsely chopped
   cooked chicken

1½ cups cooked sausage meat

¾ cup chopped green pepper

¾ cup chopped onion

2½ tablespoons chopped
   parsley

1 tablespoon chopped chives

½ cup coarse breadcrumbs

½ teaspoon grated lemon rind

½ cup Cream Sauce (p. 315)

salt to taste

pepper to taste

4 tablespoons butter or
   margarine

1 In large mixing bowl, combine chicken, sausage meat, green pepper, onion, parsley, and chives and chop until fine. Stir in breadcrumbs, lemon rind, and cream sauce. Taste for seasoning.

2 Melt butter in heavy skillet and spread hash evenly in bottom of skillet. Cook gently (low heat) until bottom of hash is brown and crusty. (Lift edge carefully with spatula to check.) Fold in half, omelette fashion, and slide onto hot platter.

YIELD: 6 SERVINGS

LOW-CALORIE,
LOW-CHOLESTEROL
CHICKEN RECIPES

Following are five chicken recipes pretty enough for a party, juicy enough for anyone, and all very low in fat and cholesterol. You can enjoy them with a clear conscience.

Chicken Chop Suey

I've always heard that chop suey was invented in America—no one ever said New England, yet it IS popular in New England. It makes a good change of pace. Serve over fluffy white rice, sprinkle with crisp Chinese noodles, and garnish with watercress sprigs.

1 cup sliced onions

1 cup chopped celery

2 tablespoons peanut oil

1 tablespoon arrowroot

1 cup chicken stock

1/2 cup bamboo shoots

6 mushrooms, sliced

1 teaspoon salt

soy sauce to taste

1 tablespoon sweet sherry

1   In large skillet (or wok), stir-fry onions and celery in peanut oil until translucent but still crisp.

2   Sprinkle arrowroot over dish, add chicken stock, and stir until sauce has thickened. Add remaining ingredients, cook several minutes to blend, and taste for seasoning.

YIELD: 4 SERVINGS

Paillard of Chicken

4 pieces skinless, boneless
    chicken breast, about 1/4
    pound each

1/2 cup old-fashioned oatmeal

salt to taste

freshly ground Tellicherry
    pepper to taste

1/4 cup skim milk

1 egg white, lightly beaten

1/2 cup chopped pistachio nuts

fresh parsley for garnish

1 lemon, quartered

Tabasco Jelly (p. 324)

1   Coat broiler rack lightly with vegetable spray. Preheat broiler.

2   Place chicken pieces on wooden board between 2 sheets of plastic wrap and pound with mallet until very thin.

3   Grind oats in food processor or blender about 1 minute. In shallow dish, combine oats with salt and pepper. In separate shallow dish, combine milk and beaten egg white.

4   Coat chicken pieces with oat mixture and shake off excess. Dip in egg mixture, then coat again with oat mixture.

5   Place chicken pieces on broiler rack. Broil about 4 inches from heat, 5 to 6 minutes on each side, until golden brown.

6 Transfer to hot plates. Sprinkle with chopped pistachios, garnish with parsley and lemon quarters, and serve with Tabasco jelly.

YIELD: 4 SERVINGS

Chicken Parmesan

1 cup old-fashioned oatmeal
1/3 cup grated Parmesan cheese
1/2 teaspoon salt
1/2 teaspoon paprika
1/4 cup skim milk
1 egg white, lightly beaten

1 pound boneless chicken
  breasts
2 tablespoons margarine
4 slices prosciutto ham
parsley

1 Coat broiler rack lightly with vegetable spray. Preheat broiler.

2 Grind rolled oats in food processor or blender about 1 minute. In shallow dish, combine oats, cheese, salt, and paprika. In separate shallow dish, combine milk and beaten egg white.

3 Coat chicken pieces with oat mixture and shake off excess. Dip in egg mixture, then coat again with oat mixture.

4 Place chicken pieces on broiler rack and dot with 1 tablespoon margarine. Broil about 4 inches from heat, 4 to 6 minutes on each side, until golden brown.

5 Sauté ham briefly in remaining margarine and put one slice on each plate. Divide chicken pieces among plates and garnish with parsley.

YIELD: 4 SERVINGS

Saffron Chicken Burgers

This recipe can be used for outdoor grilling, in which case omit the sauce and garnishes and serve on toasted buns or pita bread.

1 pound ground chicken
1 cup old-fashioned oatmeal
8 ounces plain low-fat yogurt
1/4 cup chopped Vidalia onion
2 egg whites, lightly beaten
juice of 1 lime
4 teaspoons snipped cilantro
  (or parsley)

1/2 teaspoon saffron
1 teaspoon salt
6 fluted mushrooms
2 or 3 tablespoons capers
  cilantro sprigs
parsley sprigs

1 Line broiler rack with aluminum foil and coat foil with vegetable spray. Preheat broiler.

2 Combine ground chicken, oatmeal, $1/2$ cup yogurt, onion, egg whites, half of lime juice, 2 teaspoons cilantro, saffron, and salt. Mix well and shape into 6 patties.

3 Place patties on prepared rack and broil 6 inches from heat, 5 or 6 minutes on each side, until golden brown.

4 Meanwhile, flute mushrooms and sauté in skillet coated with vegetable spray.

5 Prepare sauce by combining remaining yogurt, lime juice, and cilantro. Heat in saucepan but do not boil.

6 Serve each patty topped with sauce, 1 fluted mushroom, and a few capers. Garnish with sprigs of cilantro and parsley.

YIELD: 6 SERVINGS

Slim Chicken

1 frying chicken, about $3^{1/2}$ pounds, cut into pieces and fat removed
$1/2$ cup orange juice
$1/2$ cup pineapple juice
$1/4$ cup soy sauce

1 tablespoon vermouth
1 large clove garlic, minced
candied ginger, chopped
chopped parsley
8 glazed kumquats

1 Preheat oven to 350°.

2 Place chicken parts in single layer in shallow baking pan. In small bowl, combine remaining ingredients, except chopped parsley and kumquats, and spoon over chicken.

3 Bake 1 hour, basting with pan juices every 15 minutes. Garnish with chopped parsley and kumquats.

YIELD: 4 SERVINGS

Rock Cornish Game Hens

6 rock cornish game hens
prepared mustard
2 medium carrots
3 stalks celery
10 ounces mushrooms
4 medium shallots
1 small onion

salt to taste
about 2 tablespoons flour
chicken stock
1 tablespoon red currant jelly
bouquet garni: 1/2 teaspoon
minced oregano and 3 black
peppercorns, crushed

1 Preheat oven to 450°.

2 Rub hens with prepared mustard. Mince carrots, celery, mushrooms, shallots, and onion to make what the French call *mirepoix*.

3 Coat roasting pan with vegetable spray and add mirepoix to cover bottom of pan. Place hens on top of this mixture and sprinkle with salt.

4 Bake hens, turning occasionally, until brown, then reduce heat to 350°. Bake, breast side up, until tender.
    (When hens are cooked, leg meat is soft and bone will turn with little pressure.)

5 Remove hens from pan and keep warm. Place pan on top of stove and add flour to mirepoix and pan juices to make roux. Add chicken stock and thicken to consistency desired. (If no chicken stock is available, make it from chicken bouillon cubes or granules.)

6 Add bouquet garni and currant jelly. Allow to simmer 15 minutes, then strain through fine-mesh cheesecloth.

7 Place hens in sauce in roasting pan and return to oven, simmering at low temperature (250°) 10 minutes.

YIELD: 6 SERVINGS

Roast Duckling

Duckling should be cooked a long time in order to melt away completely the thick layer of fat that is beneath the skin, leaving the skin very, very crisp with no fat at all between it and the meat.

1 duckling, 3 to 3½ pounds	2 cloves garlic, crushed
salt to taste	(optional)
pepper to taste	½ cup lemon juice (optional)

1 Preheat oven to 350°.

2 Rub duck well inside and out with salt and pepper, adding, if desired, garlic and lemon juice.

3 Place on rack in roasting pan and prick skin to allow fat to drain. Roast about 2½ hours, basting occasionally. (Stuffed ducklings take longer than unstuffed ones.)

4 When duck is nearly done, remove from oven and remove as much fat as possible from roasting pan. Baste with juices and any marinade you wish.

YIELD: 2 SERVINGS

VARIATION – Bigarade Sauce for Roast Duckling

Roast duckling according to the instructions above. A generous rubbing of garlic and lemon juice is a great addition to this recipe, as is a sectioned orange stuffed inside.

3 oranges	2 ounces Madeira
juice of 2 lemons	1 ounce Cointreau
1 jar red currant jelly	2 teaspoons cornstarch
2 ounces brandy	

1 Use vegetable peeler to remove colored rind from oranges. With sharp knife, cut peel into long, hair-thin strips. Cut all pith away from oranges and separate oranges into sections, discarding membranes and seeds. Reserve any juice that collects.

2 In saucepan, put reserved orange juice, plus lemon juice and currant jelly. Warm until jelly dissolves. Remove from heat.

3 When duckling is done, skim fat from pan juices, then add remaining pan juices to saucepan containing dissolved jelly. Add liqueurs and cornstarch and cook, stirring, until reduced slightly. (Add 1 chicken bouillon cube and a little water if more liquid is needed.) Add orange sections for last minute of cooking. Serve sauce with duckling.

VARIATION – Bing Cherry Sauce for Roast Duckling

Roast duckling according to instructions above, but do not use garlic. When duckling is crisp and brown, remove to hot platter. Skim juices in pan, then add 1-pound can of bing cherries and their juices, 2 teaspoons cornstarch, and brandy or cherry liqueur to taste. Stir until thick and smooth. This makes enough sauce for one large duckling.

Broiled Duckling

 Very simple and very good.

1 small duck	**salt to taste**
flour	**pepper to taste**
ground ginger to taste	**melted butter**

1 Split duck. (For domestic duck, trim off extra fat.) Rub skin with flour and small amount of ginger. Let stand 2 or 3 hours.

2 When ready to roast, preheat broiler. Salt and pepper. Broil slowly, basting occasionally with melted butter.

YIELD: 2 SERVINGS

Roast Long Island Duckling

 An unusual and interesting way to cook duckling.

1 Long Island duckling	**¹/₄ cup honey**
salt	**¹/₄ cup orange juice**
1 teaspoon curry powder	**¹/₄ cup lemon juice**
1 clove garlic, chopped	**1 teaspoon curry powder**
1 teaspoon turmeric	**8 to 12 glazed kumquats**
few dashes of Tabasco sauce	

1 Preheat oven to 325°.

2 Rub duckling inside and out with salt, curry powder, garlic, and turmeric. Sprinkle with Tabasco. Stuff with Wild Rice Stuffing (p. 220).

3 Place duckling on rack in roasting pan and roast 2¹/₂ to 3 hours. When duck is nearly done, skim fat from juices in bottom of pan. For last half hour of cooking time, baste with mixture of honey, orange and lemon juices, and curry powder.

4 Serve duck quartered, arranged over mound of stuffing. Spoon pan juices over duck pieces and garnish with kumquats and chopped parsley.

YIELD: 4 SERVINGS

Roast Goose

The finest possible fare for Christmas dinner.

1 goose, about 10 pounds
salt to taste
pepper to taste
1 clove garlic, if desired
stuffing, as desired

1 cup hot cider or red wine
glazed fruit (crabapples, spiced
    pears, or stuffed prunes)
parsley or watercress sprigs

1 Wash and dry goose. (If you have doubts about the bird's youth and tenderness, parboil in water for about 1 hour before roasting. If this is required, turn goose once during boiling and dry goose after boiling.)

2 Preheat oven to 450°. Rub skin with salt and pepper and, if desired, a garlic clove. Fill cavity loosely with stuffing and fasten with skewers and string. Prick skin well to allow fat to run off during roasting.

3 Place goose on rack in roasting pan and roast 20 to 25 minutes. Reduce heat to 300° and pour off fat. Pour cider or wine over bird and roast, uncovered, about 3 more hours.

4 Serve goose on large platter garnished with glazed fruit and sprigs of parsley or watercress.

YIELD: 8 SERVINGS

Pigeon Pie

Use either squabs or game hens for this recipe.

6 pigeons
6 strips bacon
1 tablespoon butter or
    margarine
1 1/2 tablespoons flour
2 cups chicken stock

1 teaspoon Kitchen Bouquet
salt to taste
pepper to taste
3 onions, sliced
Basic Pie Crust (p. 352)

1 Preheat oven to 500°.

2 Wash and dry pigeons. Place them in baking dish with 1 strip of bacon over each. Bake 5 minutes and remove. Turn off oven.

3 Meanwhile, melt butter in large kettle over low heat, add flour, then add stock, Kitchen Bouquet, salt, and pepper and whisk together until smooth. Add pigeons and onions and simmer 1 hour.

4 While pigeons are simmering, preheat oven to 450°.

5 Place pigeons close together in pie dish, add sauce from kettle, cover with pie crust, and bake 12 to 15 minutes.

YIELD: 6 SERVINGS

Roast Turkey

 Wash turkey in cold running water. Pat inside dry with paper toweling, leaving outside moist. Stuff bird and tuck drumsticks under band of skin at tail, or tie them to tail. Preheat oven to 325°. Rub turkey with salt, white pepper, and paprika and coat bird generously with butter, margarine, or turkey fat. Place slices of fat salt pork over breast.

Place turkey, breast side up, on rack in roasting pan. Cover with cheesecloth dipped in melted butter or margarine or loose tent of aluminum foil. Baste every half hour during roasting time, using fat and drippings from pan. Remove cloth or foil for last half hour of cooking.

Turkey is done when drumstick yields slightly when pushed up and down. Meat thermometer should register 185°.

Timetable for Roasting Stuffed Turkey

Weight	Time	
6 to 8 pounds	3 to 3½ hours	Remove turkey from oven and
8 to 12 pounds	3½ to 4 hours	allow to stand on hot platter
12 to 16 pounds	4 to 5 hours	about 20 minutes before carving.
16 to 20 pounds	5 to 6 hours	
20 to 24 pounds	6 to 6½ hours	

Broiled Squad Turkey

 Serve this succulent bird with wild rice and sautéed mushrooms.

1 young turkey, about 6 pounds
salt to taste
pepper to taste

1 Have backbone removed from turkey, the back slit, and leg joints

cracked. Pin legs down with skewers to keep them in place until bird is partly cooked.

2 Preheat broiler. Coat broiler rack lightly with vegetable spray.

3 Season turkey well with salt and pepper, rub well with butter, and place split bird skin side down on broiler rack.

4 Broil 3 inches from heat, about 45 to 50 minutes, turning as needed and adding more butter if skin becomes dry. When partially cooked, turn skin side up.

   Breasts may be sliced into 6 slices each; cut leg portions as desired.

YIELD: 6 TO 8 SERVINGS

WILDFOWL

Hunter's Stew

 A rich, thick, and wonderful stew to prepare for the hunter returning proud and hungry from a successful foray. It can be varied according to the game bagged. Of course, dinner may be a bit late. . . .

2 wild ducks or 1 partridge (or even 1 rabbit), cut in serving pieces	water to cover
	salt to taste
	4 or 5 peppercorns
2 tablespoons butter or margarine	whole cloves
	1 bay leaf
1 cup cubed lean ham	1 stalk celery, diced
2 onions, chopped	Worcestershire sauce
1 carrot, diced	2 to 3 tablespoons tomato paste
1 turnip, diced	sherry or Madeira
1 soup bone, large, all fat removed	chopped fresh parsley

1 In large kettle, brown fowl (or rabbit) in butter, along with ham cubes, onions, carrot, and turnip. Add soup bone and enough water to cover. Season with salt, peppercorns, cloves, and bay leaf and simmer several hours, until meat is tender.

2 Remove meat from kettle, cover and keep warm, and simmer stew 1 hour more.

3 Remove soup bone, return meat to pot, and add celery. Simmer until celery is tender, then add Worcestershire sauce, tomato paste, sherry or Madeira (all to taste), plus chopped parsley.

4 Serve with fried croutons and add cooked barley or wild rice to stew if you wish.

YIELD: 4 TO 6 SERVINGS

Wild Duck

 A 2½-pound duck will serve two people well. If the ducks are much smaller, allow one per person. Exact times and amounts cannot be specified for these recipes, since the size of the bird can vary greatly.

Wild Duck Stuffed with Apples

 The duck (or ducks) may be roasted at 350° for about an hour to whatever state of doneness you prefer. If, like many enthusiasts, you like it rare, roast at 450° for 20 or 30 minutes.

wild ducks	butter (or margarine) or bacon
salt to taste	strips
freshly ground pepper	apples
lemon juice	granulated sugar
	applejack brandy

1 Preheat oven to desired temperature.

2 Clean and dry ducks and sprinkle inside and out with salt, pepper, and lemon juice. Rub ducks generously with butter if you do not plan to cover them with bacon strips.

3 Stuff birds with apples that have been peeled, quartered, cored, and dipped in small amount of sugar. If using bacon, place strips over ducks and tie legs together. Prick skin to allow fat to run out.

4 Place ducks on rack in roasting pan and roast to desired doneness, basting frequently with applejack. Serve with pan juices.

The Presentation of Wild Duck

This Victorian procedure for serving wild duck is a pretty and hospitable ritual that provides fine eating.

"When two birds which should have been lightly roasted come to the table the carver should score the breasts three or four times all the way down and sprinkle a little salt and black pepper over them. He then cuts a lemon in two and powders a little cayenne over each half and squeezes both halves over the birds, adds half a teaspoon of A-1 sauce and a little port wine, mixes all with the gravy of the birds and bastes them well with the sauce before carving."

(The cook, aware that this is to take place, should use a light hand with the seasonings!)

Wild Duck with Carrots and Olives

2 large wild ducks, livers reserved

3 shallots (or scallions), chopped

3 tablespoons butter or margarine

12 black olives, sliced

3 cups buttered breadcrumbs

white pepper to taste

salt to taste

ground nutmeg to taste

2 strips bacon, cut up

12 small whole onions

1 clove garlic, crushed

2 tablespoons flour

salt to taste

pepper to taste

chopped fennel, parsley, and thyme, as available

1 bay leaf

1 bunch young carrots, peeled and sliced

1 cup beef stock

1 cup Cognac

12 green olives, sliced

1 Clean ducks and pat dry. Prepare stuffing: Sauté duck livers and 2 chopped shallots in 1 tablespoon butter. Chop livers and combine with sautéed shallots, black olives, breadcrumbs, white pepper, salt, and nutmeg.

2 Stuff and truss birds.

3 In large casserole or kettle, put 2 tablespoons butter, plus bacon, onions, 1 chopped shallot, and garlic. Dust with flour and add salt, pepper, and herbs.

4 Prepare bed of sliced carrots and top with ducks. Moisten with beef

stock and simmer gently, covered, about 1½ hours. During last 20 minutes of cooking, add Cognac and green olives.

5 Arrange ducks on platter, surrounded by cooked carrots and olives. Stir sauce until thick and smooth and pour over birds.

YIELD: 6 SERVINGS

Wild Duck with Mushrooms

1 wild duck, about 2½ pounds
3 tablespoons butter or
   margarine
flour
1 cup very good red wine
1 cup chicken stock
¼ pound mushrooms, sliced
   (use morels if available)

salt to taste
freshly ground pepper to taste
1 Bouquet Garni (p. 129)
2 tablespoons tomato paste
sautéed croutons
watercress sprigs

1 Cut wild duck into pieces, reserving liver. In kettle, brown pieces in butter. When golden, dust with flour. Add wine and bouillon, then add mushrooms, salt, pepper, and bouquet garni. Cover tightly and cook over low flame until the meat is tender. Remove the duck.

2 Fifteen minutes before serving, mash liver in small amount of red wine and add to kettle, along with tomato paste. Stir sauce until reduced.

3 Arrange duck pieces on hot platter, and spoon sauce over them. Surround platter with bread croutons and garnish with watercress.

YIELD: 2 SERVINGS

Partridge in Vine Leaves

partridges, 1 per person,
   reserving giblets
salt to taste
pepper to taste
ground cloves
ground ginger
lemon juice
bacon strips

vine leaves
red wine
mushrooms, sliced and sautéed
   in butter or margarine with
   partridge giblets
heavy cream
red currant jelly
browned buttered breadcrumbs

1 Preheat oven to 450°.

2 Rub partridges with salt, pepper, ground cloves, and ground ginger and sprinkle with lemon juice. Cover each bird with 3 bacon strips and place in shallow roasting pan. Wrap birds with grape leaves and bake about 20 minutes.

3 Remove vine leaves and bacon and return birds to oven to brown, after basting well with red wine.

4 Prepare sauce by sautéing mushrooms in butter with partridge giblets. Add mushroom mixture, cream, and currant jelly to pan juices and whisk together.

5 On hot platter, prepare bed of browned breadcrumbs and top with partridges. Spoon sauce over birds and garnish with fresh vine leaves.

Pheasants in Cream with Apples

2 pheasants, 2½ to 3 pounds each, cleaned

4 tablespoons butter or margarine

2 cups tart apples, peeled and chopped

½ cup plus 1 tablespoon applejack

2 cups heavy cream

¼ cup lemon juice

salt to taste

freshly ground white pepper to taste

1 tablespoon cornstarch

parsley sprigs

1 Preheat oven to 375°.

2 Truss pheasants and brown lightly in butter in heavy skillet. Remove birds and keep warm. Sauté apples in remaining butter.

3 Spread apples in bottom of ovenproof casserole and top with pheasants.

4 Add ½ cup applejack to skillet and heat slightly, stirring to scrape up browned bits. Pour sauce over pheasants. Cover casserole and bake 45 minutes.

5 Remove casserole and add cream, lemon juice, salt, and pepper. Return to oven and bake, uncovered, 30 minutes more, basting occasionally, until birds are tender when pricked with fork. (Drumsticks should move easily.) Remove birds to hot serving platter.

6 In small bowl, combine cornstarch with remaining tablespoon applejack and blend to form paste. Place casserole on top of stove and stir paste into remaining cooking liquid. Simmer until thickened. Strain

sauce over birds and garnish platter with parsley sprigs—and birds' plumage if you have it. Serve with wild rice.

YIELD: 4 SERVINGS

Roast Pheasant

 Roast pheasant is good stuffed with Green Grape/Black Walnut Stuffing (p. 219), Wild Rice Stuffing (p. 220), or Wild Rice Oyster Stuffing (p. 219).

2 pheasants, 2½ to 3 pounds
    each

salt to taste

freshly ground black pepper to
    taste

2 bay leaves

1 carrot, sliced

1 stalk celery, sliced

1 lemon, sliced

4 strips bacon

2 tablespoons butter or
    margarine

4 ounces Cognac

1　Preheat oven to 350°.

2　Place pheasants on rack in roasting pan. Sprinkle birds inside and out with salt and pepper. In cavity of each bird, place 1 bay leaf and half of carrot, celery, and lemon. Tie legs together and clip off tips of wings.

3　Rub birds with butter and pour 2 ounces Cognac over each. Place 2 strips bacon on each bird and cover with tent of aluminum foil.

4　Roast, basting occasionally until done, about 40 minutes.

YIELD: 4 SERVINGS

Quail Pies

 These plump little birds make excellent eating, but their flesh is firm, so it should be parboiled before roasting. Prepared in individual pie dishes according to this recipe, these one-dish meals are easy work for the hostess.

4 quail

1 package frozen spinach
    soufflé, thawed

4 carrots, cut in strips and
    cooked

1 small can pearl onions

butter or margarine

minced parsley

tarragon

Basic Pie Crust (p. 352)

1 or 2 egg yolks, beaten

1 Preheat oven to 400°.

2 Parboil quail gently in salted water 45 minutes.

3 Divide spinach soufflé into 4 portions and place ¼ in bottom of each baking dish. Divide carrots and pearl onions among 4 dishes.

4 Melt butter in skillet and brown quail. Place one quail, breast side up, in each baking dish. Dot with butter and add minced parsley and a pinch of tarragon to each dish.

5 Prepare pie crust and divide into 4 parts. Roll out dough and cover pies so quail legs protrude slightly through crust. Ornament crust with cutouts dipped in beaten egg yolk. Brush pies with beaten egg yolk. Bake 40 to 50 minutes.

YIELD: 4 SERVINGS

Stuffed Quail with Olives

6 quail
1 pound ground meat (beef, veal, and sausage combined)
2 large sprigs parsley, chopped
pinch of white pepper
pinch of dry mustard
4 tablespoons butter or margarine
2 strips bacon, chopped

1 sprig thyme, marjoram, and parsley, chopped
salt to taste
pepper to taste
2 tablespoons flour
1 cup beef stock
½ cup small green olives, halved
1 cup brandy or applejack

1 In kettle, simmer whole quail 1 hour.

2 Preheat oven to 375°.

3 Combine ground meat, parsley, white pepper, and dry mustard and stuff birds with mixture. Truss with string.

4 Melt 2 tablespoons butter in large casserole and brown quail thoroughly. Remove quail.

5 In same casserole, put 2 tablespoons butter, plus bacon, herbs, salt, and pepper. Sprinkle with flour, add beef stock and quail and bake, covered, 1 hour. During last 20 minutes of cooking, add olives and brandy.

6 Remove birds from casserole and arrange on hot platter—surrounded, if desired, with wild rice.

7 On top of stove, stir sauce over low heat until smooth, then pour over quail.

YIELD: 6 SERVINGS

Roast Woodcock

 One of these little birds is needed for each serving (only the breasts have much meat). They are rich, brown, and tender and taste of the seeds and berries of the forests where they live.

Hang the birds for a day or two, then pluck and clean them, reserving the livers. Stuff the birds with peeled apples, rub them with butter and pepper, and wrap each in a strip of bacon. Roast them in a 375° oven for about 45 minutes, basting occasionally with a little brandy. Sauté the livers in butter or margarine. Serve the birds with wild rice, carrots, and the sautéed livers.

POULTRY STUFFINGS

A good stuffing not only enhances the taste appeal of a roasted fowl but also improves its appearance, as a stuffed bird looks plump and pleasant on the platter. These days, anyone can make a good regular stuffing from the packaged mixes found on the shelves of every supermarket. Here you'll find some delectable traditional stuffings.

Chestnut Stuffing

 Recommended for turkey, chicken, or goose.

1/4 pound salt pork
1 onion, chopped
2 stalks celery, minced
1 pound chestnuts, coarsely
   chopped

2 tablespoons chopped parsley
1 teaspoon poultry seasoning
6 cups breadcrumbs
1/2 cup melted butter
2 eggs, beaten

1 Sauté pork in skillet until browned. Add onions and celery and simmer 5 minutes. Add remaining ingredients and mix well.

2 Stuff bird lightly.

YIELD: ENOUGH STUFFING FOR 15- TO 18-POUND BIRD

Cornbread Stuffing

 This stuffing is good for both turkey and chicken.

3 cups stale cornbread

3 cups stale white bread

giblets of bird (or ¹⁄₂ pound sausage meat)

2 onions, chopped

3 stalks celery, chopped

¹⁄₂ pound butter or margarine

1 apple, peeled, cored, and chopped

3 sprigs parsley, minced

1 bay leaf, crumbled

1 teaspoon dried thyme

1 teaspoon dried sage

2 cloves garlic, crushed

salt to taste

pepper to taste

1 Crumble breads into large bowl.

2 Chop giblets (or use sausage meat) and sauté in skillet with onions and celery in ¹⁄₄ cup butter until lightly browned.

3 In skillet, melt remaining butter and add, with sautéed vegetable mixture, apple, herbs, and seasonings, to bread. Stir to blend well.

4 Stuff bird just before roasting.

YIELD: ENOUGH STUFFING FOR 15- TO 18-POUND BIRD

Herb Stuffing

 4 cups dry white breadcrumbs

¹⁄₂ cup melted butter or margarine

¹⁄₂ onion, minced

1 stalk celery, minced

¹⁄₄ cup parsley, minced

¹⁄₄ cup watercress, minced

¹⁄₂ teaspoon dried tarragon

pinch of dried thyme or marjoram

¹⁄₂ teaspoon salt

pinch of white pepper

1 Mix all ingredients together lightly with fork and stuff bird.

YIELD: 4 CUPS STUFFING

Roast Goose Stuffing

 This stuffing is better prepared a day ahead to give the flavors a chance to blend.

1 pound sausage meat

1 large onion, chopped

2 stalks celery, chopped

2 cups stale breadcrumbs

½ cup dried apricots and ½ cup prunes, soaked in cider or wine and cut up

3 apples, peeled, cored, and diced

1 cup nuts (chestnuts or pecans), chopped

seasonings to taste:

    salt and pepper

    sage

    bay leaf, crumbled

    chopped parsley (generous amount)

1 Cook sausage meat in skillet until lightly browned and remove to large bowl. Sauté onion and celery lightly in remaining fat.

2 In bowl with sausage meat, put breadcrumbs, chopped fruits and nuts, and seasonings.

3 Store in cool place overnight. In morning, check stuffing for taste and add seasoning if necessary—or a little cider or wine if it is too dry.

4 Stuff lightly in bird.

Watercress Saffron Stuffing

 The flavor of the saffron and the pungency of the watercress give a chicken a sprightly and delicious flavor.

½ large Spanish, Bermuda, or Vidalia onion, chopped

1 tablespoon butter or margarine

6 slices white bread, crumbled

½ bunch watercress, finely chopped

juice and rind of half a lemon

1 teaspoon salt

½ teaspoon saffron

1 Sauté chopped onion in butter. Combine with remaining ingredients and stuff lightly into bird.

Green Grape, Black Walnut Stuffing

 The elusive flavor of the black walnuts and the juicy grapes contribute to a superior stuffing for chicken, squab, or cornish game hens.

1 1/2 cups dry breadcrumbs
1/2 small onion, chopped and
   sautéed
1 sprig parsley, chopped
1 teaspoon dried tarragon
1 tablespoon sweet butter or
   margarine

1/2 cup seedless green grapes
1/4 cup black walnuts, chopped
1/2 cup dry white wine
salt to taste
pepper to taste

1 Combine all ingredients and stuff lightly into bird.

Wild Rice Oyster Stuffing

 This recipe is for two large or three medium pheasants. Lacking pheasants, this interesting stuffing may be used with chicken or capon.

3/4 cup uncooked wild rice
1/4 pound mushrooms, chopped
1 cup breadcrumbs
1 small can water chestnuts,
   sliced
1 small can smoked oysters

1 small onion, minced
salt to taste
pepper to taste
fresh or dried thyme
white wine
melted butter

1 Wash rice at least 3 times, soak several hours, and drain.

2 Combine with remaining ingredients, moistening with melted butter.

3 Stuff birds and brush with additional melted butter.

Wild Rice Stuffing

 Good for roast duck, chicken, or pheasant.

3 tablespoons chopped celery

3 tablespoons chopped onion

2 tablespoons butter or
  margarine

2 cups bread cubes

1 teaspoon salt

pepper to taste

4 fresh oranges, peeled and
  sectioned, or 2 cans
  mandarin oranges

1 teaspoon poultry seasoning

1½ cups cooked wild (or
  brown) rice

1 Sauté celery and onion in butter. Add remaining ingredients and stuff
   bird lightly. If used with duck, serve duck quartered.

8

Meats and Game

Meat is the mainstay of the meal. Properly, all the other dishes are planned around it. There is a place in menu planning for both fine cuts of meat and humbler ones. Life would be boring with nothing but roasts and chops, so this chapter has many alternative meat dishes—a curry of lamb, sweetbreads, paillard of veal, spareribs, and a meat pie all make interesting possibilities.

The judgment of meat, however, is knowledge not easily acquired by an amateur. Choose a butcher whom you like and trust and seek his advice freely.

BEEF

Roast Beef

 A prime standing rib roast of beef is the joint held in the highest esteem by the Anglo-Saxon school of cooking. A two-rib roast weighing around 4 or 5 pounds will usually serve six people. However, appetites quicken at the sight of a roast, so it is wise to have at least three ribs if you are feeding several men and four ribs for a larger group. Any leftover beef will make another perfect meal, served cold with a macaroni and cheese casserole.

Ask the butcher to remove the chine (backbone), short ribs, and backstrap and tie together the roast. If the meat has been refrigerated, let it stand at room temperature 2 or 3 hours before roasting. Preheat the oven to 325°. Rub the surface of the meat well with salt and pepper and flour and place fat side up on a rack in a roasting pan. Put a few tablespoons of water in the pan to keep the cooking juices from sticking to the pan. Insert a meat thermometer in the thickest part of the roast. Place in oven and bake about 15 minutes per pound for rare beef, or until thermometer registers 115°. For medium-rare beef, roast until thermometer registers 120° to 130°. If you like well-done beef, cook to 150°, but this is a sad waste of a fine piece of meat, as it will shrink considerably. Let the roast rest and the juices settle for 20 to 30 minutes before carving. During this time, bake the Yorkshire Pudding (p. 325) and make the gravy (below) if desired. (Many people prefer just the meat juices.) Serve the beef on very hot plates.

Roast Beef Gravy

pan drippings and 4 tablespoons fat	freshly ground black pepper to taste
4 tablespoons flour	Kitchen Bouquet or
1 1/2 cups boiling water	Worcestershire sauce
salt to taste	

1 After removing roast from pan, pour off all but 4 tablespoons fat. Place pan on top of stove and stir in flour and water over low flame. Add seasonings and cook, stirring continuously, until thick and smooth.

Fillet of Beef with Mushrooms

 An expensive cut, but every bite is delicious.

1 fillet of beef, 4 to 4 1/2 pounds, trimmed of all fat and gristle and tied	4 tablespoons sweet butter or margarine
1 teaspoon salt	3/4 pound mushrooms, cleaned and sliced
freshly ground black pepper to taste	2 ounces Madeira
2 tablespoons safflower oil	chopped parsley

1 Bring beef to room temperature. When ready to prepare, preheat oven to 450°.

2 Rub fillet with salt, then grind pepper over it and brush with oil. Place in small roasting pan and roast 25 to 28 minutes, basting twice during that time. Remove from pan, place on hot platter, cover lightly with tinfoil, and let rest about 20 minutes. The meat will be perfectly rare throughout.

3 Add butter and mushrooms to pan drippings. Cook, stirring, 10 minutes. Add Madeira and parsley and stir to combine.

4 Remove string from beef and pour sauce over it. To serve, slice diagonally.

YIELD: 8 TO 10 SERVINGS

Tournedos with Mushrooms

½ pound small white
  mushrooms, trimmed and
  cleaned
6 tablespoons sweet butter or
  margarine
salt to taste
freshly ground white pepper to
  taste

2 teaspoons flour
½ cup warm milk
4 tournedos (beef tenderloin
  slices cut 1 inch thick)
4 slices French bread, cut on
  diagonal
¼ cup port wine
watercress sprigs

1 Slice mushrooms and sauté in skillet with 2 tablespoons butter until all liquid has evaporated. Sprinkle with salt, pepper, and flour and blend well. Stir in milk and cook until smooth. Keep hot.

2 Meanwhile, quickly sauté tournedos in 2 tablespoons butter, turning until brown but still rare inside.

3 Sauté bread slices in remaining 2 tablespoons butter until evenly toasted.

4 Place each tournedos on slice of bread and arrange all on hot platter. Spoon creamed mushrooms into center of platter.

5 Prepare sauce by stirring port into pan juices. Season sauce to taste with salt and pepper and spoon over tournedos. Garnish with watercress.

YIELD: 4 SERVINGS

Eye Round Roast

This is a very simple and an economical piece of beef that can be presented with much style. Serve it with a mushroom sauce, as described, or with Bearnaise, Mustard, or Horseradish Sauce (pp. 313, 319, 318). Also serve an important vegetable, such as broccoli, asparagus, or wild rice casserole.

1 eye round of beef, about 3
  pounds
salt to taste
pepper to taste

¼ cup flour
mushrooms, sliced (optional)
lemon juice to taste (optional)
1 cup red wine (optional)

1 Let meat rest at room temperature several hours or overnight. When ready to prepare, preheat oven to 425°.

2 Rub meat well with salt, pepper, and flour and place in small roasting pan containing water about ½ inch deep. Roast 15 minutes; reduce oven temperature to 325° and roast 15 minutes more.

3 Remove meat from oven and allow to rest 15 to 20 minutes before serving. It will be rare. Carve paper thin.

4 If desired, place roasting pan on top of stove and prepare sauce by adding mushrooms, lemon juice, and wine to pan and stirring until thick and smooth.

YIELD: 6 SERVINGS

Steak Tartare

 This dish is a great favorite with its champions, but there are those who will not touch raw meat. Have a frying pan ready and let them retire to the kitchen and cook their portion if they will. The steak should be served within an hour or two of grinding. Allow ⅓ pound per person.

1½ pounds freshly ground
   sirloin or top round steak,
   all fat removed
1½ teaspoons salt
4 egg yolks

4 tablespoons finely minced
   Bermuda onion
8 teaspoons capers
1 lemon, quartered
spinach, watercress, or parsley
freshly ground black pepper

1 Add salt to ground steak and lightly mound one portion on each of 4 chilled plates. Don't overhandle the meat.

2 Make an indentation in each portion and carefully slip 1 raw egg yolk into it. Arrange 1 tablespoon onion and 2 teaspoons capers over each. Garnish each with 1 lemon quarter and fresh greens.

3 Pass pepper grinder and let each guest mix his own portion. Serve with fresh melba toast or pumpernickel spread with sweet butter, and cold beer.

   Some people like Worcestershire or Tabasco sauce in steak tartare, but these strong condiments seem to defeat the point of the dish, which is to enjoy the fresh, sweet taste of the meat.

YIELD: 4 SERVINGS

Beef Stew

Keep in mind that for some mysterious reason, all beef stews are better if refrigerated overnight (overnight can be expanded to several days, too!).

½ cup flour

2 teaspoons salt

black pepper to taste

2 pounds top round or chuck, all fat and gristle removed, cut into 1½-inch cubes

5 tablespoons butter or margarine

2 cloves garlic, mashed

1 bay leaf, crumbled

½ pound mushrooms, thickly sliced

1 cup red wine

2 tablespoons tomato paste

8 medium-small whole onions

1 medium turnip, diced

½ pound carrots, peeled and cut in strips

2 cups salted water

1 teaspoon dried thyme or 2 sprigs fresh thyme

1 Mix flour with salt and several grindings of pepper. Dredge meat in flour, coating meat on all sides and using up all flour.

2 Melt 5 tablespoons butter in large skillet and brown meat over high heat. Turn meat to brown on all sides and scrape pan from time to time to prevent flour from sticking. (This takes 10 to 15 minutes.) Near end of browning, add mashed garlic and crumbled bay leaf. When meat is browned, place in large iron casserole with tight-fitting lid.

3 Sauté mushrooms in remaining butter in skillet and add to casserole. Deglaze skillet with red wine, stirring to loosen browned bits. Add wine and tomato paste to casserole, stirring to mix well.

4 Wash and boil onions, turnip, and carrots in salted water. When vegetables are nearly soft (about 15 minutes), add to the meat in casserole. Stir in enough of the water to make a thick, smooth sauce. Sprinkle casserole with thyme.

5 Simmer casserole about 1 hour. Taste for seasoning. Arrange stew so an attractive array of vegetables is on top. Garnish with beef marrow (p. 226) and sprinkle dish with chopped parsley or other green herb. Cover casserole.

6 Fifteen or 20 minutes before serving, reheat stew slowly. Carry casserole to table and remove cover there, so all will enjoy its aroma. A bowl of hot white rice or buttered noodles makes a nice accompaniment.

YIELD: 4 TO 6 SERVINGS

Yachtsman's Stew

 A special dish from the Ocean Point Inn in Boothbay Harbor, Maine.

½ pound salt pork, diced	3 whole cloves
2 pounds beef, cubed	¼ cup chopped parsley
2 tablespoons flour	1 large bay leaf
1 teaspoon salt	¾ cup sherry or dry white
½ teaspoon pepper	wine
1½ cloves garlic, minced	6 medium potatoes, peeled and
1 large onion, chopped	quartered
1 8-ounce can tomato sauce	6 carrots, peeled and cut in
1 bouillon cube dissolved in 1	2-inch pieces
cup boiling water	1 stalk celery, chopped
12 peppercorns	

1 In deep skillet or casserole, sauté salt pork. Sprinkle beef with flour, salt, and pepper and brown in pork fat. Add remaining ingredients except sherry, potatoes, carrots, and celery. Cover and simmer 4 hours.

2 After 3 hours, add sherry or wine. Then cook potatoes, carrots and celery in saucepan until partially tender. Add to stew for last 5 minutes of cooking time.

YIELD: 8 SERVINGS

Beef Marrow

 To prepare beef marrow, have the butcher crack a pound of marrow bones lengthwise so you can easily remove the marrow with the point of a small knife. Poach the marrow in water or beef stock for 10 minutes, until it is soft and quivery. Drain the marrow and keep it warm. Slice it thinly and use it on top of your beef stew as a garnish.

Beef Tongue

 Beef tongue is a nice change and is good served with Mustard Cream Sauce (p. 319). Mustard Yogurt Sauce (p. 320), or Raisin Sauce (p. 320).

1 smoked beef tongue, 4 to 5	1 stalk celery, cut up
pounds	1 carrot, sliced
half a lemon, sliced	1 bay leaf
1 onion, studded with cloves	

1 Rinse the beef tongue, place in a casserole, and add remaining ingredients. Simmer, covered, until tender, about 3 hours. Drain and cool tongue.

2 Skin tongue and remove root.

3 Place on a hot platter and garnish with parsley or watercress. Pass one of the suggested sauces.

YIELD: 8 SERVINGS

Chili Beef

 This dish is not, of course, of New England origin, but it is so useful and economical (not to mention the fact that it is best prepared a day before it is used) that it has long ago been adopted by New Englanders. It is a favorite dish for church suppers and other gatherings. Good for young people especially. (Leftover chili may dry out a little the next day, in which case you can add a small can of tomatoes to it.)

1 cup white soldier beans	3 bay leaves, crumbled
2 teaspoons salt	1 can (16 ounces) tomatoes
3 large onions, chopped	1/2 cup chili sauce
2 pounds ground beef	8 teaspoons chili powder
1 pound ground pork	1 teaspoon oregano
2 tablespoons cooking oil	1 teaspoon cumin
4 cloves garlic, crushed	1 cup ripe olives, halved

1 Rinse beans and soak overnight in water to cover. Next day, cook beans in new water to cover and 2 teaspoons salt until almost soft.

2 While beans are cooking, brown onions and meat in oil in very large skillet.

3 In large pot, combine beans, their cooking water, meat, onions, and browned bits from skillet. Add remaining ingredients.

4 Cover pot tightly and simmer over lowest heat, stirring occasionally, 2 hours. Taste for seasoning. (If you like very hot chili, you may wish to add more chili seasonings or some dried red pepper flakes.)

5 Serve in bowls with saltines that have been crisped in oven. Pass cold sour cream and cold minced Bermuda or Spanish onions.

YIELD: 8 SERVINGS

Swedish Meatballs

2 pounds ground beef (or 1¹/₂ pounds ground beef and ¹/₂ pound ground pork)

3 slices bread

2 cups water

1 onion, minced and sautéed

2 medium potatoes, peeled, boiled, and mashed

2 teaspoons salt

¹/₈ teaspoon pepper

2 eggs

4 tablespoons butter or margarine

1 Have the butcher grind the meat a couple of times.

2 Soak bread in water.

3 Combine all ingredients in large bowl. Keep working mixture until smooth and spongy. (It is best to work mixture by hand.)

4 Heat butter in skillet. Wet a spoon and the palm of your hand and shape meat into small balls. Brown meatballs evenly in butter, shaking pan continuously to retain round shape. Remove to kettle.

YIELD: 8 MEATBALLS

Gravy for Swedish Meatballs

3 to 4 tablespoons butter or margarine

¹/₂ cup flour, sifted

3 cups beef stock

1 cup light cream

salt to taste

pepper to taste

1 Prepare gravy in same skillet in which you made meatballs. Heat butter and add flour, stirring to a golden paste. Add stock gradually, stirring briskly to prevent lumps.

2 If you prefer darker gravy, add a few drops Kitchen Bouquet or brown some sugar and add.

3 Add cream and season to taste. Simmer sauce 4 to 5 minutes.

4 Pour gravy over meatballs in kettle and cook over low heat 40 to 60 minutes. Neither overcooking nor reheating will harm this wonderful concoction.

Roquefort Cheeseburgers

1 and ¹/₂ pounds ground beef

3 ounces Roquefort cheese

salt

Bermuda onion

bacon

Shape the meat into 8 patties. Place crumbled cheese on 4 of these, top each with a plain patty, and press the edges together securely. Lightly sprinkle a skillet with salt; heat and brown the patties on both sides. Serve hot on toasted, buttered buns. A thin slice of Bermuda onion and a sprinkling of crisp bacon may be added.

YIELD: 4 SERVINGS

Halfway House Yankee Pot Roast

Interesting seasoning and long, slow cooking transforms a modest cut of meat into one of the most satisfactory of all Yankee dishes. If there are leftovers, they will taste even better the next day.

2 cloves garlic

4 tablespoons butter or

    margarine

1 pot roast, chuck or tip, 3 to 4

    pounds

salt to taste

¹/₄ cup flour

1 large onion, thinly sliced

12 whole peppercorns

12 whole allspice

1 bay leaf, crumbled

1 tablespoon grated

    horseradish

1 cup red wine

¹/₂ cup water

small whole carrots, or larger

    carrots, peeled and

    quartered (optional)

turnips, peeled and quartered

    (optional)

1 recipe dumplings (p. 322)

    (optional)

fresh dill, if available

1 Mash garlic and sauté in butter. Rub meat with salt and flour and brown well on all sides in garlic butter.

2 Place meat on bed of onion slices in large Dutch oven or any pot with tight-fitting lid. Add garlic butter, then add seasonings and pour wine over meat. Cover tightly and simmer 3 to 4 hours, until roast is tender. (A good pot roast will supply most of its own juices, but as it cooks, pour in ¹/₂ cup water to ensure an ample supply of gravy.)

3 If you want carrots and turnips with pot roast, add them to pot for last

half hour of cooking. If you want dumplings, add for last 12 minutes of cooking.

4 When roast is done, remove to hot, round platter and surround with dumplings, carrots, and turnips, if desired. Stir gravy until smooth, correcting seasoning if necessary, then pour over roast. If fresh dill is available, cut it over meat with lavish hand. (If you prefer noodles instead of dumplings, they are good with pot roast.)

YiELD: 6 TO 8 SERVINGS

Corned Beef and Cabbage

 All New Englanders have grown to love the dishes introduced to our table by New Englanders of Irish descent. Corned beef and cabbage is high on the list of favorites. Be sure to rinse the meat well in boiling water first to remove excess salt.

4 pounds corned beef	pepper to taste
cold water to cover	2 medium onions
1 sprig thyme	1 whole carrot, scraped
several sprigs parsley tied together	1 cabbage, about 2 pounds
1 onion, studded with 6 cloves	butter or margarine
	finely chopped parsley

1 Tie beef neatly, place in large pot, and cover with cold water. (No salt is needed.) Add remaining ingredients except cabbage and butter and parsley and bring to boil very slowly uncovered so you can see what is happening. Simmer very gently 3 hours, skimming as necessary.

2 Remove thyme, parsley, and clove-studded onion. Cut cabbage into 8 pieces and add to pot. Simmer 15 minutes more. Remove meat from pot, place on hot platter, and cut string. Drain cabbage and arrange around meat. Dot cabbage with butter and sprinkle with parsley. Serve with Horseradish Sauce (p. 318) or Mustard Sauce (p. 319).

YIELD: 6 TO 8 SERVINGS

New England Boiled Dinner

 A great Yankee favorite traditionally served on Mondays and Wednesdays throughout the fall and winter.

5 pounds brisket corned beef,
   rinsed in boiling water

4 peppercorns

6 small beets, unpeeled

4 medium turnips, peeled

6 carrots, unpeeled

8 potatoes, peeled

1 small cabbage, quartered

dill pickles

1 Place meat in kettle with peppercorns. Cover with cold water. Simmer
3½ to 4 hours, until meat is tender. During last hour of cooking, remove peppercorns and add beets, turnips, and carrots. In last half
hour of cooking, add cabbage and potatoes.

2 Before serving, peel beets. Serve with mustard, horseradish sauce, and
dill pickles. Pass a pepper mill.

YIELD: 8 SERVINGS

Meat Loaf

This meat loaf may be made with beef, or with a mixture of beef, veal,
turkey, or pork, or any combination of these meats.

2 pounds ground meat

4 slices bread, crumbled

1 onion, minced

4 sprigs parsley, minced

1 clove garlic, crushed

2 eggs

1 cup chili sauce or tomato
   juice

1 tablespoon salt

freshly ground black pepper to
   taste

2 strips bacon

tomato catsup (optional)

1 Preheat oven to 375°.

2 In mixing bowl, combine all ingredients (except bacon and catsup)
until thoroughly blended.

3 Coat loaf pan with vegetable spray. Pack meat mixture into pan.

4 To obtain crisp "crust" on loaf, spread catsup over top of meat. If you
prefer crisp surface all over, pat meat into loaf shape and place on
baking sheet. Arrange bacon strips over meat.

5 Bake about 45 minutes. (If you use pork, bake 1 hour.) Let meat loaf
rest 20 minutes before cutting.

6 Serve, if desired, with hot tomato or brown mushroom sauce.

YIELD: 8 SERVINGS

Presidential Corned Beef Hash

 This recipe was used at the White House during Herbert Hoover's term.

2 cups minced corned beef (no fat)

4 medium potatoes, boiled and mashed

1/2 cup hot light cream

2 rounded tablespoons butter or margarine

2 tablespoons chopped celery

2 tablespoons chopped green pepper

2 tablespoons chopped onion

salt to taste

pepper to taste

1 Preheat oven to 375°.

2 Combine all ingredients thoroughly in mixing bowl. Coat heavy skillet generously with vegetable spray. Place ingredients in skillet.

3 Brown hash (over medium heat) until the bottom is crusty.

YIELD: 4 TO 6 SERVINGS

Red Flannel Hash

 Mix the leftover meat and vegetables of a New England Boiled Dinner, chop coarsely, and moisten with a little cream. Bake in an iron skillet in melted butter in a 350° oven for about 40 minutes until nicely browned. Turn out on a hot platter, and serve with the same fixings used for the Boiled Dinner. Rhode Island Toads (p. 30) are good with this.

LAMB

Butterfly Leg of Lamb

 This recipe is for cooking on an outdoor grill. This is a good dish to serve in the summer, when your herb garden is yielding bountifully. In the winter or in bad weather, you can cook it the same way over the coals of a grate fire, or you can adapt it for cooking under the broiler of a stove. If you use the broiler, preheat it and substitute dried herbs rubbed into the meat for the fresh ones. Cook the fell (fat) side first toward the flame, then turn and cook the cut side.

1 leg of lamb, boned	sprigs of fresh herbs—parsley,
salt to taste	thyme, marjoram, mint,
pepper to taste	sage, or summer savory, as
1 or 2 cloves garlic	available

1 Have the butcher bone the leg of lamb by making one long cut on the underside. Spread meat flat. (It will resemble an irregularly shaped butterfly.) Season to taste with salt and pepper. Rub with garlic.

2 Prepare bed of fresh herbs on grill and place lamb on it. Grill meat about 30 minutes on one side, 15 minutes on other side. (It should be deliciously charred on the outside and pink in the center. Since the cut is of uneven thickness, there will be pieces of various degrees of doneness to suit a variety of tastes.)

3 Carve lamb as you would steak and serve with green vegetable—asparagus, Brussels sprouts, or broccoli with Hollandaise sauce, and baked or roast potatoes.

YIELD: 6 TO 8 SERVINGS

Lamb Curry

 One of the finest of all curries is made with lamb. Three to 4 cups of lamb cut in good-size chunks will serve six people. Make the sauce as you would for Shrimp Curry (p. 185), incorporating in it, however, any fat-free pan drippings or leftover juices from the lamb. Add the cut-up meat and season to taste. Serve with an assortment of condiments.

Lamb Hash

 Lamb that is left on the roast, and the vegetables that remain, will provide a splendid hash. Chop together the leftover lamb, some potatoes, carrots or spinach, adding a small onion to the bowl. Moisten with a little light cream or leftover meat juices from which the fat has been skimmed and fry to a crisp undercrust in as much butter as is needed. It's worth planning ahead for this hash.

Navarin of Lamb

2½ pounds lamb shoulder,
   cubed and fat removed
¼ cup flour
salt to taste
freshly ground pepper to taste
4 tablespoons butter or
   margarine
12 small onions, peeled
1 cup white wine

1 cup red wine
¾ cup beef stock
2 cloves garlic, mashed
Bouquet Garni (p. 129)
4 potatoes, peeled and
   quartered
12 small carrots, scraped and
   halved diagonally
chopped parsley

1 Dredge the meat in flour seasoned with salt and pepper.

2 In heavy pot, melt butter, then brown onions and meat. Add wines, stock, garlic, and bouquet garni and cook, tightly covered, 30 minutes.

3 Add potatoes and carrots and cook 1 hour more, until meat and vegetables are very tender.

4 Remove bouquet garni and sprinkle with chopped parsley. Serve with hot white rice.

YIELD: 6 SERVINGS

Roast Leg of Lamb

This method of cooking a leg of lamb is absolutely carefree. The meat will be evenly pink all the way through. If you like your lamb better done, cook it ten minutes longer. Use fresh rosemary, thyme, or marjoram, if you have them, but use these strong herbs discreetly. Serve with the lamb roast potatoes or wild rice.

1 6-to-7-pound leg of lamb
salt to taste
freshly ground pepper to taste

rosemary, thyme, or marjoram
   to taste (use discreetly)
1 clove garlic, slivered
1 cup red wine

1 Bring lamb to room temperature. Two and a half hours before dinner, preheat oven to 400°.

2 Rub lamb with salt, pepper, and herbs. Make small slits in lamb and insert garlic slivers.

3 Place lamb in roasting pan. Pour red wine over the lamb to keep cook-

ing juices from sticking to pan. Place pan on center rack of oven and roast 30 minutes. Turn off heat but do not open oven door for 2 hours more. At that time, the roast will be cooked through evenly. Let the roast rest for 20 minutes before serving. Garnish the shank bone with a bouquet of parsley or a paper frill.

YIELD: 8 OR MORE SERVINGS

Mixed Grill

country sausages

thick-sliced country bacon

loin lamb chops, 1½ inches thick

large tomatoes, not quite ripe

toast crumbs

chopped basil or parsley

green peppers

large mushroom caps

toast rounds

butter or margarine

watercress or parsley sprigs

1 In large skillet, brown sausages and fry bacon strips—two of each for each person to be served for dinner (one of each should be enough for lunch). Remove bacon and sausages to drain on paper toweling. Discard most of grease in skillet.

2 Brown required number of lamb chops. Remove chops to large oven-proof platter.

3 Halve tomatoes and cook briefly in same skillet. Arrange, cut side up, around chops. Sprinkle toast crumbs and chopped basil or parsley over tomatoes.

4 Sauté large sections of green pepper and mushroom caps very briefly and arrange on platter.

5 Finally, garnish platter with sausages and bacon curls and some toast rounds sautéed in butter.

6 Place platter in 150° oven—it will be ready for dinner any time within 1 hour. (Put dinner plates in oven at same time.) When ready to serve, garnish platter generously with watercress or parsley.

Vanderbilt Grill

4 thick lamb chops
butter or margarine
salt to taste
pepper to taste
4 pineapple slices, canned

2 tablespoons melted butter or
  margarine
4 large mushroom caps
4 tomato halves
grated goat cheese
basil

1 Preheat broiler. Put chops on separate broiling pan. Dot chops with butter and sprinkle with salt and pepper. Place as near as possible to broiling unit and broil until about half done, about 6 minutes.

2 Remove pan from oven. Turn over chops and dot with butter, salt, and pepper.

3 Dip 4 pineapple slices in melted butter and arrange around chops. Dip 4 mushroom caps in melted butter and place one in center of each pineapple slice. Sprinkle tomato halves with salt and pepper and place on top of the chops. Return to oven and complete broiling, about 6 minutes more.

4 Just before removing pan, sprinkle tomatoes with grated goat cheese and basil.

YIELD: 2 TO 4 SERVINGS

PORK

Baked Ham

A 15-pound ham will serve 25 or more people, depending on the number of dishes which accompany it. Ham goes well with so many things: creamed turkey; chicken and oyster pie; baked beans; white beans cooked with the ham drippings; yam pudding; spoon bread; corn fritters. A fine baked ham makes, in short, a reliable and spicy focal point of a large buffet meal. Garnish it elaborately and serve it with a well seasoned fruit sauce. Baking powder biscuits, spinach soufflé, stuffed pumpkin, and corn bread all adapt themselves to the menu.

Remove the rind from the ham with a sharp knife. Spread a piece of heavy-duty aluminum foil large enough to enclose the ham completely in a large roasting pan. This will keep your oven from getting stained and will save all of the good juices of the ham. Place the ham upon the foil, fat side up. Fold the foil carefully upward so that it will catch all of the juices of the joint. Baste with a cup or so of cider, red wine, fruit juice, or gingerale (all are good and so is a combination) and close the foil around the ham. Place in a 300° oven and bake for 20 minutes to the pound. Open the foil occasionally and baste the ham. About 30 minutes before the ham is done, remove it from the oven and score the fat side diagonally to make small diamonds. Press whole cloves into the ham at the crossing of the diamonds. Spread it with a cup of brown sugar mixed with 2 tablespoons of hot mustard. At this time use some of the juices from the foil mixed with this sauce to glaze the fruit you are preparing for the ham. Baste and return it to a 400° oven until nicely glazed.

While the ham is in the last stage of cooking, prepare some attractive fruit garnish with which to decorate it. Crabapples, kumquats, orange slices, pineapple slices, and cherries are some suggestions. Glaze them in a little of the juice, and when the ham is arranged on a large platter, fix them to the surface with cloves or toothpicks. The bone end of the leg may be decorated with a large ruffle cut from baking parchment or stiff shelf paper, or with a bouquet of parsley tied in place with a ribbon of clean white cloth. Place slices of glazed fruit around the ham and garnish it with more parsley. Serve raisin, cherry, or orange sauce (see Sauces), or chutney with it.

VARIATION – Baked Ham and Sour Cream

1 slice ham, 1 inch thick
1 teaspoon dry mustard
1 cup sour cream

1 Soak ham in lukewarm water about 1 hour. (If ham has been pre-cooked, soaking is not necessary.) Preheat oven to 350°.

2 Drain ham and sprinkle with mustard. Coat baking dish with vegetable spray. Arrange ham in baking dish and cover with sour cream.

3 Bake, basting frequently, until tender, about 1 hour.

YIELD: 4 SERVINGS

VARIATION – Baked Ham and Pineapple

1 slice ham
12 whole cloves
4 pineapple slices (canned)

pineapple syrup, from can
2 tablespoons light molasses

1 Preheat oven to 350°. Coat baking dish with vegetable spray.

2 Stud ham with cloves and place in baking dish. Arrange pineapple slices on top of ham, adding some syrup from can. Pour molasses over all.

3 Cover and bake about 1 hour, basting frequently.

YIELD: 4 SERVINGS

Boneless Pork Chops with Cranberry Sauce and Endive

 A happy wintertime combination, quickly prepared and relatively free of cholesterol and fat

4 boneless pork chops

4 small heads endive

1 cup Cranberry Sauce
  (p. 315)

4 ounces Madeira

2 teaspoons balsamic vinegar

1/4 teaspoon ground cloves

several dashes of Tabasco sauce

salt to taste

watercress

1 Trim extra fat from pork chops. Coat large iron skillet liberally with vegetable spray and place chops in skillet with endive heads. (When endive is cooked to your liking, remove from the pan and keep warm.)

2 Cover tightly and cook over low heat until chops are cooked through and no pink juice runs out when you prick chops with fork. (This will be 12 to 15 minutes per side, depending on thickness of chops.)

3 In saucepan, combine cranberry sauce, Madeira, vinegar, cloves, Tabasco sauce, and salt. Cook over low heat until hot and well blended.

4 Turn up heat under pork chops and cook until browned on each side.

5 Pour 1/4 of the cranberry sauce on each of 4 hot plates. Place 1 chop on each plate and a head of endive at side. Garnish with watercress.

YIELD: 4 SERVINGS

Ham Balls with Spiced Cherry Sauce

2 cups ground cooked ham

⅓ cup breadcrumbs

1 egg, beaten

¼ cup milk

½ cup chopped green pepper

¼ cup shortening

¼ cup hot water

1 cup cherry preserve

2 tablespoons prepared
   mustard

2½ tablespoons lemon juice

¾ teaspoon ground cloves

1　Combine ham, breadcrumbs, egg, milk, and green pepper. Shape mixture into individual medium-size balls.

2　Melt shortening in skillet over medium heat. Add ham balls and turn occasionally to brown on all sides.

3　Remove skillet from heat and add hot water. Return skillet to heat, cover, and simmer about 30 minutes.

4　Meanwhile, prepare cherry sauce. In saucepan, whisk together cherry preserve, mustard, lemon juice, and cloves. Cook over low heat, stirring frequently, and bring just to boil.

YIELD: 4 SERVINGS

Roast Pork with Apricots

1 pork shoulder, 4 to 5 pounds

2½ tablespoons chopped onion

2½ tablespoons chopped
   celery

2½ tablespoons butter or
   margarine

1 can (8 ounces) apricot halves

¼ cup apricot juice

2½ cups toasted breadcrumbs

salt to taste

pinch of nutmeg

1　Ask butcher to bone and cut pocket in pork shoulder.

2　Preheat oven to 325°.

3　Sauté onion and celery in butter 5 minutes. Add apricot juice from can, plus breadcrumbs and seasonings. Stir to combine and stuff mixture into pocket in shoulder.

4　Roast 3 to 4 hours. Remove from oven and arrange apricots on top of roast. Roast 15 minutes more. Let it rest a few minutes before carving.

YIELD: 6 SERVINGS

Stuffed Crown Roast of Pork

This treatment of pork will produce fat-free, pure white meat and crunchy, browned ribs. It is delicious, reliable, and easy to prepare—now often forgotten and therefore all the more appreciated when it appears. This is a perfect main course for a dinner party—the smells that waft forth are tempting and the finished product is memorable. Have the butcher prepare a crown roast using fourteen loin ribs of pork. Following standard procedure, he will grind the meat trimmings, stuff them in the center of the roast, then add a paper frill to each little loin.

1 crown roast of pork (14 ribs stuffed with ground pork)	salt to taste
1 small onion, minced	1 tablespoon green peppercorns
3 slices whole wheat bread, crumbed	watercress sprigs
1/2 cup minced parsley	glazed kumquats
fresh or dried sage to taste	parsley sprigs

1 Remove paper frills from loins and set aside until serving time.

2 Remove ground pork stuffing from center of crown and braise in skillet with minced onion, breadcrumbs, parsley, sage (go lightly), salt, and peppercorns until partially cooked. Stuff mixture back into center of roast. (The butcher did not plan this step, but if you don't do it, the stuffing is inclined to be heavy and possibly slightly underdone.)

3 Place Pyrex bowl (4 inches in diameter) top down on rack in roasting pan. Position roast so bowl is beneath center of crown. This will hold ribs in firm, upright position. Stuffing can be mounded stylishly high over bowl, which also serves to conduct heat evenly to center of roast.

4 About 3 hours before serving, preheat oven to 350°. Roast pork, basting occasionally, about 3 hours, until meat is thoroughly cooked and surface is golden brown. When meat is pierced with long fork, no pink juices should appear.

5 Remove roast to hot platter and allow to rest while you dish out vegetables. Garnish roast by replacing paper frills over each loin, arranging bouquet of watercress in center, and surrounding roast with kumquats and parsley.

YIELD: 8 TO 10 SERVINGS

Stuffed Pork Chops

It is convenient to bake sweet potatoes or sweet potato pudding at the same time that you bake these chops. Bake some cornbread, too, if you have a hungry family.

6 pork chops, 1½ inches thick, slit with pocket
salt to taste
pepper to taste
1 cup seasoned breadcrumbs
2 apples, peeled and diced
½ cup chopped walnuts

½ cup chopped celery
1 egg
¼ cup raisins (optional)
½ teaspoon dried oregano or thyme
1 cup light cream

1 Preheat oven to 350°.

2 Wash and dry chops and season with salt and pepper.

3 In mixing bowl, combine remaining ingredients, except cream, and stuff lightly into slits in chops. Place in baking dish and cover with cream.

4 Bake 1½ hours, or until done.

YIELD: 6 SERVINGS

VEAL

Calves' Liver

4 strips bacon
1 pound calves' liver
salt to taste
pepper to taste
paprika for garnish

1 tablespoon butter or margarine
about ½ cup beef stock
Madeira to taste
chopped parsley

1 Fry bacon in skillet until crisp, drain on paper towel, and keep warm. Pour off fat, leaving just enough to brown liver.

2 Brown liver quickly over brisk flame, then reduce heat and cook to degree of doneness you prefer. Remove to warm oven while you prepare sauce.

3 In same skillet used for browning, put butter, beef stock, and Madeira. Salt and pepper to taste. Simmer 5 minutes until reduced somewhat.

4 Arrange liver on hot plates. Pour sauce over liver, then sprinkle with crumbled bacon. Garnish with chopped parsley. This dish is good with asparagus or spinach.

YIELD: 2 SERVINGS

Creamed Sweetbreads with Mushrooms in White Rice Ring

 Easy to prepare, a light and festive main course.

4 pairs sweetbreads

2 tablespoons chopped shallots

7 tablespoons butter or
   margarine

1½ cups sliced mushrooms

9 tablespoons flour

1 cup light cream

salt to taste

freshly ground white pepper to
   taste

2 egg yolks

½ cup heavy cream

6 cups cooked white rice

parsley or watercress sprigs

1 One day in advance, blanch sweetbreads in salted water to cover, cooking them just 1 minute after water boils. Drain, transfer to bowl, cool, and weight down. Refrigerate overnight. Next day, drain again and peel off outer tissues.

2 In skillet, sauté shallots in 4 tablespoons butter, add sweetbreads, and cook gently until tender, 2 to 3 minutes. Add the mushrooms.

3 To prepare cream sauce, melt remaining 3 tablespoons butter in separate skillet over low heat. Stir in flour and gradually add light cream. Whisk until thick and smooth, about 3 minutes. Season with salt and pepper.

4 In mixing bowl, beat egg yolks until light and pale, then beat in heavy cream. Whisk egg mixture slowly into cream sauce. Add cooking juices from mushrooms.

5 Meanwhile, firmly press hot rice into oiled ring mold. Unmold onto hot platter.

6 Put sweetbreads in center of rice ring. Add sautéed mushrooms to cream sauce and pour sauce over sweetbreads. Garnish with parsley or watercress.

YIELD: 6 TO 8 SERVINGS

Paillard of Veal

4 veal chops cut from loin or
   shoulder
1/4 cup flour
salt to taste
freshly ground white pepper to
   taste
1 egg, lightly beaten

1/4 cup breadcrumbs
chopped parsley
1/2 teaspoon chopped tarragon
butter, margarine, or olive oil
4 rolled anchovies
parsley sprigs
1 lemon, quartered

1 Cut away all fat and gristle from chops. Place each chop between sheets of plastic and pound with mallet until very thin.

2 Dip chops first in flour, then in beaten egg, then in breadcrumbs seasoned with chopped parsley and tarragon.

3 Heat butter in skillet until very hot and quickly sauté each chop on both sides until crisp and golden.

4 Transfer chops to hot plates or hot platter, garnish with anchovies and parsley, and serve with lemon quarters.

YIELD: 4 SERVINGS

Stuffed Glazed Shoulder of Veal

1 boned veal shoulder
12 dried apricots
1/2 pound sausage meat
1 pound chestnuts, boiled and
   peeled
5 pears, peeled, cored, and
   diced

4 tablespoons butter or
   margarine
1/4 cup port wine or fruit juice
salt to taste
pepper to taste
8 to 10 strips bacon
2 tablespoons apricot jam

1 Wipe veal with damp cloth. Soak apricots in water 30 minutes, then drain and chop.

2 Preheat oven to 300°.

3 In skillet, fry sausage meat until lightly browned. Drain on paper toweling and set aside.

4 Chop chestnuts and combine with apricots and pears. Sauté fruit mixture slowly in butter until tender, about 12 minutes.

5 Combine sautéed fruits in mixing bowl with sausage meat, wine, salt, and pepper and pack stuffing into cavity of veal. Roll veal and sew or tie securely.

6 Place shoulder on rack in roasting pan and cover with bacon strips. Roast until done, allowing 40 to 50 minutes per pound.

7 Thirty minutes before meat is done, spread with apricot jam. Bake until golden glaze is formed.

YIELD: 8 SERVINGS

Vealburgers in Mustard Cream

 These are as quick and easy as anything you can prepare, yet delicate and still unusual. Since the veal is tender, the interior should be rare and juicy, the exterior crusty brown. The meat needs only a little onion juice for seasoning. The sauce is smooth and very sharp.

2 tablespoons onion juice	$^1/_2$ cup Dijon-style mustard
2 pounds good-quality ground veal, with little fat	$^1/_2$ cup heavy cream or yogurt
	1 tablespoon lemon juice
6 tablespoons sweet butter or margarine	6 rolled anchovies
	watercress or parsley sprigs

1 Mix onion juice with veal and shape into 6 cylindrical patties about 1$^1/_2$ inches thick, flat on tops and bottoms and straight on sides.

2 Melt butter in skillet and sauté patties over brisk heat, turning until nice crust forms on all sides and patties have reached desired state of doneness.

3 Remove meat to warm platter while preparing sauce. Stir mustard, cream, and lemon juice into pan juices. Blend well.

4 Pour sauce onto hot platter and arrange patties on it. Top each pattie with rolled anchovy, garnish with watercress or parsley, and serve.

YIELD: 4 OR 5 SERVINGS

Veal Chops with Mushroom Sauce

 This recipe may also be used for veal scallops.

4 veal chops

2 tablespoons butter or
  margarine

2 tablespoons olive oil

2 tablespoons sherry

1 tablespoon flour

1/2 pound mushrooms, sliced

salt to taste

pepper to taste

dash of lemon juice

Worcestershire sauce to taste

1/2 cup sweet or sour cream

1 In skillet, sauté chops in butter and oil until golden. Remove from pan. Keep warm.

2 Add sherry and flour to pan juices, then add mushrooms and sauté until brown.

3 Add salt, pepper, lemon juice, and Worcestershire sauce to mushroom mixture. Return chops to skillet.

4 Just before serving, remove chops from skillet and stir in cream.

Veal Kidneys in Mustard Sauce

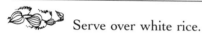 Serve over white rice.

6 tablespoons butter or
  margarine

8 to 10 veal kidneys, fat
  removed

3 leeks, washed thoroughly and
  minced

1 cup dry vermouth

4 tablespoons Dijon-style
  mustard salt to taste

black pepper to taste

1 In large skillet, heat 3 tablespoons butter until foam starts to subside. Add kidneys and cook, uncovered, until nicely browned, about 10 minutes. Remove kidneys to hot platter.

2 Add minced leeks, remaining butter, and vermouth and cook until leeks are soft. Stir in mustard and season with salt and pepper.

3 Slice each kidney into 3 pieces and return to the skillet. When heated through, divide kidney slices among 4 hot plates and serve with sauce.

YIELD: 4 SERVINGS

Veal Vaduz

2 tablespoons butter or
  margarine
1 can (8 ounces) whole onions,
  drained and well rinsed
1 medium onion, coarsely
  chopped
2 pounds lean veal scallopini,
  cut into 1" x 2¹/₂" strips
¹/₂ teaspoon salt

1¹/₂ tablespoons paprika
2 tablespoons minced parsley
2 tablespoons dry white wine
¹/₂ to ³/₄ cup chicken stock
2 tablespoons capers, with
  juice
1 small dill pickle, cut into
  strips (optional)
1 cup sour cream

1 Melt butter in heavy skillet, add whole onion, and sauté gently, turning until evenly browned. Remove onions. Set aside and keep warm.

2 In same skillet, lightly brown chopped onion; add meat and brown lightly. Add salt, paprika, parsley, wine, and about ¹/₄ cup stock. Cover tightly and cook over low to medium heat 45 minutes, or until veal is tender. Stir occasionally and add stock from time to time when necessary.

3 When meat is tender, stir in capers, whole onions, pickle strips (if desired), and sour cream. Heat thoroughly over low heat. Do not allow to boil. Serve over noodles.

YIELD: 4 TO 6 SERVINGS

Vitello Tonnato

  Exceptionally good for dinner in the summertime.

3 pounds boneless veal, loin, or
  shoulder chop (firmly tied)
6 tablespoons olive oil
1 medium carrot, chopped
1 medium onion, chopped
1 rib celery, chopped
Bouquet Garni (p. 129)
dash of salt
1 can (6¹/₂ ounces) tuna fish,
  with oil
1 tin (2 ounces) anchovies,
  with oil

3 tablespoons lemon juice
³/₄ cup mayonnaise
freshly ground white pepper to
  taste
Tabasco sauce
capers
black olives (small Greek ones
  if possible)
tomatoes, peeled and cut in
  wedges
parsley sprigs

1   In large saucepan, brown veal on all sides in olive oil. Add vegetables and bouquet garni. Cover with water, add salt, and simmer gently 2 hours. Cool meat in broth, then chill veal.

2   In blender or food processor, purée tuna fish and anchovies with olive oil and lemon juice. Beat puréed mixture together in mixing bowl with mayonnaise and season to taste with salt, white pepper, and Tabasco sauce. Chill.

3   At serving time, remove veal from refrigerator, cut off strings, and slice carefully to keep it from falling apart.

4   Arrange veal slices on round platter. Pour chilled sauce over veal slices and garnish with capers and black olives. Surround dish with tomato wedges and parsley sprigs.

YIELD: 6 SERVINGS

RABBIT

Baked Rabbit in Mustard Sauce

1 rabbit, about 4 pounds, cut
   into 8 neat pieces
2 tablespoons white vinegar
1/2 cup flour
salt to taste
freshly ground pepper to taste
4 tablespoons butter or
   margarine
1 onion, finely chopped

2 cloves garlic, minced
6 mushrooms, sliced
2 1/2 cups meat stock
1 tablespoon tomato paste
1/2 cup white wine
2 tablespoons dry mustard
1/2 cup sour cream
fresh tarragon or parsley sprigs

1   Soak rabbit pieces in cold water with vinegar 2 hours. Drain and pat dry.

2   Preheat oven to 325°.

3   Dust rabbit pieces with flour seasoned with salt and pepper. Melt butter in skillet, and when it sizzles, brown rabbit well. Remove from skillet.

4   Add onion and garlic to skillet. Cook a few minutes and add mushrooms. Cook 2 minutes.

5 Remove skillet from heat and add remaining flour, 1 cup stock, and tomato paste. Stir until smooth. Add the remaining stock and wine and return to heat. Stir continuously over low flame until sauce bubbles.

6 Combine mustard and sour cream and stir into sauce. Return rabbit to skillet. Turn rabbit in sauce to coat it. Add small sprigs of tarragon.

7 Transfer rabbit and sauce to earthenware casserole and cover. Bake 1 hour, until the rabbit is quite tender. Remove from oven, sprinkle with chopped tarragon, and serve.

YIELD: 4 SERVINGS

Fried Rabbit

 Because of its active life, the rabbit has very little fat, so use plenty of shortening and baste frequently to keep the meat from becoming dry. Serve with Lapin Cream Gravy (below).

1 rabbit, about 4 pounds, cut into 8 neat pieces	4 tablespoons butter or shortening
1/4 cup flour	juice of half a lemon
salt to taste	thyme sprigs
freshly ground black pepper to taste	paprika
	lemon slices

1 Wash rabbit pieces and drain, but do not dry. In paper bag, place flour seasoned with salt and pepper and shake rabbit pieces in flour, one or two at a time, to coat.

2 Melt butter to depth of about 1/4 inch in heavy skillet. Over high heat, brown rabbit evenly on all sides.

3 Reduce heat and squeeze lemon juice over rabbit. If pan is dry, moisten with water. Sprinkle thyme over rabbit. Cover skillet and cook slowly 1 hour or more, until rabbit is tender. For crisp skin, uncover skillet for last 10 minutes of cooking.

4 Sprinkle paprika over rabbit pieces, remove to hot platter, and garnish with lemon slices.

YIELD: 4 SERVINGS

Lapin Cream Gravy

Serve with rabbit.

For each cup of gravy desired, use 2 tablespoons rabbit drippings, 1 and ½ tablespoons flour, and 1 cup milk. Blend drippings and flour thoroughly in the skillet, add milk gradually, and stir until thickened. Add seasoning to taste, herbs, or a little wine. You'll find a few sliced mushrooms a tasty addition.

Hasenpfeffer

 This is an old German recipe. Noodles and sauerkraut are good with it.

1 rabbit, about 4 pounds, cut into 8 neat pieces	dash of ground mace
1½ cups cider vinegar	2 medium onions, sliced
1 teaspoon whole cloves	½ cup flour
3 bay leaves	salt to taste
2 teaspoons granulated sugar	pepper to taste
1½ teaspoons salt	6 tablespoons butter or
½ teaspoon peppercorns	margarine
1 teaspoon juniper berries	6 to 8 gingersnaps

1 Combine vinegar, seasonings, and sliced onions with enough water to cover rabbit in covered crock. Marinate in refrigerator 1 or 2 days.

2 Remove, drain, and dry rabbit pieces. Dust with flour seasoned with salt and pepper. Brown well in hot butter in heavy skillet. Cover and simmer 1 hour or longer, until very tender.

3 Remove rabbit to hot platter. Strain gravy, skim it, and thicken with finely crushed gingersnaps.

YIELD: 4 SERVINGS

VENISON

Formerly, venison was available only in hunting season, when your family hunter brought home a deer or a generous friend shared one with you. In recent years, however, venison farms and ranches have become numerous, raising deer from a strain of European origin. Now available year round, this venison is somewhat milder and more tender than the wild variety.

Venison is low in fat and cholesterol, a joy to those who like lean red meat. You need to cook the better cuts—saddles and steaks—over high heat in butter to sear in the juices. The less tender cuts lend themselves to slow, moist cooking—meat loaves, stews, and pot roasts.

Venison may be cooked and served in much the same way as beef, except that you have to use butter or some other fat in the cooking, since venison is much leaner than beef. Meat from older, larger animals should be tenderized by marinating in cider, red wine, or the marinade given below. Steaks will need about six hours of marinating time, while the less tender parts may require one or two days.

Marinated Venison Steak

 Moose steaks may also be prepared according to this recipe.

4 venison steaks	1 tablespoon pickling spices
1 clove garlic, minced	2 cups water
2 cups claret	4 tablespoons butter or
8 black peppercorns	margarine
1 bay leaf, crumbled	8 mushrooms, sliced
1 medium onion, chopped	parsley sprigs

1 Marinate steaks in wine, seasonings, and water 5 to 6 hours. Refrigerate while marinating.

2 Sauté steaks quickly in butter on hot griddle until seared on both sides and done to your liking. Remove to hot platter and dot with butter.

3 On same griddle, sauté mushrooms briefly in butter, pour over venison, and garnish with parsley.

YIELD: 4 SERVINGS

Roast Venison

 This recipe is good only for small, young deer and is not recommended for larger animals, whose meat will be tougher and more gamey.

1 roast of venison, about 4 pounds	freshly ground pepper to taste
paprika to taste	1 cup Burgundy wine
salt to taste	2 tablespoons chopped basil
	2 tablespoons melted butter

1 Preheat oven to 325°.

2 Rub venison with paprika, salt, and pepper and place in small roasting pan with small amount of water.

3 Roast 1³/₄ to 2 hours, basting with Burgundy during last half hour of cooking.

4 Remove to hot platter, dot with melted butter, and sprinkle with chopped basil.

YIELD: 6 SERVINGS

Venison Pâté

 This pâté is of a firmer consistency than the meat loaf. Serve it hot with mushroom sauce or cold on lettuce leaves with melba-thin buttered rye toast.

1 bay leaf

4 strips bacon

2 pounds ground venison

3 slices white bread, crumbled

1 onion, finely chopped

1 cup roasted chestnuts, coarsely chopped

2 tablespoons juniper berries

4 parsley sprigs, finely chopped

2 eggs

²/₃ cup port wine

¹/₂ teaspoon dried rosemary

1 clove garlic, minced

2 teaspoons salt

freshly ground pepper to taste

1 Preheat oven to 350°.

2 Place bay leaf in bottom of loaf pan and line pan with bacon strips.

3 Combine remaining ingredients thoroughly with fork or hands and press firmly into loaf pan. Bake 50 minutes to 1 hour.

4 Remove to cool place and cover with plastic wrap. Place brick or other heavy weight on top to pack meat firmly.

5 Drain overnight and chill, or reheat.

YIELD: 1 LOAF

Venison Meat Loaf

 This is very good served hot with a mushroom sauce to which you can add the juices from the loaf pan.

1 bay leaf	1 clove garlic, minced
4 strips bacon	1 cup tomato juice
2 pounds ground venison	2 teaspoons salt
4 slices white bread, crumbled	freshly ground pepper to taste
1 onion, chopped	1/2 teaspoon ground mace
1 stalk celery, chopped	2 eggs

1 Preheat oven to 350°.

2 Place bay leaf in bottom of loaf pan and line pan with bacon strips.

3 Combine remaining ingredients thoroughly with fork or hands and press firmly into loaf pan. Bake 50 minutes to 1 hour.

YIELD: 1 LOAF FOR 6 TO 8 PEOPLE

Venison Stroganoff

 A woodsy feast made with wild mushrooms and juniper berries and served on wild rice. Stew meat may be used instead of steaks but must be cooked longer. This dish is best prepared in the morning so that it can season during the day.

2 pounds venison steaks, cut in 1/2-inch strips	salt to taste
4 tablespoons flour	freshly ground white pepper to taste
5 tablespoons sweet butter or margarine	8 ounces morels or other wild mushrooms, sliced
1 medium Vidalia or Spanish onion, quartered and thinly sliced	2 tablespoons juniper berries
	1/2 cup beef stock
	1 cup sour cream
1 clove garlic, minced	1 tablespoon tomato purée

1 Roll venison strips in flour to coat lightly.

2 In large skillet, melt 2 tablespoons butter and brown half of venison over high heat. Set aside. Repeat with 2 tablespoons butter and remaining venison.

3 Melt remaining butter in skillet and add onions, garlic, salt, and pepper. Sauté, covered, over low heat, 10 to 15 minutes. Add mushrooms during last minute of cooking.

4 In mixing bowl, combine juniper berries, stock, sour cream, and to-

mato purée and add to onion mixture in skillet. Stir to blend over low flame.

5 Add browned venison strips and heat together 3 to 5 minutes.

YIELD: 4 TO 6 SERVINGS

9

Vegetables

One of the great advantages of present-day cookery over the cooking of the past is, surely, our wonderful vegetables. As a child in New England I can remember how limited our winter table was—carrots, potatoes, turnips, hubbard squash, spinach, beets, celery (which was never cooked), onions, and creamed canned corn. That was about it. Now vegetables go flying merrily around—endive arrives daily from Belgium, tiny green beans and morels from France, ripe tomatoes from Israel, cucumbers from Mexico, and we take for granted the fresh peas, snow peas, broccoli, asparagus, lettuce, and watercress that fly up every day from Florida and the mushrooms that are grown in cellars in Pennsylvania.

We have learned, also, how to treat these vegetables with proper respect. These are the rules of thumb: Whenever possible, buy them and serve them the same day. Cut away any tough parts. Remove the skins of the asparagus and brocoli stems with a vegetable peeler and split the thick stems of the broccoli. Cut the vegetables into small pieces and cook as briefly as possible, in rapidly boiling water, to attain a nice consistency. They will retain their color and their individual character. Save the water in which the vegetables are cooked for broth. It is rich in vitamins.

Often the vegetables are best served hot with just a bit of salt, pepper, and butter. If you are following a low-fat, low-cholesterol regime, Butter Buds are a wonderful solution.

 ## The Birthplace of Our Vegetables

Potatoes came from far
   Virginia;
Parsley was sent us from
   Sardinia;
French beans, low grown on the
   earth,
To distant India trace their
   birth;
But scarlet runners, gay and
   tall,

That climb upon your garden
   wall—
A cheerful sight to all around—
In South America were found.
The onion traveled here from
   Spain;
The leek from Switzerland we
   gain,
Garlic from Sicily obtain.
Spinach in far Syria grows;

Two hundred years ago or
more,
Brazil the artichoke sent o'er,
And Southern Europe's sea
coast shore
Beet root on us bestows.
When 'Lizabeth was reigning
here
Peas came from Holland and
were dear.
The south of Europe lays its
claim
To beans, but some from Egypt
came.
The radishes both thin and
stout,

Natives of China are, no doubt;
But turnips, carrots, and sea
kale,
With celery so crisp and pale,
Are products of our own fair
land;
And cabbages—a goodly tribe
Which abler pens might well
describe—
Are also ours, I understand.

AMICUS
*(Goldthwaite's Geographical
Magazine)*

Artichokes

 Artichokes are a great help in winter menu planning, as they ship well and are at their best at that time. They are often served as a separate course, either at the beginning of the meal or as a salad course. Serve one for each person on a large plate so there will be room for the discarded leaves.

Select firm green artichokes and trim off the stem and the small, tough leaves at the bottom so they will stand upright. Boil them, covered, in salted water to which lemon juice has been added, for 35 to 45 minutes, or until an outer leaf pulls off easily. Serve hot, with melted butter or Hollandaise Sauce (p. 317), or cold with Sour Cream Sauce (p. 308) or Roquefort Mayonnaise (p. 308). If you serve them hot, each guest removes the choke or thistly center after finishing the outside leaves. If you serve artichokes cold, remove the inner "meatless" leaves and the choke beforehand with a sharp-edged teaspoon. Then chill the artichokes and spoon sauce into the center of the vegetable.

Sautéed Artichokes

 Wonderful but a little untidy. Not for parties.

Select 1 small artichoke per person. Clean and quarter the artichokes and remove the chokes with a sharp paring knife. Cook until tender (about 20 minutes) in a large, covered skillet in olive oil, garlic, and salt. Serve with lemon wedges.

Asparagus

 Asparagus is the first welcome vegetable of spring and one of the best. Select large stalks with tightly closed buds. Stand them in a bowl of water until cooking time. Serve on a hot platter with melted butter and lemon juice, with Hollandaise Sauce (p. 317) or Cheese Sauce (p. 316), or covered with breadcrumbs sautéed in sweet butter. Nobody ever says this, but if you like asparagus really green and edibly soft, add a small pinch of baking soda to the cooking water.

2 pounds asparagus, at room
   temperature
2 quarts salted water

1 Cut off and discard tough ends of asparagus stalks and remove most of the skin with a vegetable peeler.

2 In skillet large enough to accommodate stalks, heat water to furious boil. Drop in asparagus and continue cooking, uncovered, until water boils rapidly again. Boil 8 to 10 minutes. Serve immediately.

YIELD: 4 SERVINGS

Asparagus on Toast

 If you wish to make asparagus a complete meal—and at least once each spring, you ought to—prepare it with one of the sauces suggested for fresh asparagus. Serve it on hot buttered toast, allowing 2 pounds of asparagus for three people.

Asparagus au Gratin

2 pounds fresh asparagus   **salt to taste**
¼ cup grated Cheddar cheese   **pepper to taste**
⅓ cup melted butter or   **paprika to taste**
   margarine

1 Cook the asparagus 10 to 15 minutes. Drain. Preheat broiler.

2 Coat an ovenproof dish with vegetable spray and place asparagus in dish. Sprinkle with grated cheese and pour melted butter over all. Season with salt, pepper, and paprika.

3 Place under broiler until cheese is browned.

YIELD: 4 SERVINGS

Asparagus Amandine

2 pounds fresh asparagus
¹/₂ cup melted butter or
   margarine
¹/₃ cup sliced almonds

¹/₃ cup breadcrumbs
salt to taste
pepper to taste

1 Cook the asparagus 10 to 15 minutes. Drain. Preheat broiler.

2 Coat an ovenproof dish with vegetable spray and place asparagus in dish. Sprinkle with almonds, breadcrumbs, salt, and pepper. Pour melted butter over all.

3 Place under broiler until top is browned.

YIELD: 4 SERVINGS

Asparagus Tips with Ham

A simple but elegant luncheon or supper dish to serve with hot buttered rolls or popovers. Vary it by adding a little curry to the sauce.

2 pounds asparagus
4 large, lean slices ham
2 cups Cheese Sauce (p. 316)

1 Preheat oven to 400°.

2 Cook asparagus 10 to 15 minutes. Drain.

3 Wrap each ham slice around 3 or 4 cooked asparagus stalks. Coat baking dish with vegetable spray.

4 Place ham-wrapped asparagus in baking dish and pour cheese sauce over all. Bake 5 or 6 minutes, or until browned.

YIELD: 4 SERVINGS

Green Beans

One of the most wonderful crops of summer, green beans are easy to raise and yield abundantly all summer long. Pole beans, which have a slightly "beanier" flavor, may be used in the same recipes. It is wise to have a couple of rows of each type in even the smallest garden. In winter, frozen green beans serve many useful purposes, combining well with almost all other vegetables and vegetable garnishes and complementing almost any dish. Green beans frozen whole seem to have the best flavor.

Remove ends of beans, and strings if there are any. If the beans are small, leave them whole; otherwise, snap them into 1-inch lengths or French-cut them into long, thin strips. Wash the beans, then cook them in a small amount of rapidly boiling water until just tender and still green—10 to 15 minutes, depending upon their size. Serve at once with butter. (A pound of green beans makes 4 servings.)

You can also serve green beans with: almonds, slivered or sliced and browned in butter; water chestnuts, sliced very thin, and a pinch of dill or oregano; sliced new potatoes garnished with crisp crumbled bacon; mushrooms and a little cream; lima beans, with or without almonds.

Green Beans Country Style

2 large onions, sliced
1 teaspoon salted water
2 pounds string or pole beans (as fresh and young as possible)
1 heaping tablespoon flour

3 tablespoons butter or margarine, melted
1/2 cup heavy sweet cream or sour cream
1 teaspoon chopped fresh basil
freshly ground black pepper to taste

1 Boil onion slices a few minutes in salted water. Add beans (cut large beans in half but leave smaller ones whole) and cook briskly 10 to 15 minutes, letting most of the water evaporate.

2 Add flour, butter, cream, basil, and pepper. Reduce heat to low and stir until sauce is thick. (An acceptable substitute may be made with frozen whole beans and dried basil.)

YIELD: 6 TO 8 SERVINGS

Green Bean Casserole

1½ pounds fresh green beans,
French cut
salt to taste
pepper to taste
flour (for dusting)
onion rings, shaved paper thin,
from medium onion

2 tablespoons butter or
margarine
½ cup light cream
¼ cup grated Swiss cheese
¼ cup buttered breadcrumbs

1 Preheat oven to 400°.

2 Cook green beans until nearly done. Let cooking liquor reduce to a few tablespoons. Remove beans and reserve bean liquor.

3 Place beans in shallow casserole and sprinkle with salt and pepper. Dust with flour. Cover beans with layer of onion rings.

4 In saucepan, prepare light sauce of butter, 1½ tablespoons flour, and bean liquor. Pour sauce over beans, then pour cream over all and sprinkle with grated cheese. Top with buttered breadcrumbs and few dots of butter.

5 Bake until bubbly, about 10 to 15 minutes.

YIELD: 6 SERVINGS

Purée of Lima Beans and Watercress

This smooth, bright-green purée makes an interesting use of our old friend the lima bean. In menu planning, you can sometimes use it as a substitute for potatoes.

1 package frozen lima beans
lightly salted water
½ bunch watercress
¼ cup heavy cream

1 tablespoon butter or
margarine, softened
white pepper to taste

1 Cook lima beans in boiling salted water until tender. Drain.

2 Wash watercress and remove large stems.

3 In blender or food processor, purée vegetables together until very smooth. Add cream and butter and purée again.

4 Season to taste with salt and white pepper.

YIELD: 4 OR 5 SERVINGS

Harvard Beets

3 tablespoons butter or
   margarine
1 tablespoon cornstarch
1¹/₂ cups beet liquor
¹/₂ cup brown sugar
¹/₄ cup cider vinegar

salt to taste
ground cloves to taste
ground nutmeg to taste
12 medium cooked beets,
   whole or cut up

1 Melt the butter in a saucepan over low heat. Blend in cornstarch and stir in beet liquor. Cook, stirring constantly, until smooth and thick.

2 Add the brown sugar and vinegar, then add salt, cloves, and nutmeg to taste. When sauce is well mixed, add beets and serve hot.

YIELD: 6 SERVINGS

Beets in Cream Sauce

12 medium cooked beets,
   whole or cut up
³/₄ cup sour cream
¹/₄ cup sweet cream
juice of half a lemon

¹/₂ teaspoon dry mustard
¹/₂ teaspoon salt
white pepper to taste
chopped fresh dill for garnish

1 Heat beets in top of double boiler. Add remaining ingredients and mix together—gently, to avoid breaking beets.

2 Serve hot, garnished with dill. (If fresh dill is not available, use chopped fresh parsley or chopped fresh chives.)

YIELD: 4 SERVINGS

Beets in Orange Sauce

Boiled baby beets taste good in a sauce made by adding 1 tablespoon orange juice and some grated orange rind to the butter or margarine in which they are served. (A pound of beets makes 4 or 5 servings.)

Beet Greens

Prepare the same way you fix fresh spinach (p. 283).

Beets and Beet Greens in Cream

Here the young savory beet greens count as much as the beets. Dig a few handfuls of very small beets and gather enough leaves to make an equal quantity. (A fresh bunch of beets from the market will do, too.)

1 bunch young beets, with
   greens
pinch of granulated sugar
2 tablespoons butter or
   margarine
1 small onion, minced

salt to taste
pepper to taste
1 tablespoon lemon juice
1/2 cup sweet or sour cream
1 hard-boiled egg

1 Boil the beets separately from the greens and skin them.

2 Rinse greens but do not dry. Discard all tough stems, then put in saucepan. Add sugar, butter, and minced onion. (Do not add more water.) Cook slowly, covered, until tender. Remove cover and boil away any remaining liquid.

3 Add beets, chopped quite fine. Add salt, pepper, and lemon juice and heat through. Stir in cream.

4 Serve garnished with sieved hard-boiled egg.

YIELD: 4 SERVINGS

Broccoli

One of the most delicious of all vegetables, broccoli must be cooked immediately before serving to preserve its bright green appearance. Since it is a rather special vegetable, broccoli is very well suited to be served separately as a first course. Keep the kitchen door closed because of its strong smell.

Purée of Broccoli

1 head broccoli
salted water
about 3 tablespoons butter or
   margarine

about $1/4$ cup heavy cream or
   yogurt
juice of half a lemon

1 Clean the broccoli. With a small knife, remove florets within 1 inch or
so of their stems. Boil florets rapidly in salted water until bright green
and tooth-tender. Drain and set aside.

2 Cut tough ends from rest of broccoli, pare stems, and cut in pieces. Boil
stems rapidly in salted water until tender but still green. (Stems need to
cook longer than florets.) Drain.

3 Put cooked stems in food processor fitted with steel blade. Purée, adding some butter and cream until the mixture is smooth and light.

4 In separate saucepans, reheat florets and puréed stems. Spoon purée
into hot serving dish and arrange florets on top. Squeeze lemon juice
over all and brush with small amount of melted butter.

YIELD: 4 OR 5 SERVINGS

Brussels Sprouts and Celery Casserole

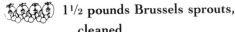
$1 1/2$ pounds Brussels sprouts,
   cleaned
hearts of 1 bunch celery
few drops of lemon juice
2 cups Cream Sauce (p. 315)

1 cup sour cream
$1/2$ cup buttered breadcrumbs
$1/2$ cup sliced almonds
chopped fresh parsley for
   garnish

1 Preheat oven to 350°. Coat ovenproof casserole with vegetable spray.

2 Boil the vegetables in salted water and lemon juice about 15 minutes,
or until almost tender. Drain.

3 Spread vegetables in the prepared casserole. Whisk together cream
sauce and sour cream and pour over vegetables. Combine breadcrumbs, almonds, and parsley and sprinkle on top.

4 Bake 15 minutes, until golden.

YIELD: 6 TO 8 SERVINGS

Steamed Cabbage

1 small cabbage, 1½ to 2
   pounds
1 tablespoon butter or
   margarine

salt to taste
freshly ground white pepper to
   taste

1 Remove any soiled or tough outer leaves of cabbage. Cut the cabbage in 8 pieces and remove the core. Halve each piece.

2 Steam cabbage with butter and ½ cup water in tightly covered saucepan until tender but still crisp and green. (To make creamed cabbage, add 1 cup cream sauce thinned with a little milk.)

YIELD: 6 SERVINGS

Red Cabbage Black Forest

Perfect on a cold night with turkey, beef, or game.

1 small head red cabbage
4 tablespoons red wine vinegar
2 tablespoons granulated sugar
1 teaspoon salt

freshly ground pepper to taste
½ cup chestnuts, broken into
   pieces
butter or margarine to taste

1 Wash the cabbage and shred finely. Place in a large pot with water, vinegar, sugar, salt, and pepper. Cover closely and steam, stirring occasionally, until cabbage is just soft. Drain.

2 Add chestnuts and butter and heat together thoroughly.

YIELD: 8 OR MORE SERVINGS

Carrots and Fresh Mint

1 pound fresh young carrots
3 tablespoons water
3 tablespoons butter or
   margarine
salt to taste

freshly ground pepper to taste
few crumbs of brown sugar
3 or 4 small mint leaves,
   shredded

1 Combine carrots (sliced, or left whole if small) with water and butter in a saucepan. Cook, covered, until tender.

2 Remove cover and add salt, pepper, and brown sugar. Stir to allow any extra liquid to steam away.

3 Add mint leaves. (Mint flavor should be elusive, so don't use too much.) Heat together and serve.

YIELD: 4 SERVINGS

Glazed Carrots

 1 pound carrots
1 cup salted water
1/2 teaspoon salt

3 tablespoons butter or margarine
2 tablespoons granulated sugar
1/2 teaspoon ground ginger

1 Scrape carrots. (If young and small, use whole; otherwise, slice.)

2 Boil salted water in shallow saucepan and add carrots. Cover and cook 15 minutes. Remove cover and continue cooking until water has evaporated.

3 Add the butter, sugar, and ginger to saucepan. Shake and toss carrots over heat until shiny and golden brown.

YIELD: 4 SERVINGS

Purée of Carrots

 Made in the blender, these carrots are light as air.

1 pound carrots
2 tablespoons butter or margarine
2 tablespoons light cream

salt to taste
white pepper to taste
pinch of ground mace

1 Clean, scrape, and cut up the carrots. Cook in just enough water to cover until carrots are very tender and water has boiled away.

2 Purée carrots in blender or food processor with butter and cream. Season and reheat.

YIELD: 4 SERVINGS

Creamed Carrots in Chicken Stock

1 pound carrots, peeled
2 cups chicken stock
3 tablespoons butter or
   margarine
3 tablespoons flour
juice of half a lemon
salt to taste

cayenne pepper to taste
1 tablespoon chopped fresh
   parsley
1 tablespoon chopped fresh
   chives
1 egg yolk
1/2 cup light cream

1 Clean carrots. (Leave whole if small, or cut larger carrots as desired, first removing any tough core.) Cook carrots in 1 cup chicken stock until tender.

2 In a separate saucepan, melt butter, then stir in flour. Gradually stir in remaining chicken stock and lemon juice. Add salt and cayenne and cook over low heat, stirring until sauce is thick.

3 Add the carrots, parsley, and chives. Mix the egg yolk with cream and add to saucepan. Reheat but do not boil.

YIELD: 4 SERVINGS

Carrot Ring

A very useful recipe and an easy, attractive way to offer several vegetables at once for a buffet or large gathering. You can fill this ring with cauliflower, Brussels Sprouts, and green peas, or you can fill it with one vegetable and surround it with another. Creamed mushrooms are excellent.

1 cup boiled carrots, puréed in
   blender or food processor
1 teaspoon grated onion
salt to taste
paprika to taste
celery salt to taste

1 cup thick Cream Sauce
   (p. 315)
4 eggs, separated
1 teaspoon cream of tartar
chopped fresh parsley for
   garnish

1 Preheat oven to 350°.

2 Combine the carrots with the onion, salt, paprika, celery salt, and cream sauce. Cool.

3 Beat in egg yolks, one at a time. Put egg whites in separate bowl with cream of tartar and beat until stiff. Fold into carrot mixture.

4 Coat ring mold with vegetable spray. Fill mold two-thirds full.

5 Place the mold in larger pan in water halfway up side of mold and bake about 45 minutes, or until firm. Unmold immediately. Garnish with chopped parsley.

YIELD: 4 SERVINGS

Carrots and Parsnips

 A simple but excellent combination.

1 pound carrots	**butter or margarine to top**
1 pound parsnips	**pepper to taste**
fresh parsley for garnish	

1 Cut equal quantities of the carrots and parsnips into shoestring sticks.

2 Place carrots in boiling water; after 1 or 2 minutes, add parsnips, which cook more quickly.

3 When vegetables are tender, top with a pat of butter and serve garnished with parsley and pepper.

YIELD: 8 SERVINGS

Cauliflower

 For this recipe, you will need a large, white cauliflower with fresh green leaves.

1 large cauliflower	**2 tablespoons buttered**
melted butter or margarine	**breadcrumbs or nut crumbs**
1 tablespoon lemon juice	

1 With a sharp knife, carefully remove cauliflower from its green leaves, keeping both intact. Turn cauliflower over and cut several large gashes in stem. Wash and place in large pan of boiling salted water. Cover pan and steam until cauliflower is tender, about 20 minutes.

2 Meanwhile, trim base of plant so it will sit flat. Trim leaves neatly and steam in separate pot until leaves turn bright green.

3 Place cauliflower on steamed leaves on large, round, hot platter. Pour melted butter, lemon juice, and buttered crumbs over vegetable. Or serve with Hollandaise Sauce (p. 317) or Cheese Sauce (p. 316).

You can create a fine effect by surrounding the cauliflower with buttered whole carrots or beets, or a combination of the two.

YIELD: 6 SERVINGS

Braised Celery

1 bunch celery

6 tablespoons butter or
    margarine

2 beef bouillon cubes

$^1/_4$ cup slivered almonds

salt to taste

white pepper to taste

chopped fresh parsley for
    garnish

1 Clean the celery, discarding tops and any tough stalks. Cut stalks, hearts, and root into 3-inch pieces.

2 In a large skillet, heat butter until bubbling. Dissolve bouillon cubes in butter, then add celery, almonds, salt, and pepper. Cook until celery and almonds are brown and glazed with beef-flavored butter.

3 Garnish with chopped parsley and serve.

YIELD: 4 SERVINGS

Creamed Celery Hearts

4 scallions, minced

3 tablespoons butter or
    margarine

1 clove garlic, crushed

4 cups celery hearts, cut in
    1-inch pieces

salt to taste

white pepper to taste

$^1/_3$ cup chicken stock

2 egg yolks

2 tablespoons heavy cream

$^1/_3$ cup Madeira

1 teaspoon chopped fresh dill

1 Sauté the scallions in butter until golden. Add garlic, celery, salt, pepper, and chicken stock. Simmer, covered, about 15 minutes, or until celery is just tender.

2 Stir together the egg yolks, cream, and Madeira and add to celery. Continue to cook over low heat, stirring constantly until sauce thickens. (Do not let it boil.)

3 Serve sprinkled with chopped dill.

YIELD: 6 SERVINGS

Creamed Celery and Chestnuts

 A useful winter dish.

4 cups sliced celery	1 can (11 ounces) whole
8 tablespoons butter or	chestnuts, drained
margarine	salt to taste
1/4 cup flour	white pepper to taste
1 cup light cream	cayenne pepper to taste
1 cup sliced mushrooms	1 1/2 cups half-inch bread cubes

1 Cook celery in salted water, covered, until tender but still crisp. Drain, reserving 1 cup of cooking liquid.

2 In saucepan, melt 4 tablespoons butter, stir in flour, and gradually stir in reserved celery liquid and cream. Cook over low heat until mixture bubbles and thickens. Simmer 5 minutes more.

3 Add celery, mushrooms, and chestnuts to sauce. Season to taste.

4 Sauté bread cubes in remaining butter. Turn vegetable mixture into serving dish and sprinkle with sautéed bread cubes.

YIELD: 6 SERVINGS

Corn on the Cob

 Serve corn as soon as possible after it is picked. If it must wait a few hours, shuck it and cover with cold water.

In a large kettle, bring to a boil enough water to cover corn. Add 1 tablespoon sugar for each quart of water. Boil corn 3 to 5 minutes. It will be very tender. Serve with butter and salt.

Succotash

 M'sickquatash, the Algonquian Indian word for "corn boiled whole," became the succotash of the earliest settlers. This was one of the easiest Indian recipes adopted by the Pilgrims, and the hearty mixture was usually sweetened with bear fat. As time went on, succotash developed into a more elaborate dish made with large white beans, hulled corn, salt pork, and onion. The modern version is a lot lighter! Succotash is one of the great New England dishes. Simple but perfect. If you wish, you can add a teaspoon of finely minced green or red pepper—rather like confetti.

2 cups corn kernels, scraped from cob	3 tablespoons butter or margarine, softened
milk from corn kernels (liquid from scraping corn off husk)	2/3 cup light cream
1 1/2 cups lima beans	1 tablespoon flour
	salt to taste
	white pepper to taste

1 Stir together the corn, milk from kernels, beans, butter, and cream. Sprinkle flour over mixture so it will not be lumpy. Cook in a double boiler for about 8 minutes, stirring until well blended. Sauce should not be thick. Add salt and pepper to taste.

YIELD: 4 SERVINGS

Corn Oysters for Summer

 Corn oysters are delicious served with fried chicken, ham, or grilled bacon. At breakfast, serve them with maple syrup.

2 cups corn kernels, scraped from cob	1 tablespoon melted butter or margarine
milk from corn kernels	salt to taste
2 eggs, well beaten	freshly ground white pepper to taste
1/2 cup flour	

1 Mix together all the ingredients and set aside 10 or 15 minutes.

2 Drop by tablespoonfuls onto well-greased hot griddle. (These "fritters" should be the size of large oysters.) Turn, brown on all sides, and serve.

YIELD: 4 SERVINGS

Corn Oysters for Winter

2 cups canned creamed corn	1 tablespoon melted butter or margarine
2 eggs, well beaten	salt to taste
2 teaspoons baking powder	freshly ground white pepper to taste
1/2 cup flour	

1 Mix together all the ingredients. Drop by teaspoonfuls onto well-greased hot griddle. (These "fritters" should be the size of large oysters.) Turn, brown on all sides, and serve.

YIELD: 4 SERVINGS

Cucumbers in Hollandaise Sauce

 Unusually tasty. The deep green, white, and yellow hues of the dish are very appetizing.

2 seedless cucumbers, unpeeled   Hollandaise Sauce (p. 317)
1 tablespoon butter or
   margarine

1 Cut the cucumbers crosswise into 1½-inch lengths. Quarter each piece lengthwise and trim each quarter piece into an olive-shaped oval, removing seeds and reserving trimmings for other uses (such as cucumber soup).

2 In a skillet over low heat, melt butter and sauté cucumber pieces, stirring, 4 to 5 minutes, until just tender.

3 Serve in heated bowl masked with Hollandaise Sauce.

YIELD: 4 SERVINGS

Sautéed Cucumber Rings

 2 cucumbers, peeled   **salt to taste**
butter or margarine   **white pepper to taste**

1 Remove ends of cucumbers and cut cucumbers in half crosswise. Remove seeds with apple corer.

2 Slice cucumbers in thin rings (the thickness of a silver dollar) and pat dry with paper toweling.

3 Melt the butter in a skillet and sauté cucumber rings until translucent. Add salt and pepper.

YIELD: 2 SERVINGS

Dandelion Greens

 Wash the greens, keeping only the tenderest leaves. Cover with cold water until ready to use. Remove leaves from water and shake to remove most of the water. Cook with 1 tablespoon butter in covered saucepan until soft. Season with salt, pepper, and lemon juice.

Fried Dandelion Blossoms

 Very few people realize the nutritious value of dandelion blossoms. This unusual recipe is believed to have originated in Germany, whence it was brought over by the pioneers.

Pick any amount of dandelion blossoms close to the bud (no stems) and soak in salt water 20 minutes. Rinse well and squeeze out any excess water. Roll well in flour and sauté blossoms in enough butter to keep from burning. Keep heat low and brown well, turning blossoms to brown on all sides. Add salt and pepper to taste. Use as a vegetable.

Panned Escarole

2 heads escarole
3 tablespoons butter or
  margarine
2 medium onions, very thinly
  sliced

salt to taste
white pepper to taste
2 tablespoons heavy cream
crushed cornflakes to top

1 Wash and pick over the escarole, then cut crosswise in narrow strips.
2 Melt butter in large saucepan or skillet and add escarole and onion. Cover and cook over low heat about 10 minutes. Season with salt and pepper and stir in cream.
3 Remove to warm serving bowl and top with cornflake crumbs.

YIELD: 6 SERVINGS

Fiddlehead Ferns

 Fiddlehead ferns, if you know where to find them, are the first delicacy of spring, appearing even before asparagus. (In some parts of New

England, they are now available in specialty food shops and large supermarkets.) To cook them, plunge fiddleheads briefly in rapidly boiling water. Serve with butter, salt, and, if you like, lemon juice. You can also add chopped almonds, or serve the ferns on hot buttered toast. The ferns are also delicious chilled and served as a salad or appetizer with vinaigrette.

Braised Leeks

 Leeks make a good first course served hot on buttered toast, or chilled and served with French Dressing (p. 309).

12 leeks
3 tablespoons butter or
  margarine
2 cups beef stock, or 2 beef
  bouillon cubes dissolved in 2
  cups water

salt to taste
white pepper to taste
1/2 teaspoon dried thyme
chopped fresh chives for
  garnish

1 Wash leeks thoroughly and trim off roots and most of tops (save tops for soup). Put in large skillet with butter, stock, salt, pepper, and thyme. Cook, covered, until tender, about 15 minutes. Garnish with chives if desired.

YIELD: 3 OR 4 SERVINGS

Mushrooms in Cream

 These may be served as an accompaniment to an entrée, or over buttered toast as a lunch or supper dish.

4 tablespoons butter or
  margarine
1 onion, chopped
1 pound mushrooms, sliced
salt to taste

freshly ground white pepper to
  taste
1/2 teaspoon paprika
juice of half a lemon
2 tablespoons flour
3/4 cup light cream

1 Melt the butter in a skillet and sauté onion until transparent. Add mushrooms and sauté briefly. Add salt, pepper, paprika, lemon juice, and flour. Cook 5 minutes before stirring in cream.

YIELD: 4 TO 6 SERVINGS

Mushroom Puffs

Serve these puffs with meat.

1 pound fresh mushrooms	1 cup milk
1/2 cup butter or margarine	1 cup light cream
3 rounded tablespoons flour	1 egg, beaten
1 teaspoon salt	1/2 cup breadcrumbs

1 Wipe mushrooms, trim stems, and chop finely.

2 Melt butter in skillet and sauté mushrooms.

3 In a saucepan, dissolve flour and salt in milk and cream. Add sautéed mushrooms and cook until very thick, stirring constantly.

4 Spread mushroom mixture in flat pan to cool. When cool, form into balls about the size of a walnut. (Smaller balls can be served as appetizers.)

5 Dip balls in beaten egg, then in breadcrumbs. Fry in deep fat (at 370°) until brown.

YIELD: 6 TO 8 SERVINGS

Timbale of Mushrooms

1 cup chicken stock	1 tablespoon chopped fresh
1/2 cup light cream	parsley
4 eggs	1/2 pound mushrooms, chopped
1/2 teaspoon salt	2 tablespoons butter or
1/2 teaspoon paprika	margarine
pinch of ground mace	

1 Preheat oven to 350°.

2 Whisk together the stock, cream, eggs, salt, paprika, mace, and parsley. Set aside.

3 Sauté mushrooms in butter with a dash of salt and add to egg mixture.

4 Coat 1-quart mold with vegetable spray. Pour mushroom and egg mixture into mold and bake 30 minutes, or until knife inserted in center comes out clean.

YIELD: 6 SERVINGS

Mushrooms with Wine and Dill

 A recipe from the "Beacon Hill Wednesday Night Buffet" group.

3 cups thinly sliced mushrooms
6 tablespoons butter or
   margarine
salt to taste

cayenne pepper to taste
3 tablespoons sherry
1 tablespoon finely chopped
   fresh dill

1 In a skillet, sauté mushrooms in very hot butter 3 to 4 minutes. Add salt and cayenne, then add sherry and dill. Heat through. This can be served over toast points.

YIELD: 6 SERVINGS

Glazed Onion Rings

6 tablespoons butter or
   margarine
6 large Bermuda or Spanish
   onions, sliced ½ inch thick
¾ cup Madeira

2 tablespoons chopped fresh
   parsley
salt to taste
white pepper to taste

1 Melt the butter in a heavy skillet and toss onions in butter. Add ½ cup Madeira and cover pan. Cook onions over medium heat until tender, 15 to 20 minutes.

2 Remove cover and let wine reduce to glaze. Stir in remaining Madeira. Add chopped parsley and season with salt and pepper.

3 Serve with grilled steak.

YIELD: 6 SERVINGS

Glazed Onions

 Prepare the same way you fix Glazed Carrots (p. 264), substituting small, peeled, white onions for the carrots.

Braised Parsnips

1 pound parsnips
3 tablespoons butter or
   margarine
salt to taste

white pepper to taste
ground nutmeg
finely chopped fresh parsley
   for garnish

1 Clean and scrape young, freshly dug parsnips and cut in half lengthwise.

2 Melt butter in a skillet, add the parsnips, salt, pepper, and nutmeg and cook, covered, over low heat until tender.

3 Serve garnished with chopped parsley.

YIELD: 4 SERVINGS

Glazed Parsnips

Prepare the same way you fix Glazed Carrots (p. 264), substituting young parsnips, peeled and halved, for the carrots.

Parsnip Griddlecakes

6 cooked parsnips
1 egg, well beaten
3/4 teaspoon salt

1 tablespoon melted butter or
   margarine
2 tablespoons flour

1 Mash the parsnips, add egg, and beat until light. Season with salt and butter and fold in flour.

2 Drop the batter by spoonfuls onto greased hot griddle. Brown, turn, and brown other side.

YIELD: 6 TO 8 GRIDDLECAKES

Fresh Peas

One pound of peas in the shell will yield about 1 cup, or 2 medium servings. Allow 1 tablespoon of butter or margarine for each cup of peas.

Put 2 large lettuce leaves in a double boiler. On leaves, place butter, then shelled peas. Salt and pepper lightly and cover with another lettuce leaf. Steam gently about 20 minutes. (In winter, you can treat tiny frozen peas the same way. If you like, add small, parboiled pearl onions.)

Snow Pea Mixture

¹/₄ pound snow peas	1 tablespoon water
1 cucumber, peeled	¹/₂ teaspoon granulated sugar
1 cup tiny fresh or frozen peas	salt to taste
2 tablespoons butter or	white pepper to taste
margarine	1 endive

1 Wash the snow peas and remove stems and strings, if any. Shell peas, or, if using frozen peas, bring to room temperature.

2 Halve and seed the cucumber. With small melon-ball cutter, cut out round balls.

3 Melt butter in a skillet with water and add snow peas, cucumber, and peas. Cook until peas are bright green. Add sugar, salt, and pepper. Slice endive into mixture and cook together a few minutes more.

YIELD: 4 SERVINGS

Roquefort-Stuffed Peppers

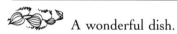 A wonderful dish.

4 medium green peppers	¹/₂ cup milk
³/₄ cup Roquefort cheese	1 tablespoon butter or
³/₄ cup soft breadcrumbs	margarine
³/₄ cup mayonnaise	

1 Preheat oven to 350°.

2 Cut a half-inch slice from top of each pepper and remove seeds and membrane.

3 Make the filling by mixing crumbled cheese with breadcrumbs, mayonnaise, and milk.

4 Fill peppers and dot with butter. Place peppers in baking dish, then

put baking dish in larger pan in ½ inch of hot water. Bake 30 to 40 minutes, or until peppers are tender when pierced with fork but still slightly crisp.

YIELD: 4 SERVINGS

Baked Potatoes

There are a number of ways to embellish the baked potato. A little sour cream, finely chopped chives, mashed anchovies, crumbled bacon—all delicious, but don't use them all at once!

Scrub potatoes well and rub with a little butter or margarine. Maine, Long Island, and Idaho potatoes are all good, though we favor the first. Bake on the center rack of the oven at 425° for 45 minutes to an hour, depending upon the size of the potatoes. When the potatoes are light and mealy when pricked with a fork, break them open and put a large piece of butter in each. Sprinkle with salt, pepper, paprika, and chopped parsley. Serve piping hot. If your potatoes must be cooked in an oven whose temperature is adjusted to bake some other dish, they may be cooked just as well at a lower temperature, but they must cook correspondingly longer.

Accordion Potatoes

The recipe for these crispy potatoes, of real Yankee ingenuity, comes from Watch Hill, Rhode Island.

4 medium baking potatoes
½ cup melted butter or
  margarine
1 tablespoon vegetable oil
1 teaspoon salt

few grindings of white pepper
½ cup grated Cheddar cheese
  (optional)
paprika

1 Preheat oven to 425°.

2 Slice the potatoes thinly, accordion-style, not cutting through potatoes. (Place a potato on a cutting board and put the handle of a wooden spoon next to it. With a sharp knife, make thin slices through the potato, at right angles to the spoon handle. The handle will keep you from cutting all the way through.)

3 In shallow bowl, combine melted butter, oil, salt, and pepper. Roll po-

tatoes in mixture and place in roasting pan. If desired, sprinkle with cheese.

4   Bake 40 to 50 minutes. Sprinkle with paprika before serving.

YIELD: 4 SERVINGS

 ## Potato Ribbons

Even more addictive than potato chips, potato ribbons were a favorite snack of President James A. Garfield's. Mrs. Arthur Emmons, source of this recipe, says, "The recipe is over a hundred years old and was used in the Ballou home in Ohio by Eliza Ballou, President Garfield's mother and my own great-great-great aunt, who fried her potato ribbons in the old iron kettle hung in the fireplace."

Cut 4 pared, medium potatoes in 3/4-inch slices. Pare round and round in very long ribbons. Fry them in hot lard or drippings until crisp and browned. Dry them on paper towels. Some will turn out to look like roses, and they are both attractive and delicious filled with creamed chicken, tuna, or peas. Or just pile the ribbons on a hot dish and season with salt.

Stuffed Baked Potatoes

 3 large oval potatoes
2 tablespoons butter or
    margarine

salt to taste
white pepper to taste
1/2 cup warm light cream

1   Preheat oven to 450°. Bake potatoes 40 minutes, or until soft.

2   Remove the potatoes from oven (but do not turn off oven). Cut potatoes in half lengthwise and scoop out insides. Mash with butter, salt, pepper, and cream.

3   Refill potato shells with mashed mixture. Bake 5 to 6 minutes, until brown.

YIELD: 6 SERVINGS

VARIATION – Baked Potato

Add 1/2 cup grated Parmesan or Cheddar cheese and 1 tablespoon finely chopped chives or green pepper to potato mixture.

Mash anchovies with potato (1 anchovy per serving).

Add 2 tablespoons each of fresh basil, tarragon, and parsley to potato mixture.

Serve as a main course smothered in Creamed Dried Beef (p. 45) and accompanied by Fried Salt Pork (p. 45).

Colcannon

 A versatile Irish specialty.

6 medium boiled potatoes

4 tablespoons butter or
   margarine

1 small head cabbage, about a
   pound, trimmed, washed,
   and shredded

1 onion, minced

salt to taste

black pepper to taste

parsley for garnish

chives for garnish

1 Drain and mash the boiled potatoes with 2 tablespoons butter.

2 Cover the cabbage with boiling salted water, add the onion and cook until just tender. Drain and add to the potatoes.

3 Season to taste with salt and mix in the remaining butter. Mound on a hot platter and garnish with chopped parsley and chives. Sometimes a hollow is made in the mound and more butter is melted and poured into it.

YIELD: 6 SERVINGS

Potatoes Hashed in Cream

 6 baked potatoes

2 cups heavy cream

salt to taste

butter or margarine

2 tablespoons grated Cheddar
   cheese paprika

1 Bake the potatoes in their skins at least 24 hours before using; 36 hours is even better. Refrigerate.

2 When ready to serve, peel potatoes, cut into cubes, and place in top of a double boiler. Cover with cream and add salt. Cook, uncovered, 1 hour.

3 Preheat oven to 325°.

4 Put potatoes and cream in shallow casserole and dot with butter. Sprinkle with grated Cheddar cheese and paprika. Bake 30 minutes.

YIELD: 6 TO 8 SERVINGS

Roasted Potatoes

 A marvelously tasty and effortless addition to the main course when you are roasting a joint of meat (pork, beef, or lamb).

8 potatoes, peeled or unpeeled   **meat drippings**
salted water

1 Cut and trim potatoes to about the size of golf balls. Boil or steam in salted water until nearly done. Dry potatoes in clean towel.

2 Place in pan containing drippings (or in with meat), brush well with drippings, and roast well in hot oven (400°) about 15 minutes. (If you put potatoes in with meat roasting at lower temperature, they will take longer to cook.)

Potato Puff

3 tablespoons light cream
2 tablespoons butter or
  margarine
dash of ground nutmeg
salt to taste
white pepper to taste

2 cups hot mashed potatoes
3 egg whites (reserve 1
  tablespoonful)
minced fresh parsley, a
  sprinkle
dash of paprika

1 Preheat oven to 375°.

2 Add cream, butter, nutmeg, salt, and pepper to hot potatoes. Beat until very light.

3 Beat egg whites to stiff froth and fold into potato mixture.

4 Coat ovenproof dish with vegetable spray. Pile potatoes lightly in prepared dish and brush with reserved egg white. Brown in oven 12 to 15 minutes. Before serving, sprinkle with parsley and paprika.

YIELD: 6 SERVINGS

New Potatoes in Cream

12 small new potatoes
1 bunch scallions
dusting of flour
1 cup milk
1 cup light cream

1 tablespoon butter or
   margarine
salt to taste
white pepper to taste
chopped fresh dill or parsley, a
   sprinkle

1 Scrub the potatoes and cut in quarters. Scrub scallions and cut into 1-inch pieces.

2 Put potatoes and scallions in saucepan and dust with flour. Add milk, cream, butter, salt, and pepper. Cook, covered, over low heat, 20 to 30 minutes, stirring occasionally. Before serving, sprinkle generously with dill or parsley.

YIELD: 6 SERVINGS

Aroostock Savory Supper

You can use your own judgment as to how much to make of this old-fashioned dish. It is crusty and succulent.

Preheat oven to 250°. Coat a baking dish with vegetable spray and line the bottom with sliced raw onions. Fill dish with thin slices of Maine potatoes. Sprinkle with salt and pepper. Add water to almost cover. Put cubes of salt pork on top. Cook 3 hours.

Oven Potato Chips

4 potatoes
ice water
melted butter or margarine

salt to taste
white pepper to taste

1 Preheat oven to 350°.

2 Scrub and peel the potatoes and cut into slices 1/4 inch thick. Soak slices in ice water to cover 1 hour, then drain well on paper towels.

3 Dip slices in melted butter and arrange in one layer in large, shallow pans. Sprinkle with salt and pepper.

4 Bake 25 to 30 minutes, stirring occasionally until chips are nicely browned.

YIELD: 4 SERVINGS

Buttered Red Radishes

 One of spring's earliest crops. If you cook red radishes quickly, they will not lose their color.

1 bunch red radishes   salt to taste
1 tablespoon butter, margarine,
   or Butter Buds

1 Clean radishes and slice into thin rounds.

2 Melt butter in skillet and sauté radishes briefly. Salt lightly and serve.

YIELD: 4 SERVINGS

Ratatouille

 An excellent dish, particularly useful for a buffet party—it keeps warm for a long time and does not lose in appearance by waiting.

1 large eggplant   fresh oregano
2 green peppers   dash of Tabasco sauce
3 onions   salt to taste
1/2 pound mushrooms   pepper to taste
1/4 cup olive oil   1 can (16 ounces) tomatoes, or
1 tablespoon fresh basil   fresh tomatoes in season

1 Preheat oven to 350°.

2 Cut up vegetables and mix with oil, seasonings, and tomatoes. Peel eggplant if you prefer.

3 Coat large casserole with vegetable spray. Put vegetable mixture in casserole (juice should just be visible around edges of vegetables) and bake 1 hour.

YIELD: 12 SERVINGS

Scallions on Toast

12 scallions

2 slices buttered toast

2 tablespoons melted butter or margarine

1 Cook scallions in boiling water 15 to 20 minutes, until tender. Drain.

2 Arrange scallions on toast and pour melted butter over all.

YIELD: 2 SERVINGS

Spinach

Freshly picked spinach deserves special treatment.

Trim stems of spinach and wash it several times. Lift it from the water, letting it drain briefly in your hands, and toss it into large pot. Cover pot tightly and cook spinach over low heat 5 minutes. The leaves should wilt but retain their color and shape. Uncover and raise the heat to boil away the water. Chop spinach coarsely, just enough so the leaves are manageable on a fork. Add salt and pepper, a little sour cream, and a few drops of lemon juice. (A pound of spinach makes 3 servings.)

Tomato Spinach Soufflé

A pretty and easy vegetable combination

1 package frozen spinach soufflé

4 medium tomatoes

1 Partially defrost spinach soufflé.

2 Preheat oven to 325°.

3 Cut tomatoes in half. Arrange on baking sheet and spread spinach soufflé over each half.

4 Bake 10 to 15 minutes, until puffed and slightly brown.

YIELD: 8 SERVINGS

Baked Squash

Turban, hubbard, and butternut squash are all traditional.

1 squash (about 2 pounds)
about ¼ cup brown sugar
salt to taste

pepper to taste
1 teaspoon lemon juice
butter or margarine to top

1 Preheat oven to 375°.

2 Cut the squash into quarters and remove the seeds and fiber. Put ¼ inch of water in baking pan and arrange squash quarters in pan. Sprinkle each quarter with brown sugar, salt, pepper, and lemon juice. Dot with butter.

3 Bake, covered with aluminum foil, 30 minutes. Uncover, baste (adding more butter if necessary), and bake 30 minutes more, or until tender.

YIELD: 4 SERVINGS

Stuffed Acorn Squash

 This makes a nice supper dish.

2 acorn squashes
salt to taste
pepper to taste
butter or margarine

1½ cups chopped ham
½ cup cooked rice
1 tablespoon milk or cream
4 strips bacon

1 Preheat oven to 375°.

2 Cut the squash in half and remove the seeds and fiber. Season with salt and pepper and dot with butter.

3 Bake 30 minutes, then remove from oven.

4 Combine ham and rice and moisten with small amount of milk or cream. Fill squash halves with ham mixture. Cut bacon strips in two and place crosswise over each squash half. Bake 10 to 15 minutes more.

YIELD: 4 SERVINGS

Lady Slipper Summer Squash

 6 small summer squashes
1 cup sour cream
½ teaspoon curry powder
½ teaspoon ginger

salt to taste
white pepper to taste
2 tablespoons grated Parmesan cheese, a sprinkle

1 Preheat oven to 375°.

2 Cut squash in two lengthwise.

3 Combine sour cream with curry powder, ginger, salt, and pepper and spread over each squash half.

4 Put small amount of water in baking pan and arrange squash halves in pan. Bake, covered, 20 to 30 minutes, or until done. Sprinkle with Parmesan cheese.

YIELD: 6 SERVINGS

Baked Sweet Potatoes with Apples

3 large apples, peeled, cored, and sliced

3 tablespoons butter or margarine

3 large sweet potatoes, boiled, skinned, and sliced

1 teaspoon salt

1/2 cup maple syrup

marshmallows or crumbled cornflakes (optional)

1 Preheat oven to 350°.

2 Melt 2 tablespoons butter in skillet and sauté apple slices until light brown. Slice potatoes.

3 Coat the baking dish with vegetable spray and arrange apples and potatoes in alternate layers. Sprinkle with salt. Pour syrup over dish and dot with butter.

4 Bake 35 minutes. (Before dotting this dish with butter, you can crumble cornflakes over all, or top with a layer of marshmallows.)

YIELD: 6 SERVINGS

Sweet Potato Orange Pudding

A dish to be served with ham. Children love this pudding topped with marshmallows.

1 1/2 cups grated raw sweet potatoes

3/4 cup orange juice

1 teaspoon grated orange rind

1/4 cup granulated sugar

1/2 teaspoon salt

1/4 teaspoon ground cinnamon

1/8 teaspoon ground cloves

1/2 cup melted butter or margarine

6 to 8 marshmallows (optional)

1 Preheat oven to 350°. Coat casserole with vegetable spray.

2 Mix together all ingredients and pour into prepared casserole. Cover with aluminum foil and bake 35 minutes.

3 Reduce oven heat to 325° and remove foil. (If desired, arrange layer of marshmallows over top of casserole.) Bake 30 minutes more. When pudding is done, knife inserted in center will come out clean.

YIELD: 6 SERVINGS

Nottingham Yam Pudding

A family recipe, this light and airy dish is almost a soufflé.

⅓ cup butter or margarine	½ cup sherry
1¼ cups brown sugar	salt to taste
4 egg yolks, well beaten	1 teaspoon ground nutmeg
5 medium sweet potatoes, boiled, peeled, and mashed	¼ teaspoon ground mace
	2 egg whites, beaten stiff

1 Preheat oven to 350°.

2 Cream together the butter and sugar. Mix in beaten egg yolks, mashed sweet potatoes, sherry, salt, nutmeg, and mace. Fold in egg whites.

3 Coat the casserole with vegetable spray. Pour potato mixture into prepared dish and bake 40 minutes.

YIELD: 8 SERVINGS

Tomatoes in Cream

6 large tomatoes, skinned and sliced	white pepper to taste
1 tablespoon flour	3 tablespoons butter or margarine
1½ tablespoons granulated sugar	1 cup light cream
salt to taste	chopped fresh basil, dill, or parsley, a sprinkle

1 Preheat oven to 375°. Coat shallow baking dish with vegetable spray.

2 Arrange tomato slices in prepared dish. Dust with flour and sugar, season with salt and pepper, and dot with butter. Pour cream over casserole.

3 Bake, covered, about 10 minutes, until tomatoes are tender but not soft. Sprinkle with chopped herbs and serve.

YIELD: 6 SERVINGS

VARIATION – **Tomatoes au Gratin**

Prepare Tomatoes in Cream, and when tomatoes are cooked, sprinkle surface with ¼ cup grated Parmesan cheese and place under broiler to brown.

Glazed Turnips

 Prepare the same way you fix Glazed Carrots (p. 264), substituting peeled white, purple-topped turnips for the carrots.

Wild Rice Casserole

 This recipe and the one below are excellent served with game of all kinds. Today wild rice is very expensive, but there are, fortunately, excellent products that combine brown and wild rice and closely approximate the once-plentiful wild rice.

1 cup wild rice	½ cup sliced olives (green and
4 or 5 strips bacon	black)
2 onions, chopped	salt to taste
2 stalks celery, chopped	pepper to taste
3 tablespoons butter or	marjoram or thyme to taste
margarine	½ cup buttered breadcrumbs
2 tablespoons chopped parsley	

1 Preheat oven to 350°.

2 Boil rice until done. Fry strips of bacon until crisp, then drain and crumble.

3 Sauté onion and celery in butter until slightly soft.

4 In casserole, combine all ingredients except breadcrumbs. (If dish is not moist enough, add small amount of broth.) Cover casserole generously with buttered breadcrumbs. Bake 15 to 20 minutes.

YIELD: 6 SERVINGS

Wild Rice and Mushrooms in Sour Cream

1 pound mushrooms, coarsely sliced	pinch of ground mace
3 tablespoons butter or margarine	1/2 cup red wine
salt to taste	1 cup sour cream
white pepper to taste	1 cup wild rice
	crumbled crisp bacon
	parsley sprigs for garnish

1 Sauté mushrooms in butter with salt, pepper, mace, and red wine. When mushrooms are tender, add sour cream and heat through.

2 Meanwhile, cook and season rice and fry bacon.

3 Put mushrooms on large hot platter and surround with mounds of wild rice. Cover with crumbled bacon and garnish with parsley.

YIELD: 6 SERVINGS

Zucchini with Almonds

1/4 cup whole blanched almonds	1/2 onion, minced
4 tablespoons butter or margarine	1 pound zucchini (small ones are best), sliced diagonally
1 teaspoon salt	pepper to taste

1 Sauté almonds in butter in large skillet. Add salt, onion, and zucchini slices. Add a few grindings of pepper and cook, stirring, over medium heat, until zucchini is tender—about 5 minutes.

YIELD: 4 TO 6 SERVINGS

Zucchini Cutlets

3 zucchini squashes	2 rounded tablespoons grated Romano cheese
1/4 teaspoon salt	1 1/4 cups seasoned breadcrumbs
freshly ground pepper to taste	
2 eggs, beaten	chopped fresh or dried parsley, a sprinkle
3 tablespoons cooking oil	

1. Cut the ends from zucchini, peel, and cut into strips (1 inch wide, 4 inches long, ³/₄ inch thick).

2. Add salt and pepper to beaten eggs and set aside. Combine cheese and breadcrumbs and set aside.

3. Heat the cooking oil in a large skillet until hot. Dip zucchini slices first in egg, then in breadcrumb mixture, and brown on all sides in oil. Turn gently to avoid breaking slices and add more oil if necessary. Drain.

4. Arrange zucchini on heated platter, sprinkle with parsley, and serve as is or with a tomato sauce.

YIELD: 6 SERVINGS

Cheese Zucchini Crisps

These are also delicious served with cocktails.

¹/₃ cup cornflakes, crumbled

2 tablespoons grated Parmesan cheese

¹/₂ teaspoon salt

¹/₄ teaspoon minced garlic

4 small unpeeled zucchini, quartered

¹/₄ cup melted butter or margarine

1. Preheat oven to 375°. Coat baking sheet with vegetable spray.

2. Combine the cornflake crumbs, cheese, and seasonings and place in paper bag. Dip zucchini strips in melted butter, then shake gently in bag of crumbs to coat them.

3. Bake about 10 minutes, until crisp.

YIELD: 4 SERVINGS

Baked Zucchini

1 clove garlic

4 tablespoons olive oil

3 or 4 young zucchini, sliced into thin rounds

¹/₂ pound mozzarella cheese, thinly sliced

¹/₄ cup grated Parmesan cheese

salt to taste

freshly ground pepper to taste

1 bunch parsley, coarse stems removed

¹/₂ cup crumbs made from Italian or French bread

1 Preheat oven to 350°.

2 Rub 8-inch baking dish with split garlic clove and pour in 2 table-spoons oil. Add layers of zucchini, mozzarella, and Parmesan, salt, pepper, and parsley.

3 Cover with breadcrumbs, drizzle remaining olive oil over baking dish, and bake 40 minutes.

YIELD: 4 SERVINGS

10

Salads and Salad Dressings

A salad of greens is often the perfect accompaniment to either luncheon or dinner—with meats (hot or cold), birds, fish, omelets, and soufflés. There are leafy varieties galore—Boston, Bibb, cos (romaine), red lettuce, chicory, watercress, radicchio, endive, arugula, mâche (also called lamb's lettuce), and more. Choose the best available and examine the leaves carefully, discarding the outside leaves if they are bruised or tough. (Endive is removed from its outer leaves before it is packed, so it does not need washing, only wiping with a paper towel.)

Salad greens can be served alone or combined with all sorts of vegetables, fruits, meats, seafood, and chicken to make a salad that is the mainstay of a meal. Add hot breads or toast and you're all set. This is an ideal time for popovers, hot biscuits, muffins, scones, and cornbread.

There are a number of salad dressings here, too. They can be varied to suit the components of the salad, and a summer garden can yield a tantalizing variety of herbs and young vegetables. Salads are great for experimentation.

GREEN SALADS

Salad of Greens

 When greens are at their best, fresh from the garden or the market, it's best to dress them simply. Wash them thoroughly in cold water, place them in the basket of a lettuce dryer, and rinse again. Spin the lettuce dryer to remove every drop of water. This should be done four or five times. You don't want any water in the bottom of your salad bowl. Just to make sure, pat the greens with paper towels.

Choose a mixture of greens or only one kind; for a change, add some chopped herbs or tomatoes or cucumbers or a few chopped nuts.

If you like garlic, rub the bowl with a split garlic clove before you prepare your salad dressing. Then make the dressing—olive, safflower, or corn oil; a good vinegar or lemon juice; a little mustard, if you like; and salt and pepper. Use delicate oils that will not submerge the taste of the greens. Mix oil with a good vinegar according to how tart you wish the dressing. Or, for an interesting change, try a recipe sometimes used by the French—a combination of cream and lemon juice instead of oil. It's splendid!

This is a good place to note that, contrary to the old theory, a wooden bowl *should* be washed after each use. If not, it will become rancid. But why not use a glass bowl? It's prettier and shows off the salad better.

Asparagus Vinaigrette

 This is as tasty as it is pretty!

2 pounds asparagus	**basic vinaigrette**
10 long, thin strips red pepper	**1 tablespoon Dijon-style**
3 long, thin strips yellow	**mustard**
pepper	**peppercorns**

1 Cook the asparagus according to directions on page 256. During the last 2 minutes of cooking, add pepper strips to asparagus pot.

2 Prepare a large, shallow dish of ice water, and when vegetables are crisp-tender, remove with tongs and plunge into water to preserve color. Remove vegetables to a clean towel and dry thoroughly.

3 Prepare a basic vinaigrette, then whisk in mustard. Marinate asparagus in vinaigrette, turning once to coat thoroughly. Chill.

4 At serving time, divide asparagus among 4 individual plates. Arrange 2 strips red pepper in an X pattern across each asparagus bunch. Dice remaining red and yellow pepper strips and arrange, together with peppercorns, to resemble confetti at bottom of asparagus spears.

YIELD: 4 SERVINGS

Cucumber Salad

2 medium cucumbers, peeled
   and thinly sliced
1 small onion, thinly sliced
salt to taste
pepper to taste
white vinegar

1 teaspoon olive oil
1 tablespoon sour cream
   (optional)
finely minced parsley, chives,
   or mint (optional)

1   If cucumbers have large seeds, spoon out seeds. Place cucumbers and onions in bowl and sprinkle with salt and pepper. Add vinegar to cover and marinate in refrigerator at least 3 hours.

2   Drain salad well and add oil and, if desired, sour cream and herbs. Arrange in serving dish and return to refrigerator until ready to serve.

Endive Salad with Brie or Camembert

Endive is a wonderful winter vegetable, arriving clean and fresh from Belgium and so carefully packed that not a leaf is wasted. I like to choose the short, fat heads.

1 pound endive
Watercress Dressing (p. 311)
1/2 pound Brie or Camembert
   cheese

1 ounce toasted walnuts or
   pistachio nuts, coarsely
   chopped

1   Sliver endive and toss it lightly but thoroughly in dressing. Arrange on the salad plates, alternating endive slivers with Brie or Camembert slivers. Toss nuts in salad dressing and sprinkle over salad.

YIELD: 4 OR 5 SERVINGS

Green Beans Vinaigrette

1 pound fresh green beans, as
   small as possible
1 clove garlic (optional)
few thin slices of Spanish,
   Bermuda, or Vidalia onion
olive or other salad oil

balsamic vinegar
salt to taste
freshly ground pepper to taste
pinch of dry mustard
3 strips crisp bacon, crumbled
   (optional)

1 Remove stems from beans. Cut in two, diagonally, if they are large. Cook 4 or 5 minutes in rapidly boiling water.

2 Prepare large, shallow dish of ice water, and when beans are crisp-tender, drain quickly in sieve and plunge into ice water to preserve color and crispness. Shake beans dry, then pat dry completely with paper toweling. Chill.

3 At serving time, rub bowl with garlic clove, if desired, and toss beans and onion in oil, vinegar, and seasonings until thoroughly coated. Garnish, if you like, with crumbled bacon.

YIELD: 4 OR 5 SERVINGS

MAIN-DISH SALADS

Chef's Salad

 Very popular for luncheon, this salad is one of the best. Fresh tarragon is very important to its flavor. If you can't find it, substitute tarragon vinegar.

1 clove shallot, chopped
2 tablespoons extra-virgin olive oil
2 tablespoons safflower oil
1 tablespoon white wine vinegar or raspberry vinegar
salt to taste
freshly ground white pepper to taste
1 head Boston lettuce, washed, dried, and torn in pieces
1 head Bibb lettuce, washed, dried, and separated

½ bunch watercress, washed, dried, and tough stems removed
1 cup julienne strips chicken
1 cup julienne strips tongue
1 cup julienne strips mildly cured ham (York, Polish, or Danish)
1 cup julienne strips mild cheese (Emmenthaler or Muenster)
2 sprigs tarragon, minced
1 large tomato, peeled, seeded, and cut in eighths

1 Rub large salad bowl with cut shallot. Put oils, vinegar, salt, and pepper in bowl, mix, and add greens. Toss lightly until thoroughly coated with dressing.

2 Arrange meats and cheese in 4 separate piles on bed of greens. Garnish with tarragon and tomato wedges. Just before serving, toss salad once more, adding more oil or vinegar if needed.

YIELD: 5 OR 6 SERVINGS

Bacon-and-Egg Salad

 This salad is wonderful combined with Victoria House Dressing (p. 311). Combine the ingredients in a quantity sufficient for the size of your group.

young spinach leaves, washed and dried

hard-boiled eggs

strips of boiled or baked ham

plenty of crisp bacon

chopped pistachio nuts

1 fresh pear, peeled, cored, and sliced

croutons of whole wheat bread rubbed with garlic and browned in olive oil

Caesar Salad

 This ever-popular salad has a unique and appealing combination of ingredients. I like the addition of rolled anchovies as a garnish, but this is a personal taste.

1 clove garlic

1 teaspoon salt

freshly ground pepper to taste

$\frac{1}{3}$ cup olive oil

juice of 1 lime

1 tablespoon red wine vinegar

1 egg, boiled 1 minute

Worcestershire sauce to taste

2 medium heads romaine lettuce, washed, dried, crisped, and torn into bite-size pieces

1 cup freshly made bacon-garlic croutons

freshly grated Parmesan cheese

rolled anchovies (optional)

1 Rub a salad bowl with garlic clove. Add the salt, pepper, oil, lime juice, vinegar, egg, and Worcestershire sauce. Whisk together until creamy. Add lettuce and croutons and toss. Add cheese and toss again. Serve immediately, garnished, if desired, with anchovies.

YIELD: 4 OR 5 SERVINGS

Chicken Salad

3 whole chicken breasts or 1
   whole chicken
½ teaspoon salt
3 peppercorns
1 slice onion
1 bay leaf
inside stalks of 1 bunch celery,
   chopped
1 teaspoon each parsley,
   tarragon, and chives,
   chopped

2 tablespoons capers
1 cup Mayonnaise (p. 307)
salt to taste
white pepper to taste
sliced ripe olives, if desired
salad greens, dressed
tomato wedges, avocado slices,
   or watercress sprigs

1 Place chicken in a kettle with enough water to cover. Add salt, peppercorns, onion, and bay leaf and cook until tender. Let chicken cool, then
remove skin and cut into large cubes.

2 In large bowl, combine chicken with celery, herbs, capers, mayonnaise,
salt, white pepper, and olives (if desired). Mix carefully but thoroughly
and mound on large platter on bed of dressed greens. Garnish as desired with tomatoes, avocado slices, or watercress sprigs.

YIELD: 6 SERVINGS

VARIATION – Hawaiian Chicken Salad

Add 1 cup diced, fresh pineapple and about 2 tablespoons macadamia
nuts to salad.

VARIATION – Chicken Salad Supreme

Add 1 cup white grapes and toasted slivered almonds or chopped pistachio nuts to salad.

Another Chicken Salad

For me, this one is the best! It's ideal when you have part of a roast
chicken left over. Otherwise, use meat from chicken breasts cooked for
the salad. Preparation time is only a few minutes. Try to save a little of
the chicken essence from the bottom of the roasting pan. It is delicious
mixed into the salad.

1 head Boston lettuce, washed, dried, and torn in pieces

1½ cups warm strips of cooked chicken

1 large, ripe tomato, peeled, seeded, and sliced

¼ pound goat or feta cheese, sliced

12 black olives, sliced

4 tablespoons olive oil

1 tablespoon balsamic vinegar

salt to taste

freshly ground black pepper to taste

1 Mix all ingredients thoroughly in large bowl.

YIELD: 4 SERVINGS

Warm Grilled Chicken Salad

This is an excellent change from the typical chicken salads, and it is very, very good.

2 whole chicken breasts

1 or 2 cloves garlic (optional)

1 teaspoon olive oil

salt to taste

freshly ground pepper to taste

½ teaspoon lemon juice

¼ cup dry white wine

1 head Boston or buttercrunch lettuce, washed and dried

1 tablespoon olive oil

1 teaspoon balsamic vinegar

2 ripe Anjou pears, peeled, cored, and sliced

12 spears asparagus, peeled

2 ripe tomatoes, peeled, sliced, and seeded

chopped watercress leaves

1 Preheat grill.

2 Wash and pat dry chicken breasts. Rub with garlic, if desired, then with olive oil, salt, pepper, and lemon juice.

3 Put chicken pieces on grill to brown them. At same time, preheat oven to 350°. When chicken is grilled on both sides, remove pieces to baking pan. Add wine and bake 10 to 15 minutes, basting occasionally, until done. Keep warm in oven until needed.

4 Dress lettuce in oil, vinegar, salt, and pepper and arrange on individual serving plates. Dress pears, asparagus, tomatoes, and watercress in same mixture and set aside.

5 Cut chicken meat from bones in plump slices and arrange on lettuce.

Skim fat from chicken juices in baking pan and pour juices over chicken. Arrange pears and vegetables around edges of plates.

YIELD: 4 TO 6 SERVINGS

Lobster Salad

 This salad can also be made with crabmeat or tiny shrimp instead of lobster meat.

salad greens, lightly coated
    with French Dressing
    (p. 309)
3 cups cooked lobster, cut into
    large pieces
chopped hearts of 1 bunch
    celery
3 hard-boiled eggs, chopped

1 teaspoon chopped chives
1/2 teaspoon chopped dill
1 cup Mayonnaise (p. 307)
1 tablespoon lemon juice
tomato slices, watercress
    sprigs, stuffed eggs, as
    desired

1 Prepare bed of salad greens on large platter.

2 Combine lobster, celery, eggs, herbs, mayonnaise, and lemon juice. Mound on greens and garnish, as you wish, with tomato, watercress, and/or stuffed eggs.

YIELD: 6 SERVINGS

Meat-and-Potato Salad

 A fine, hearty salad that uses up those choice morsels of leftover beef. This is another salad you can expand according to the size of your luncheon crowd.

fresh young lettuce, clean and
    dry
rare roast beef or steak (all fat
    removed), in julienne strips
cold potatoes (skins on), sliced

cucumbers, peeled and
    chopped
oil, vinegar, salt, and pepper to
    taste
finely minced dill or chives

Midsummer Fruit Salad

An eye-catching summer luncheon dish. Try serving it with blueberry popovers and sweet butter.

1 pint strawberries
1 pint raspberries
1 pint blueberries
3 kiwifruit
2 ripe peaches
2 ripe pears
2 tablespoons raspberry
   vinegar
$^{1}/_{2}$ cup plus 2 tablespoons
   extra-virgin olive oil

1 head Boston lettuce, washed,
   dried, and torn in pieces
2 heads Bibb lettuce, washed,
   dried, and separated
salt to taste
freshly ground pepper to taste
6 round slices goat cheese
pistachio nuts, chopped, for
   garnish

1 Keeping fruit in separate bowls, wash and dry berries, slice strawberries, peel and slice kiwifruit, peaches, and pears.

2 Whisk together vinegar and $^{1}/_{2}$ cup oil and marinate each fruit separately. Refrigerate fruit in bowls while preparing rest of salad.

3 Toss lettuces in oil and vinegar mixture, season with salt and pepper, and arrange on 6 large individual plates.

4 Sauté cheese slices in olive oil until warm and partially melted. Place 1 cheese round in center of each plate.

5 Arrange berries and other fruits in separate mounds on each plate, varying textures and colors. Sprinkle with chopped pistachio nuts and serve.

YIELD: 6 SERVINGS

Mixed Vegetable Salad

1 cup small string beans,
   halved if necessary
1 cup halved or quartered baby
   carrots
1 cup fresh peas
1 cup cauliflower florets
1 head garden lettuce, washed
   and dried

basic vinaigrette
Green Mayonnaise (p. 308)
salt to taste
freshly ground pepper to taste
1 cup julienne strips lean ham
2 ripe tomatoes, peeled and
   quartered
$^{1}/_{4}$ cup small black pitted olives

1 Cook beans, carrots, peas, and cauliflower separately in 4 small saucepans until just tender. Drain and chill until needed.

2 Toss lettuce in vinaigrette dressing and arrange in bottom of large
   salad bowl.

3 Mix cooked vegetables together with enough mayonnaise to coat well.
   Season with salt and pepper and mound in salad bowl. Garnish with
   ham strips, tomato wedges, and black olives.

YIELD: 6 TO 8 SERVINGS

Salade Niçoise

 This hearty Mediterranean salad is always a hit. It has a number of
variations, but this is my favorite combination.

1 large clove garlic	3 small new potatoes, boiled
3 to 4 tablespoons olive oil	and quartered
1 tablespoon balsamic vinegar	$^1/_2$ pound small green beans,
salt to taste	cooked crisp-tender
freshly ground pepper to taste	1 can (6 ounces) tuna packed
1 head Boston lettuce, washed,	in oil, drained
dried, and torn in pieces	1 tin (2 ounces) anchovies,
$^1/_2$ bunch watercress, washed,	with oil
dried, and tough stems	1 tablespoon capers
removed	$^1/_2$ cup unpitted Greek black
1 head endive, separated	olives
1 large handful basil leaves,	2 hard-boiled eggs, coarsely
washed and dried	chopped
2 scallions, sliced	2 large ripe tomatoes, peeled,
few slivers red pepper	cut in eighths, and seeded

1 Rub large salad bowl heavily with garlic. If desired, mince remainder
   of clove into bowl. Whisk in olive oil, vinegar, salt, and pepper.

2 Add lettuce, watercress, and endive, tossing until each leaf is coated
   with dressing. Add remaining ingredients, reserving a few olives and
   tomato wedges, and toss again. Add more oil or seasonings if needed.

YIELD: 4 TO 5 SERVINGS

Salmon Salad

2 cups cooked salmon

1 cup chopped cucumber, drained

1 teaspoon chopped parsley

1 teaspoon minced onion

½ cup celery, sliced

½ teaspoon salt

⅛ teaspoon pepper

½ cup Green Mayonnaise (p. 308)

salad greens, dressed

½ cup bacon-garlic croutons

1 teaspoon capers (optional)

1 Flake salmon. Add cucumber, parsley, onion, celery, salt, and pepper and mix carefully but thoroughly. Blend in green mayonnaise.

2 Mound on bed of dressed salad greens and garnish with bacon-garlic croutons and capers if desired.

YIELD: 6 SERVINGS

Scampi Salad

This is delicious served with cold saffron rice and Green Beans Vinaigrette (p. 293).

1 clove garlic

1¼ pounds large shrimp, peeled, deveined, washed, and dried

olive oil

salt to taste

freshly ground pepper to taste

3 cups basil or arugula leaves, washed and dried

3 large tomatoes, peeled, cut in eighths, and seeded

1 tablespoon balsamic vinegar

1 Rub large skillet with garlic and in it sauté shrimp in 2 tablespoons olive oil until just pink. Season with salt and pepper.

2 Toss basil and tomatoes in oil and vinegar to taste, salt and pepper. Arrange on platter or in bowl, topped by shrimp.

YIELD: 4 SERVINGS

Spinach Salad Supreme

A delicious luncheon salad that can be expanded or contracted according to the number of guests.

fresh spinach leaves	avocados, peeled, stoned, and
garden lettuce	sliced
hard-cooked eggs, peeled and	Green Goddess Salad Dressing
quartered	(p. 310)
fresh tomatoes, peeled, cut into	
wedges, and seeded	

1 Remove stems from spinach leaves. Wash spinach and lettuce thoroughly and dry leaves in lettuce dryer. Wrap leaves in clean, dry towel and place in refrigerator to crisp.

2 Meanwhile, prepare other ingredients. When ready to serve, combine spinach, lettuce, eggs, tomato wedges, and avocado slices and toss carefully but thoroughly with salad dressing.

YIELD: 4 SERVINGS

Stuffed Tomatoes

4 large, ripe tomatoes, peeled	salad greens
2 cups chicken, lobster, or	basic vinaigrette
crabmeat salad	capers

1 Scoop out tomato centers and drain.

2 Fill tomatoes with salad, piling it high on top.

3 Dress salad greens with basic vinaigrette and arrange on 4 individual plates. Place 1 stuffed tomato on each plate and garnish with capers.

YIELD: 4 SERVINGS

Trout Salad

1 medium trout	Green Sauce (p. 317)
herb vinegar	4 hard-boiled eggs, peeled and
lettuce leaves	quartered

1 Boil trout in slightly salted water to cover. Drain.

2 Remove bones and skin and break fish into flakes. Marinate in vinegar 2 hours. Drain.

3 Arrange lettuce leaves on 4 individual plates and divide trout among

them. Serve with mayonnaise and garnish with hard-boiled egg wedges.

YIELD: 4 SERVINGS

HEARTY SALADS

Hot New Potato Salad

10 small new potatoes

2 eggs

1/2 pound lean bacon

1 clove garlic, mashed

1 shallot, finely chopped

1 tablespoon chopped fresh dill

1 tablespoon chopped fresh chives

1 tablespoon chopped fresh tarragon

2 tablespoons dry white wine

2 tablespoons olive oil

salt to taste

freshly ground pepper to taste

1 head garden lettuce, washed, dried, and torn in pieces

1/2 cup basil leaves, washed and dried

1 tablespoon white wine vinegar

1 tablespoon capers

1 Wash potatoes and boil in salted water until tender, 15 to 20 minutes.

2 Meanwhile, hard-boil eggs and fry bacon until crisp. Drain bacon on paper towels.

3 Drain potatoes, peel and slice eggs. Slice potatoes and combine with garlic, shallot, and herbs. Add sliced eggs and toss with white wine and oil, salt and pepper.

4 Toss lettuce and basil in mixture of oil, vinegar, salt, and pepper. Arrange lettuce in bottom of bowl and spoon in potato salad. Garnish with crumbled bacon and capers and serve while still quite warm.

YIELD: 5 OR 6 SERVINGS

Old Dutch Cole Slaw

 This excellent cole slaw may be varied from time to time with grapes, slivered almonds, or a pinch of dry mustard.

1 young cabbage
1 cup heavy cream or yogurt
½ cup granulated sugar
½ cup white vinegar

1 teaspoon salt
white pepper to taste
watercress sprigs

1 Shred cabbage into large bowl and set aside.

2 Beat together cream, sugar, vinegar, salt, and pepper until mixture is consistency of thin whipped cream.

3 Just before serving, combine sauce with shredded cabbage. Garnish with watercress.

YIELD: 6 SERVINGS

Tortellini Salad

1 pound tortellini, spinach or
    meat filled
3 large tomatoes, peeled, cut in
    eighths
1 clove garlic
about 2 cups basil leaves,
    washed and dried

¼ cup pitted black olives,
    sliced
2 tablespoons pignolia nuts
2 to 3 tablespoons olive oil
1 to 2 tablespoons balsamic
    vinegar
salt to taste
freshly ground pepper to taste

1 Cook tortellini as directed on package. Cool.

2 Rub large salad bowl with cut garlic clove. Put tortellini, tomato wedges, basic leaves, olives, and nuts in bowl and toss together, adding enough oil and vinegar to coat everything well. Season with salt and pepper.

YIELD: 4 SERVINGS AS MAIN COURSE

Wild Rice Salad

 Very good with cold meats.

2 cups cooked wild rice

4 tablespoons French Dressing (p. 309)

1/2 cup sliced mushrooms

1/2 cup sliced pecans

1/2 cup green grapes, halved

1 tablespoon chopped chives

1 tablespoon chopped parsley

1 Combine all ingredients in bowl and serve at room temperature.

YIELD: 4 SERVINGS

MOLDED SALADS

Crisp Cucumber Aspic

 Mrs. Griswold Frelinghuysen of Woodstock, Vermont, perfected this appetizing summer dish.

2 thin cucumbers, 1 peeled, 1 unpeeled

2 tender stalks celery, minced

1/2 green pepper, minced

1 tablespoon grated onion

chopped herbs, dill, chives, or parsley, as available

1 teaspoon salt

1 tablespoon granulated sugar

1/4 cup lemon juice

1/4 cup white vinegar

2 envelopes unflavored gelatine softened in 1/2 cup cold water

2 cups boiling water

2 or 3 drops green food coloring

lettuce leaves

1 Slice seedless end parts of both cucumbers, using about half of each cucumber. Remove seeds from center sections and dice remaining cucumber.

2 In large bowl, combine diced and sliced cucumber. Add celery, green pepper, onion, chopped herbs, salt, sugar, lemon juice, and vinegar and mix thoroughly.

3 Add gelatine softened in water, boiling water, and food coloring.

4 Pour mixture into 1-quart mold and chill until set.

5 When ready to serve, arrange lettuce leaves on large platter and on individual plates. Unmold aspic onto platter. Cut wedge-shaped servings and serve with Sour Cream Dressing (box on p. 308).

Health Salad

1 envelope unflavored gelatine

2 cups orange juice or canned
   pineapple juice

2 cups shredded raw carrots

1/2 cup shredded cabbage

1 cup finely chopped pineapple

lettuce leaves, dressed

1 Prepare gelatine, using boiling pineapple or orange juice for liquid required. Add vegetables and fruit and pour into 1-quart mold. Refrigerate until gelatine is set, stirring once before it sets so fruit and vegetables do not settle on bottom of mold.

2 Arrange dressed lettuce leaves on platter and unmold salad.

Jellied Roquefort Cheese Mousse

This mousse is particularly good served with the fresh fruits of summer and mixed greens from the garden. It can be used as the main course for luncheon on a hot day or, as part of a buffet, it can be molded in a loaf pan and sliced or be served to spread on crackers.

1 envelope unflavored gelatine

1/4 cup cold water

1 cup whipped cream

1/2 cup Roquefort or blue
   cheese

8 ounces cream cheese (or
   cottage cheese, whipped
   smooth)

1/4 teaspoon salt

1 teaspoon onion juice

1/4 teaspoon paprika

2 pears, cut in wedges

watercress sprigs

1 Stir together gelatine and cold water and dissolve in double boiler.

2 In mixing bowl, combine cheeses and seasonings with small amount of unwhipped cream until well blended. Add cheese mixture to gelatin, then fold in whipped cream.

3 Pour mixture into 1 1/2-quart mold and chill. (A ring mold is particularly nice.)

4 Unmold onto platter and surround with pear wedges (or other fruit) sprinkled with French Dressing (p. 309). Put watercress sprigs in center of ring.

Quick Tomato Aspic

2 envelopes unflavored gelatine
$^{1}/_{2}$ cup cold tomato juice
$3^{1}/_{2}$ cups hot tomato juice
4 tablespoons lemon juice
$^{1}/_{2}$ teaspoon salt

$^{1}/_{2}$ teaspoon Worcestershire
sauce
$^{1}/_{4}$ teaspoon celery salt
lettuce leaves

1 Soften gelatine in cold tomato juice. Add hot tomato juice and stir to dissolve gelatine. Add remaining ingredients and pour into 1-quart mold or individual molds.

2 Chill until set. Unmold onto bed of lettuce leaves. Serve with yogurt or Roquefort Mayonnaise (p. 308).

YIELD: 6 SERVINGS

SALAD DRESSINGS

Mayonnaise

Mayonnaise often is called the mother of sauces. It is easy to make if you remember to have the ingredients at room temperature and to move slowly but steadily in adding the oil to the egg yolks. Good commercial mayonnaise is nice to have on hand for emergency sandwich making, but it bears only a faint resemblance to homemade mayonnaise. It seems to me that a fine salad of chicken or cold asparagus or cold fish deserves only the best of sauces.

1 egg yolk, at room
temperature
1 teaspoon salt
$^{1}/_{2}$ teaspoon dry mustard

$^{1}/_{4}$ teaspoon paprika
2 tablespoons white vinegar or
lemon juice
1 cup fine olive or salad oil

1 Rinse small bowl with hot water and wipe dry. In bowl, beat together egg yolk, salt, mustard, and paprika. Add 1 tablespoon vinegar and beat again. Beat in oil, few drops at a time, until $^{1}/_{4}$ cup is used, then add remaining oil rapidly. As mixture becomes thick, add remaining vinegar. Chill before use.

Note: If oil is added too rapidly, mayonnaise will curdle. To remedy this, beat curdled mixture slowly into second egg yolk. Mayonnaise may be made in an electric blender or beater. Just be sure to add oil slowly at first.

YIELD: ABOUT 1¼ CUPS MAYONNAISE

VARIATION – Anchovy Mayonnaise

Beat in anchovy paste or mashed anchovies.

VARIATION – Green Mayonnaise

Add ¼ cup puréed raw spinach or watercress to mixture.

VARIATION – Roquefort Mayonnaise

Beat in 1 ounce Roquefort cheese and 1 mashed garlic clove.

VARIATION – Russian Dressing

Add ¼ teaspoon paprika, 1 ounce red caviar, and 3 tablespoons chili sauce.

VARIATION – Shrimp Dip

Mix mayonnaise half and half with sour cream and add curry powder to taste. Serve as a dip with cooked, chilled, fresh shrimp.

VARIATION – Sour Cream Mayonnaise

Mix mayonnaise half and half with sour cream and add 1 teaspoon horseradish and 1 tablespoon capers.

Anchovy Roquefort Salad Dressing

 While the young greens of summer need little adornment, the lettuce that is available in the wintertime sometimes is improved with a rather tangy dressing. This one is the recipe of my husband, John Davies Stamm, and it is particularly welcome when salad greens need a little extra inspiration. A half head of lettuce served with this, cottage cheese, and melba toast makes a splendid lunch that is low in calories.

2 or 3 anchovies

4 or 5 tablespoons Roquefort cheese, softened

¼ cup olive oil

juice of half a lemon

1 clove garlic

salt to taste

freshly ground black pepper to taste

few chopped pecans

1 Mash together anchovies, cheese, oil, lemon juice, garlic, and salt, or whirl in blender or food processor.

2 Pour dressing over lettuce, adding pepper and garnishing with pecans.

YIELD: 2 SERVINGS

French Dressing

2/3 cup olive oil or other salad oil

1/3 cup white vinegar or lemon juice

1 teaspoon salt

freshly ground pepper, black or white, to taste

1 clove garlic, crushed (optional)

1 Shake all ingredients together in screw-top jar and store in refrigerator.

YIELD: ABOUT 1 CUP DRESSING

Sour Cream Dressing

Here's a delicious recipe—just as it was written in Newfane, Vermont, more than a hundred years ago.

Put the yolks of two hard-boiled eggs in a soup plate and rub them very smooth. Add a saltspoon of salt and 1/2 saltspoon of pepper. Then rub in sour cream, as much as you would oil. It will get very thick. Now thin it out with vinegar and add a little sugar (this could be put in at the same time as the salt and pepper). Don't have the lettuce wet. The number of eggs depends on the quantity of dressing desired. Chop the whites of the eggs and sprinkle them on top when the salad is ready to serve.

Green Cheese Sauce

This may be used as a thick dressing for greens or other salads, or served to spread on crackers. The color is beautiful.

2 cups cottage cheese

2 ounces blue or Roquefort cheese

2 tablespoons sour cream

1/4 bunch watercress, chopped

1 clove garlic

1 Whirl all ingredients together in blender or food processor at high speed until light and smooth. Chill before serving.

YIELD: ABOUT 2 CUPS DRESSING

Green Goddess Salad Dressing

 Said to have been General Dwight Eisenhower's favorite salad dressing, this concoction turns a greens salad into a work of art. To make a light meal, add it to a can of tuna fish or chopped ham and sautéed croutons.

1 clove garlic, crushed

2 tablespoons scallions, chopped

1 tablespoon anchovy paste

1/2 cup sour cream

1 cup mayonnaise

2 tablespoons tarragon vinegar

1/2 tablespoon lime juice

1 drop green food coloring

black pepper to taste

1 Combine all ingredients in blender or food processor and chill 2 to 3 hours to blend flavors.

YIELD: ABOUT 1 1/2 CUPS DRESSING

Parmesan Salad Dressing

 This is good with any salad greens, but especially with Bibb or Boston lettuce

1 rounded teaspoon butter or margarine

2 slices bread

1 egg, at room temperature

salt to taste

1/2 clove garlic, mashed

dash of cayenne pepper

1/2 cup olive or salad oil

white vinegar

1/2 cup grated Parmesan cheese

1 Preheat oven to 250°.

2 Melt butter in iron skillet. Cut bread into tiny cubes and sauté in butter. Place skillet in oven, stirring croutons occasionally until browned. Set aside.

3 Meanwhile, in mixing bowl, beat egg with salt, garlic, and cayenne. Add oil, a few drops at a time, beating until thick. Add vinegar and beat well, then mix in cheese.

4 Pour dressing over lettuce and toss. Add croutons at last moment just before serving.

YIELD: ABOUT 1 CUP DRESSING

Victoria House Dressing

 This dressing is very thick, almost like mayonnaise.

1 egg	1 clove garlic
1 ounce Roquefort cheese	1/2 cup olive oil
juice of half a lemon	1/2 cup sour cream or heavy
1/2 teaspoon salt	cream
1/4 teaspoon dry mustard	

1 Bring all ingredients to room temperature.

2 Put egg, cheese, lemon juice, salt, mustard, and garlic in container of blender or food processor. Whirl or process at low speed, then pour in oil very slowly. Add cream and whirl or process until blended. Chill.

YIELD: ABOUT 1 1/2 CUPS DRESSING

Watercress Dressing

 This dressing must be made in an electric blender or food processor. The specks of watercress will coat the lettuce and lend their flavor to it. The dressing is also good on endive.

1/2 cup olive oil	1/2 clove garlic
1 tablespoon cider vinegar	salt to taste
1/2 bunch watercress, coarse	1/4 cup blanched almonds,
stems removed, washed and	slivered
thoroughly dried	

1 Whirl oil, vinegar, watercress, garlic, and salt in blender or food processor until thoroughly smooth and light.

2 Garnish salad with slivered blanched almonds.

YIELD: ABOUT 1 CUP DRESSING

11

Sauces and Accompaniments

As every serious cook knows, the proper sauce adds the finishing touch to many an entrée or dish of vegetables. Indeed, certain sauces form the basis of a great many recipes. (For dessert sauces, see chapter on desserts.)

Barbecue Sauce

 This sauce may be stored in the refrigerator. Reheat it before using (to melt the butter). You can use it successfully with all sorts of meats—steaks, spareribs, hot dogs, or chicken.

3 tablespoons butter or
  margarine
1 cup sweet vermouth
¹/₃ cup catsup
1 teaspoon salt
¹/₂ teaspoon celery salt

¹/₄ cup soy sauce
¹/₄ cup Worcestershire sauce
juice of 1 lemon
juice of half an onion
1 clove garlic, crushed

1 Melt butter in saucepan. Add remaining ingredients and stir until blended.

YIELD: ABOUT 2 CUPS

Béarnaise Sauce

Serve with steaks and chops. Béarnaise—which is similar to Hollandaise sauce—also enhances filet mignon and good hamburger.

3 egg yolks

3 tablespoons wine vinegar

3 tablespoons dry white wine

2 teaspoons chopped shallots
  or scallions

1/2 cup butter or margarine

juice of half a lemon

salt to taste

1 teaspoon chopped fresh
  tarragon or 1/2 teaspoon
  dried tarragon

1 In top of double boiler, over hot (not boiling) water, whisk together egg yolks, vinegar, wine, and shallots.

2 Add butter, 1/3 at a time, stirring after each addition.

3 Finally, add lemon juice, salt, and tarragon. Stir constantly until thick.

YIELD: ABOUT 1 CUP

Bread Sauce

This mild sauce is perfect with pheasant or other wildfowl. You can also serve them with Tabasco Jelly (p. 324) or venison jelly.

2 cups milk

3 slices white bread, crusts
  removed and reserved

1 small onion

6 whole cloves

1 teaspoon salt

pinch of cayenne pepper

3 tablespoons butter or
  margarine

1 Put milk in top of double boiler. Break in bread. Stud onion with cloves and add onion to bread and milk. Cook gently, covered, 30 minutes, stirring occasionally.

2 Remove onion and whisk sauce until smooth, while adding salt, cayenne, and 2 tablespoons of the butter.

3 Make crumbs from reserved bread crusts and sauté in remaining tablespoon of butter.

4 Pour sauce into hot sauceboat and sprinkle with browned crumbs.

YIELD: 2 CUPS

Brown Mushroom Sauce

 Serve with venison, beef, or lamb—it is even good with hash.

4 tablespoons butter or
  margarine
1/2 pound mushrooms, sliced
1 teaspoon onion juice
3 tablespoons flour

1 cup beef stock
salt to taste
paprika to taste
dash of Worcestershire sauce
2 tablespoons sherry

1 Brown mushrooms in butter. Add onion juice and flour. Stirring constantly, add beef stock gradually. Stir until thick.

2 Add salt, paprika, Worcestershire sauce, and sherry and serve hot.

YIELD: 1 1/2 CUPS

Caper Sauce

 For lamb or fish.

2 tablespoons butter or
  margarine
2 tablespoons flour
1 cup chicken stock
1 teaspoon dry mustard

1 teaspoon Worcestershire
  sauce
juice of half a lemon
1 egg yolk
1/2 cup light cream
3 tablespoons capers, drained

1 Melt butter in skillet or saucepan over low heat. Stir in flour. Gradually add chicken stock, then add mustard, Worcestershire sauce, and lemon juice. Stir until thick and smooth.

2 Remove skillet from heat and add egg yolk, cream, and capers. Again stir until smooth. Serve at once. (If sauce is to be reheated later, be sure it does not boil.)

YIELD: 1 1/2 CUPS

Clambake Sauce

1 pound butter or margarine

1 tablespoon salt

1 teaspoon Tabasco sauce

1 pint (8 ounces) tarragon
vinegar

juice of 1 lemon

1/2 bottle (2 1/2 ounces)
Worcestershire sauce

1 Melt butter in saucepan and whisk in remaining ingredients. Cover
and let simmer 5 to 10 minutes, until well blended and thickened.

YIELD: ABOUT 4 CUPS

Cranberry Sauce

2 cups water

2 cups granulated sugar

4 cups cranberries, washed

1 Boil together water and sugar 5 minutes.

2 Add cranberries and cook gently, uncovered, without stirring, until
thick. Chill.

YIELD: ABOUT 4 CUPS

Crème Fraîche

1 cup heavy cream

1 teaspoon buttermilk

1 In a small bowl, add heavy cream to buttermilk. Stir well, cover, and
leave in warm place overnight. The cream will acquire the lovely consistency of that in Paris. Sweeten a tad with sugar if desired.

YIELD: 1 CUP

Cream Sauce

This basic sauce, used in a great many dishes, can be doubled or
halved as needed.

4 tablespoons butter or
margarine

4 tablespoons flour

1 cup milk

1 cup light cream

salt to taste

white pepper to taste

1 Melt butter in skillet or saucepan over low heat and whisk in flour. Add milk gradually and stir until thick and smooth.

2 Add cream and simmer 5 minutes to cook flour. Season with salt and pepper.

YIELD: 2 CUPS

VARIATION – Cheese Sauce (Sauce Mornay)

Stir 1 cup diced Cheddar cheese and a dash of dry mustard or cayenne pepper into 2 cups of cream sauce and cook until cheese has melted.

Cucumber Yogurt Sauce

½ cucumber, peeled and seeded	finely chopped fresh dill
1 tablespoon finely minced onion	1 tablespoon dry vermouth
	½ pint low-fat plain yogurt

1 Mince cucumber, press with paper towels to remove as much liquid as possible, and place in mixing bowl.

2 With a fork, mix cucumber with remaining ingredients and chill.

YIELD: 1½ CUPS SAUCE

Cumberland Sauce

For ham—and also good with venison.

1 lemon	2 teaspoons shallots, finely chopped and blanched
1 orange	2 tablespoons wine vinegar
1 cup ham drippings, free of fat	½ teaspoon ground ginger
2 tablespoons prepared mustard	salt to taste
1 cup port or Madeira wine	pepper to taste
1 cup red currant jelly	cayenne pepper to taste

1 Grate rinds of lemon and orange, then squeeze juice from fruit.

2 Combine rind and juice with remaining ingredients and cook until well blended. Season to taste.

YIELD: 3 CUPS

Egg Sauce

Excellent with fish.

4 tablespoons butter or
   margarine

4 tablespoons flour

2 cups milk

1 teaspoon onion juice

juice of half a lemon

salt to taste

white pepper to taste

2 hard-boiled eggs, finely diced

1 Melt butter in skillet or saucepan and blend in flour. Add milk gradually over low heat.

2 Add onion juice, lemon juice, salt, and pepper and cook 10 minutes, stirring until thick and smooth.

3 Stir in diced eggs.

YIELD: 2 CUPS

Green Sauce

This zestful sauce can be served at room temperature with hot fish or shrimp or cold with cold fish or shrimp, mousses or salads.

1 egg, at room temperature

1/4 bunch parsley, chopped

1/4 bunch watercress, chopped

1/2 green pepper, sliced

1 slice onion

1/2 clove garlic

grated rind and juice of 1 lime

2 tablespoons capers, drained

3/4 cup olive oil

salt to taste

freshly ground pepper to taste

1 Combine the egg, greens, vegetables, and lime in food processor or blender. Gradually drizzle in oil. Season with salt and pepper.

YIELD: 1 CUP

Hollandaise Sauce

A classic sauce for artichokes, asparagus, broccoli, and cauliflower.

3 egg yolks

1 tablespoon cold water

1/2 cup butter (do not use
   margarine)

juice of half a lemon

salt to taste

dash of cayenne pepper

1   In top of double boiler, over hot (not boiling) water, whisk together egg yolks and water until fluffy.

2   Add butter, $^1/_3$ at a time, stirring after each addition.

3   Finally, add lemon juice, salt, and cayenne. Stir constantly until thick.

　　　If, through carelessness, the sauce becomes too hot and curdles, you can save it if you remove it quickly from the heat and add to the sauce either 1 tablespoon cold cream or 1 tablespoon very hot water or 1 ice cube. If you use the ice cube, remove it when the sauce becomes smooth and take great care in reheating the sauce. Hollandaise sauce is really very easy to make, but you are warned—it is also easy to destroy.

YIELD: ABOUT 1 CUP

Horseradish Sauce

$^1/_2$ cup heavy cream, whipped
2 tablespoons white vinegar

3 tablespoons grated fresh horseradish, squeezed dry

1   Mix together all ingredients and serve with roast or corned beef.

YIELD: $^3/_4$ CUP

Lemon Herb Sauce

For fish.

$^1/_2$ cup sweet butter or margarine, softened
1 tablespoon grated lemon rind
$^1/_2$ teaspoon finely chopped fresh chives

$^1/_2$ teaspoon finely chopped fresh basil
$^1/_2$ teaspoon finely chopped fresh dill
1 teaspoon finely chopped fresh parsley

1   Cream together all ingredients and spread on cooked fish.

YIELD: ABOUT 1 CUP

Lobster Coral Sauce

For boiled or steamed lobster. When you buy lobster, ask for 1 or 2 females so you'll have the opportunity to make this lovely coral sauce.

2 tablespoons butter or	2 anchovies
margarine	1/4 cup lobster coral
2 tablespoons flour	freshly ground white pepper to
1 cup light cream	taste
1 tomato, skinned, seeded, and	1 ounce Cognac or kirsch
chopped	

1 Make a cream sauce with butter, flour, and cream.

2 Purée together tomato, anchovies, and lobster roe and add to cream sauce. Add pepper and cook sauce until smooth. At last minute, add Cognac or kirsch. Sauce will be rosy red.

YIELD: 1 CUP

Mustard Cream

 You can vary the texture and flavor of the sauce according to the type of mustard used.

1 jar (8 ounces) Dijon-style,	8 ounces Crème Fraîche
grainy, or green peppercorn	(p. 315)
mustard	

1 Whisk together mustard and cème fraîche and serve hot or cold.

YIELD: 2 CUPS

Mustard Sauce

 This sauce is very spicy and good on all meats and fish.

2 tablespoons butter or	1 cup heavy cream
margarine	2 teaspoons dry mustard
2 tablespoons flour	1 teaspoon Worcestershire
1/2 cup beef stock	sauce

1 Blend butter and flour over low heat and gradually add beef stock and cream. Stir until thick. Add mustard and Worcestershire sauce and serve hot.

YIELD: 1 1/2 CUPS

Mustard Yogurt Sauce

 An extremely tasty and agreeable sauce for those on a low-fat/low-cholesterol diet. You can use either grainy or smooth mustard.

$1/2$ cup plain low-fat yogurt $1/2$ cup Dijon-style mustard

1 To serve cold, whisk yogurt and mustard together.

2 To serve hot, heat slowly (not to a boil) over low flame, stirring continuously to prevent the sauce from separating.

YIELD: ABOUT 1 CUP

Plum Sauce

 Try this with venison, roast lamb or cold birds or pâté.

1 pound firm ripe red plums   6 tablespoons sugar
$1^{1}/4$ cups white wine vinegar   1 teaspoon Dijon mustard
4 cloves

1 Wash and pit the plums. Stew them in the vinegar with the other ingredients until tender.

2 Remove the cloves and process the mixture in a blender or food processor until smooth. If you find the sauce too tart add a little more sugar.

YIELD: $2^{1}/2$ CUPS

Raisin Sauce

 Good for ham or tongue. If you are baking a ham, you will want to add some of its juices to the sauce.

1 cup brown sugar $1/2$ cup fruit vinegar
1 tablespoon dry mustard   2 to 3 cups liquid—pan juices,
1 tablespoon flour   white wine, or Madeira
$1/2$ cup raisins   salt (optional)

1 Mix together brown sugar, dry mustard, and flour in saucepan. Stir in remaining ingredients and cook slowly until sauce is thick and slightly clear.

YIELD: 3 CUPS

Tartar Sauce

 Very popular with hot fish dishes.

1 1/2 cups mayonnaise

4 shallots, finely chopped

1 dill pickle, finely chopped

1 tablespoon capers, drained
and finely chopped

1 tablespoon finely chopped
fresh parsley

1 tablespoon finely chopped
fresh tarragon

1 teaspoon dry mustard

1 tablespoon lemon juice

1/2 teaspoon granulated sugar

salt to taste

freshly ground white pepper to
taste

1 Combine the first 9 ingredients in a mixing bowl. Add salt and pepper
to taste.

YIELD: 2 CUPS

Velouté Sauce

 4 tablespoons butter or
margarine

4 tablespoons flour

1 1/2 cups chicken stock

1/2 cup light cream

salt to taste

freshly ground white pepper to
taste

pinch of ground nutmeg

1 In a saucepan, melt butter over low heat and blend in flour. Gradually
add chicken stock and cream, stirring constantly. Stir until thick and
smooth.

2 Season with salt, pepper, and nutmeg.

YIELD: 2 CUPS

White Wine Sauce

 This sauce is a culinary masterpiece. Use it with all kinds of white
saltwater fish fillets—sole, flounder, sea bass, and halibut. Pour it over
fillets that have been poached in court bouillon. The whipped cream in
the sauce causes it to brown quickly when placed in a hot oven or
under the broiler.

2 tablespoons butter or margarine	½ cup court bouillon
2 or 3 shallots or scallions, finely minced	½ cup light cream
	1 tablespoon flour
2 sprigs parsley	2 egg yolks, beaten
pinch of dried tarragon	¼ cup heavy cream, whipped
1 bay leaf	juice of half a lemon
½ cup dry white wine	salt to taste
	white pepper to taste

1 Melt butter in saucepan, add shallots and herbs, and cook slowly until shallots are soft.

2 Add wine and court bouillon and cook about 5 minutes to reduce liquid by about one-third.

3 Add ½ cup cream and the flour and beat with wire whisk. Cook until sauce is smooth and slightly thickened. Strain sauce.

4 Mix sauce with egg yolks and return saucepan to stove over very low heat. Beat constantly until sauce becomes thick. Do not allow to boil.

5 Remove sauce from stove and carefully fold in whipped cream and lemon juice. Add salt and white pepper to taste.

6 Pour sauce over fish and place in very hot oven or under broiler until sauce is lightly browned.

YIELD: 2 CUPS

SIDE DISHES

Dumplings

 To be served with stew or pot roast.

2 cups flour	½ teaspoon salt
4 teaspoons baking powder	1 scant cup milk

1 Sift together dry ingredients and add milk gradually.

2 Drop by spoonfuls and cook with pot roast or stew during last 12 minutes of cooking.

YIELD: 6 TO 8 LARGE DUMPLINGS

Peach Chutney

Skin, pit, and cut in cubes enough peaches to make 1 quart. (The number will depend entirely upon their size.) If you have a mango handy, include it.

1 quart cut-up peaches

2 cups raspberry vinegar

3 cups dark brown sugar

1/3 cup dried currants

2 cloves garlic, finely chopped

2 ounces fresh ginger, finely chopped

1/2 cup diced red pepper

1 Sterilize three 6-ounce jars.

2 Combine all ingredients in heavy saucepan over low heat. Cook 2 hours, stirring occasionally.

3 Pour chutney into prepared jars and seal.

YIELD: 3 JARS (6 OUNCES EACH)

Pickled Walnuts

Excellent served with game.

1/2 cup brown sugar

2 cups maple syrup

1 cup cider vinegar

1/2 teaspoon ground cloves

1/2 teaspoon ground ginger

1/2 teaspoon ground mace

grated rind of 1 lemon

1 pound English walnuts, shelled

4 ounces dark rum

1 Sterilize 6 jars.

2 Boil together all ingredients except walnuts and rum. Cook until sauce is well thickened, about 10 minutes.

3 Add nuts and rum and simmer 10 minutes more.

4 While still hot, seal in jars.

YIELD: 6 JARS

Preserved Grape Leaves

Grape leaves are good with various sorts of game, but since they are nipped by the first frost, you will need to pickle them early in September so they will be on hand when you have wildfowl on the menu.

Tie medium-size perfect grape leaves in firm rolls of a dozen or so, throw them into rapidly boiling salted water (4 tablespoons salt to 2 quarts water), and remove them after about 30 seconds. Store them in the brine in sterile jars.

Quick Brandied Peaches

 Pleasant to serve with a ham or turkey.

1 can (29 ounces) cling peach halves	2 sticks cinnamon
1/2 cup brandy	julienne strips of orange and lemon rind
1/4 cup dark brown sugar	whole cloves
1/8 cup tarragon white wine vinegar	

1 Drain peaches, reserving syrup.

2 In saucepan, combine 1/2 cup peach syrup with brandy, sugar, vinegar, and cinnamon sticks and simmer 5 minutes.

3 Stud peaches with cloves and heat in sauce. Serve warm.

Tabasco Jelly

 Good with game or steak.

1 jar (8 ounces) red currant jelly	1 teaspoon Tabasco sauce
	1/2 teaspoon lemon juice

1 Melt jelly in top of small double boiler. Season with Tabasco and lemon juice. Cook briefly to reduce.

2 Remove from heat and chill in jelly jar or small mold.

3 To serve, dip mold or jar quickly in hot water and unmold.

YIELD: ABOUT 1 CUP

Yorkshire Pudding

 The classic accompaniment to roast beef.

about ¼ cup roast beef pan
drippings, after skimming
off fat

2 eggs

1 cup milk

1 cup flour

¼ teaspoon salt

1 Set oven at 450°.

2 Prepare batter by combining eggs, milk, flour, and salt. Do not overbeat—sauce should be lumpy.

3 Put some pan drippings in a baking pan. Pour batter into pan with drippings.

4 Place pan in oven and bake about 30 minutes. When done, pudding will be puffy and golden brown. Cut in squares and arrange around roast.

12

Desserts

Yankees have a tremendous sweet tooth, so this chapter is necessarily long. There are so many recipes to choose from that it has been a difficult task to decide which are the most delicious and most typical. Many here are rich, but I have also included a number of recipes that are lighter yet still intriguing, recipes that are low or lacking in fat and cholesterol. They end the meal happily, too, and it is nice to be able to walk away from the table with a light step.

Many of these recipes lend themselves to a variety of interpretations. Blueberry Cobbler can become Cherry Cobbler, Apple Crisp can become Rhubarb Crisp, or Heavenly Pie can be flavored with apricot instead of lemon. Here is a sampling of the kinds of desserts that Yankees love.

FRUIT DESSERTS

From the time that the first pink rhubarb stalks are pushing up in the garden until the last red cranberries are taken from the bog, Yankees have a dozen homey, heavenly ways to prepare the fruits of the garden or berry patch. Some of them involve plenty of sugar and thick cream! Others are easy on the waistline of the present day.

Deep-Dish Rhubarb Pie

 Very easy to make, very good. Serve with lightly whipped cream.

Crust

6 tablespoons butter or
   margarine
3/4 cup flour
2 teaspoons baking powder

1/4 teaspoon salt
3/4 cup granulated sugar
1 cup milk

Filling

4 cups rhubarb, cut in 1-inch
pieces
1¼ cups granulated sugar

2 tablespoons lemon juice
½ teaspoon ground cinnamon

1 Preheat oven to 350°. In 3-quart soufflé dish, melt butter in oven. Remove dish.

2 Prepare the crust by sifting together flour, baking powder, salt, and ¾ cup sugar. Stir milk into dry ingredients until just wet but not thoroughly blended. Pour mixture into soufflé dish over melted butter. Do not stir.

3 Prepare filling by tossing rhubarb with 1¼ cups sugar, lemon juice, and cinnamon. Place fruit on top of batter in soufflé dish. Do not stir.

4 Bake 60 or 70 minutes, until crust has risen through rhubarb and is golden brown and bubbly.

YIELD: 8 SERVINGS

Strawberry Rhubarb Cream

1½ cups finely diced rhubarb
½ cup granulated sugar
2 tablespoons crème de cassis
or sweet vermouth

1 pint strawberries, sliced
(reserve 4 for garnish)
1 cup plain nonfat yogurt

1 Combine the rhubarb, sugar, and cassis in enameled saucepan, cover tightly, and bring to boil. Reduce heat and cook 5 minutes. Add strawberries and cook 10 minutes longer, until mixture is reduced and thickened.

2 Transfer the mixture to a bowl, and when sauce has stopped steaming, place in freezer until thoroughly chilled, 40 to 50 minutes.

3 Combine fruit with yogurt and chill in refrigerator until needed. (If you watch it very carefully, you can return the mixture to the freezer until it reaches almost ice cream-like consistency—with excellent results.)

4 At serving time, top each portion with a strawberry.

YIELD: 4 SERVINGS

Strawberry Shortcake

A very old shortcake recipe, and the proper way to make it. If you wish, add 1 tablespoon sugar to the shortcake ingredients.

1 quart strawberries (reserve a few for garnish)	$^1/_2$ teaspoon salt
2 cups flour	$^1/_3$ cup (scant) shortening
3 teaspoons baking powder	$^3/_4$ cup milk
	heavy cream or whipped cream

1 Preheat oven to 425°. Coat baking sheet with vegetable spray.

2 Crush strawberries slightly, sweeten to taste, and set aside.

3 Sift together flour, baking powder, and salt. With forks or fingers, blend shortening into dry ingredients. Little by little, stir in milk to form soft dough. Turn onto floured board and pat into a single large layer 1 to $1^1/_2$ inches thick.

4 Put batter on prepared baking sheet. Bake 15 to 18 minutes. Cool slightly.

5 Split shortcake carefully and butter both halves. Put prepared berries between layers and on top of cake.

6 Garnish with whole berries and serve warm with thick cream. Or, if you prefer, cover with lightly whipped, unsweetened cream.

YIELD: 6 SERVINGS

VARIATION – Raspberry or Peach Shortcake

Prepare Raspberry Shortcake and Peach Shortcake the same way you fix Strawberry Shortcake. They are just as good, maybe better.

Strawberry Soufflé

1 tablespoon butter or margarine	$1^1/_2$ ounces Cointreau or kirsch
1 tablespoon flour	few drops of red food coloring
1 package (10 ounces) frozen strawberries, or $1^1/_2$ cups sliced, sweetened, fresh strawberries	4 or 5 eggs, separated, plus 1 extra egg white
	whipped cream

1 Bring all ingredients to room temperature. Preheat oven to 400°. Coat soufflé dish with vegetable spray.

2   Over low heat, mix together butter and flour. Add strawberries and stir together to make thick sauce. Add liqueur and food coloring.

3   Separate eggs, adding yolks one by one to strawberry sauce. Beat whites in clean, dry bowl until stiff, then fold gently and lightly into strawberry mixture. Turn into soufflé dish.

4   Place soufflé dish in oven and reduce heat immediately to 375°. Bake 30 minutes. Serve with whipped cream and, if you wish, fresh strawberry sauce.

YIELD: 4 SERVINGS

Raspberry Crumble

3 cups crushed raspberries
1 1/4 cups granulated sugar
juice of half a lemon

1/4 cup butter or margarine, softened
3/4 cup flour
pinch of salt

1   Preheat oven to 350°. Coat 1-quart soufflé dish with vegetable spray.

2   Sprinkle raspberries with half of sugar, add lemon juice, and stir well. Place in prepared soufflé dish.

3   Blend butter with remaining sugar, flour, and salt and spread over raspberries. Bake 40 minutes.

YIELD: 4 SERVINGS

Blueberry Oatmeal Crisp

Serve the crisp warm with whipped cream, vanilla ice cream, or Cheddar cheese. Tasty with apples, too (use 3 or 4 tart cooking apples).

1 quart blueberries
1/2 cup butter or margarine
3/4 cup firmly packed brown sugar

3/4 cup quick-cooking oatmeal
1/2 cup flour
1 teaspoon ground cinnamon

1   Preheat oven to 350°. Coat shallow 1 1/2-quart quiche dish or pie plate with vegetable spray.

2 Arrange blueberries in prepared dish. Melt butter and stir in sugar, oatmeal, flour, and cinnamon. Mix well and sprinkle over blueberries

3 Bake 45 minutes, until crust is golden brown and blueberries are soft.

YIELD: 6 SERVINGS

Blueberry Cobbler

shortcake (see Strawberry
   Shortcake, p. 328)
2 tablespoons milk
1 quart blueberries

1 cup granulated sugar
1 teaspoon grated orange rind
butter or margarine

1 Preheat oven to 375°. Coat 2-quart casserole with vegetable spray.

2 Make soft shortcake dough, increasing the milk by 2 tablespoons.

3 Wash berries and shake dry. Mix with sugar and orange rind and place in prepared casserole. Spread dough over berries and dot with butter.

4 Bake 35 to 40 minutes and serve hot with whipped cream or ice cream.

YIELD: 6 TO 8 SERVINGS

VARIATION – Blackberry Cobbler

Prepare Blackberry Cobbler the same way you fix Blueberry Cobbler, substituting blackberries for blueberries and adding 1 teaspoon cornstarch.

Peach Soufflé

2 cups peach pulp
2 tablespoons lemon juice
1/2 cup granulated sugar

8 eggs, separated
1/4 teaspoon salt
1/2 pint whipping cream

1 Preheat oven to 350°. Coat soufflé dish with vegetable spray.

2 Put peach pulp in bowl and add lemon juice, sugar, beaten egg yolks, and salt. Fold in stiffly beaten egg whites.

3 Place mixture in prepared dish and bake 40 minutes. Serve with whipped cream.

YIELD: 6 SERVINGS

Brown Betty

8 tart apples, peeled and sliced
1/4 cup brown or granulated
  sugar
freshly grated nutmeg to taste
juice and grated rind of half a
  lemon

about 4 slices buttered
  homemade bread, crumbled
1/2 cup hot water
cream or Hard Sauce (p. 368)

1 Preheat oven to 325°. Coat 1-quart soufflé dish with vegetable spray.

2 Sprinkle apple slices with sugar, nutmeg, lemon juice, and rind. Place alternate layers of apples and breadcrumbs (ending with crumbs) in prepared dish.

3 Pour hot water over dish. Cover dish and bake 1 hour, removing lid for last 10 minutes. Serve hot with pitcher of rich cream or hard sauce.

YIELD: 4 OR 5 SERVINGS

Apple Pandowdy

8 slices white bread, cut into
  fingers and crusts removed
1/2 cup melted butter or
  margarine
6 large green cooking apples,
  peeled, cored, and sliced

1/2 cup dark brown sugar
1/2 teaspoon ground cinnamon
1/2 cup cider
1/2 pint whipping cream

1 Preheat oven to 350°. Coat 1 1/2-quart soufflé dish with vegetable spray.

2 Dip two-thirds of bread fingers in melted butter and line bottom and sides of prepared baking dish. Fill center with apple slices. Combine brown sugar and cinnamon and sprinkle over apples.

3 Dip remaining bread fingers in melted butter and place on top of dish. Sprinkle with additional brown sugar.

4 Cover dish and bake 1 hour, removing lid for last 15 minutes. Serve hot with whipped cream.

YIELD: 6 SERVINGS

President George Bush's Apple Crisp

As American as apple crisp.

4 cups peeled, cored, and
   sliced apples (Granny
   Smiths or other tart apples)
1/4 cup orange juice
1 cup granulated sugar
3/4 cup flour

1/4 teaspoon ground nutmeg
1/2 teaspoon ground cinnamon
1/3 cup butter or margarine, cut
   up
whipped cream

1 Preheat oven to 375°. Coat 9-inch pie plate with vegetable spray.

2 Arrange apple slices in pie plate and pour orange juice over them.

3 In mixing bowl, combine sugar, flour, and spices. With pastry blender
  or 2 knives, cut in butter until mixture resembles coarse crumbs.

4 Sprinkle topping over apples and bake 45 to 55 minutes, until topping
  is browned. Serve warm with whipped cream.

YIELD: 4 SERVINGS

Cranberry Crunch

Serve with ice cream or whipped cream for dessert or leave plain for
snacks. You can also make this with apricot jam.

2 1/2 cups old-fashioned oatmeal
1 cup flour
1 cup butter or margarine, at
   room temperature

1 cup light brown sugar
2 cups Cranberry Sauce
   (p. 315)

1 Preheat oven to 375°. Spray rimmed baking sheet (10″ x 14″) with
  vegetable spray.

2 In large bowl, mix together oatmeal, flour, butter, and brown sugar.
  Use fingers to blend dough until it is crumbled to pea size.

3 Pat half of dough firmly onto baking sheet. Spread cranberry sauce
  over dough. Sprinkle remaining dough crumbs over top of sauce. Pat
  gently but firmly.

4 Bake 30 to 40 minutes. Cut into squares while still warm.

YIELD: 16 SQUARES

Cranberry Roly-Poly

Serve warm with Hard Sauce (p. 368) or lightly whipped cream. This can also be made with other fillings—jellies or jams.

2 cups sifted flour
3 teaspoons baking powder
1/2 teaspoon salt
4 tablespoons shortening
2/3 cup milk

2 tablespoons melted butter or
   margarine
2 cups Cranberry Sauce
   (p. 315)

1 Preheat oven to 425°. Coat baking sheet with vegetable spray.

2 Sift together dry ingredients and cut in shortening with pastry blender or 2 knives. Add milk and stir until mixture forms soft biscuit dough.

3 Roll out dough on lightly floured board to 1/4-inch thickness. Brush with melted butter and cover with cranberry sauce. Roll up dough with its filling, jelly roll fashion, and place on prepared baking sheet, seam side down.

4 Bake 25 to 30 minutes and serve warm.

YIELD: 6 SERVINGS

WINTER DESSERTS

Some of these desserts are light, some lusty. When the snow piles higher and higher and the days are short, a rich sweet warms the ending of the day as much as a roaring fire.

Chestnut Cream

This dish is approximately 150 years old and is one that has been passed down from generation to generation. Puréed chestnuts are available in cans and are imported from France and Italy.

1 cup granulated sugar
1 cup water
1 can (16 ounces) puréed
   chestnuts

1 teaspoon vanilla extract
1 cup heavy cream, whipped
Chocolate Curls (below)

1 Combine sugar and water and cook about 10 minutes.

2 Mix chestnut purée and sugar syrup, and allow to cool. Add vanilla and whipped cream. Chill. Garnish with whipped cream with chocolate curls.

YIELD: 6 SERVINGS

Chocolate Curls

Place 1 square of semisweet chocolate in warm place (a gas oven with pilot light burning is satisfactory) until chocolate has just softened slightly. Shave it with a vegetable peeler or small, sharp knife—longer strokes make longer curls. Use to decorate cakes and other desserts.

Heavenly Pie

Heavenly it is.

1½ cups granulated sugar
¼ teaspoon cream of tartar
4 eggs, separated, at room
  temperature

3 tablespoons lemon juice
1 tablespoon finely grated
  lemon rind
1 pint heavy cream

1 Preheat oven to 275°. Coat 9-inch Pyrex pie plate with vegetable spray.

2 Sift 1 cup sugar with cream of tartar. Beat egg whites until stiff but not dry, gradually adding sugar mixture while continuing to beat.

3 Spread meringue in prepared pie plate and bake 1 hour. Cool.

4 Beat egg yolks slightly, stir in remaining sugar, plus lemon juice and rind, and cook in top of double boiler until thick. Cool.

5 Whip cream. Combine lemon mixture with half of whipped cream. Spread on pie and cover with remaining whipped cream.

YIELD: 6 SERVINGS

Angel Pie

½ cup confectioners' sugar
4 egg whites, beaten stiff
½ pint heavy cream

⅔ cup sifted granulated sugar
1 teaspoon vanilla extract
Chocolate Curls (above)

1 Preheat oven to 350°. Coat 9-inch Teflon pie plate with vegetable spray.

2 Beat confectioners' sugar into beaten egg whites and pour into prepared pie plate. Bake 45 minutes, then cool.

3 Whip cream, flavor with sifted sugar and vanilla, and spread on top of pie. Garnish with chocolate curls. Chill before serving.

YIELD: 6 SERVINGS

Forgotten Torte

 An absolutely magic meringue dish baked by the good fairy. You can make a lemon custard with 4 of the leftover egg yolks (as in the recipe for Heavenly Pie). There are many possibilities. Fill the center with any fruit you choose, mixed with whipped cream.

6 egg whites, at room temperature	1/2 pint heavy cream, whipped and sweetened
1/2 teaspoon cream of tartar	2 teaspoons powdered cocoa (optional)
1/4 teaspoon salt	Chocolate Curls (p. 334)
1 1/2 cups granulated sugar	(optional)
1 teaspoon vanilla extract	slivered almonds (optional)
1/4 teaspoon almond extract	

1 Preheat oven to 450°. Coat bottom of 9-inch tube pan with vegetable spray.

2 Beat egg whites with cream of tartar and salt until foamy. (With an electric beater, use medium speed.) Gradually add sugar, beating mixture well and continuously until meringue forms stiff, glossy peaks. Beat in vanilla and almond extracts.

3 Spread meringue evenly in tube pan, place on center rack of oven, and turn off heat immediately. Let stand overnight, with oven door closed.

4 Next morning, torte will be done. Loosen sides with sharp knife and unmold onto serving platter. (It will settle a bit.)

5 Serve cake frosted with whipped cream. If desired, flavor whipped cream with cocoa and sprinkle with chocolate curls.

YIELD: 8 TO 10 SERVINGS.

Marmalade Pudding

 This pleasant dessert cooks itself while you are eating dinner and makes a light but warm conclusion to the meal.

Pudding

6 egg whites

6 tablespoons granulated sugar

3 large tablespoons orange marmalade

1 teaspoon orange extract or Cointreau

Sauce

6 egg yolks, beaten until thick and lemon colored

1 1/4 cups confectioners' sugar

2 ounces sherry or Cointreau

1 cup whipped cream

slivered almonds

1 Beat egg whites with sugar (adding sugar very gradually) until stiff but not dry. Fold in marmalade and orange extract.

2 Butter or coat with vegetable spray the top pan of 2-quart double boiler and scoop in pudding. Steam 1 1/4 hours over constantly boiling water.

3 Just before serving, prepare sauce. In top of separate double boiler, put egg yolks, confectioners' sugar, and sherry or Cointreau. Mix well. At last moment, fold in whipped cream and pour over pudding. Sprinkle with slivered almonds.

YIELD: 8 SERVINGS

Blitz Torte

 You can assemble and serve this cake as is or put strawberries and whipped cream on top and between the layers.

1 cup sifted cake flour

1 teaspoon baking powder

1/8 teaspoon salt

1/2 cup shortening

1 cup plus 1 teaspoon granulated sugar

3 eggs, separated

1 teaspoon vanilla extract

4 tablespoons milk

1/2 teaspoon ground cinnamon

1/2 cup almonds, blanched and sliced

1 Preheat oven to 375°. Coat two 9-inch Teflon cake pans with vegetable spray.

2 Sift together flour, baking powder, and salt.

3 Cream the shortening with ¹/₂ cup sugar until fluffy, then add well-beaten egg yolks, vanilla, milk, and sifted dry ingredients.

4 Beat egg whites until stiff but not dry and ¹/₂ cup sugar gradually, beating until whites hold sharp peak.

5 Put dough in the prepared cake pans and spread egg-white mixture over them. Combine cinnamon with 1 teaspoon sugar and sprinkle over egg-white mixture. Then sprinkle slivered almonds over all. Bake 25 to 30 minutes

YIELD: 8 SERVINGS

Boston Cream Pie

2 cups sifted flour
2¹/₂ teaspoons baking powder
¹/₂ teaspoon salt
¹/₃ cup butter or margarine
    softened

1 cup granulated sugar
1 teaspoon vanilla extract
2 eggs
¹/₂ cup milk
confectioners' sugar

Cream Filling

³/₄ cup granulated sugar
¹/₃ cup flour
¹/₈ teaspoon salt
2 cups milk, scalded

2 eggs or 4 egg yolks, lightly
    beaten
1 teaspoon vanilla extract

1 Preheat oven to 350°. Coat two 8-inch Teflon cake pans with vegetable spray.

2 Sift together the flour, baking powder, and salt. Cream butter until light and gradually add sugar. Beat in vanilla and eggs alternately with milk. Beat well.

3 Turn into prepared layer-cake pans and bake 30 minutes.

4 Prepare the filling by first combining sugar, flour, and salt. Gradually add scalded milk. Cook in double boiler, stirring constantly until mixture thickens, about 15 minutes.

5 Add eggs and cook 2 or 3 minutes more. Cool and add vanilla. (For richer filling, add 2 tablespoons butter or margarine.)

6 Assemble pie by spreading filling between layers. Sprinkle top with confectioners' sugar.

YIELD: 8 SERVINGS

VARIATION – **Banana Cream Pie**

Prepare Banana Cream Pie the same way you fix Boston Cream Pie, adding 1 thoroughly mashed banana to cream filling.

VARIATION – **Washington Pie**

Prepare Washington Pie the same way you fix Boston Cream Pie, substituting cherry jam for the filling.

Velvet Cheesecake
with Sour Cream Topping

 The ancient Greeks made excellent cheesecake—the best of all was said to have come from the island of Samos. Today every country has its own version. This American adaptation is creamy, light, and smooth. (It may also be glazed with melted strawberry or apricot jam.)

1 package (6 ounces) zwieback, rolled into fine crumbs

2 cups cottage cheese

2 large eggs, separated

$1/2$ cup granulated sugar

4 tablespoons melted butter or margarine

juice and grated rind of half a lemon

pinch of ground cinnamon

$1/2$ teaspoon vanilla extract

2 tablespoons cornstarch

2 tablespoons light cream

Sour Cream Topping

1 cup sour cream

1 tablespoon granulated sugar

$1/2$ teaspoon vanilla extract

1 Preheat oven to 350°. Coat 9-inch springform pan with vegetable spray.

2 Press zwieback crumbs onto sides and bottom of prepared pan. Bake 5 minutes and cool.

3 Beat cottage cheese until smooth. Add beaten egg yolks, sugar, butter, lemon rind and juice, cinnamon, and vanilla. Blend cornstarch with light cream and add to cottage cheese mixture. Beat well and fold in well-beaten egg whites.

4 Spoon mixture over crust in pan and level with knife. Bake 25 minutes, or until cake feels firm to the touch for 1 inch around edges. (Center will firm up as it cools.) Remove cake and cool 10 minutes.

5 Raise oven temperature to 400°. Spread sour cream topping over cake and bake 8 minutes more. Cool cake in draft-free place. When cold, cover with aluminum foil and chill several hours.

YIELD: 8 SERVINGS

No-Bake Cheesecake

3 tablespoons melted butter or margarine

3/4 cup graham cracker crumbs

2 tablespoons granulated sugar

1/4 teaspoon ground cinnamon

1/4 teaspoon ground nutmeg

Filling

2 envelopes unflavored gelatine

1 cup granulated sugar

dash of salt

2 eggs, separated

1 cup milk

1 teaspoon lemon rind

1 tablespoon lemon juice

1 teaspoon vanilla extract

3 cups creamed cottage cheese

1 cup heavy cream, whipped

1 Coat 9-inch springform pan with vegetable spray. Combine melted butter, graham cracker crumbs, 2 tablespoons sugar, cinnamon, and nutmeg. Press 1/2 cup crumb mixture into prepared pan.

2 In saucepan, combine gelatine, 3/4 cup sugar, and salt. In bowl, beat egg yolks and milk together and stir into gelatine mixture. Cook over low heat, stirring constantly, until gelatine dissolves and mixture thickens slightly, 3 to 5 minutes.

3 Remove saucepan from heat and stir in lemon rind and juice and vanilla.

4 Chill, stirring occasionally, until mixture mounds slightly when dropped from a spoon.

5 Beat cottage cheese until smooth and stir into gelatine mixture.

6 In mixing bowl, beat egg whites until stiff. Gradually add remaining 1/4 cup sugar and beat until very stiff. Fold into gelatine mixture. Fold in whipped cream.

7 Turn into prepared pan and sprinkle with remaining crumb mixture. Chill until firm, 2 to 3 hours.

YIELD: 10 SERVINGS

Dessert Waffles

 Serve warm with a scoop of vanilla ice cream and hot fudge sauce.

1²/₃ cups cake flour	¹/₂ teaspoon salt
¹/₃ cup powdered cocoa	¹/₂ cup buttermilk
¹/₃ cup granulated sugar	6 tablespoons melted butter or
1¹/₂ teaspoons baking powder	margarine
1 teaspoon baking soda	2 eggs, separated

1 Sift together dry ingredients. Stir in buttermilk and butter.

2 Beat egg whites until they hold soft peaks. Beat egg yolks until lemon colored. Stir yolks into batter, then gently but thoroughly fold in whites.

3 To prevent overflow, pour into hot waffle iron only enough batter to partially fill each compartment. Close iron and bake until steam is no longer visible.

YIELD: 6 WAFFLES

Cold Apricot Soufflé

 A light and lively party dessert.

1 pound dried apricots	¹/₂ pint heavy cream, whipped
about 1 tablespoon granulated	4 egg whites
sugar	Chocolate Curls (p. 334)
1 tablespoon apricot brandy	

1 Soak apricots in water and cook about 2 hours, until soft. Drain off water.

2 Add sugar and apricot brandy and purée mixture in food processor or blender until smooth and light.

3 Whip cream to fairly stiff peaks and fold half into apricot purée. Chill.

4 Just before serving, beat egg whites until stiff and fold into purée. Then fold in remaining whipped cream, barely mixing, to create a pretty marbleized effect.

5 Pile soufflé lightly in cold serving dish and garnish with chocolate curls.

YIELD: 8 TO 10 SERVINGS

Cold Apricot Whip

A pretty and easy party dessert.

1 pound dried apricots	1/2 pint heavy cream
sugar to taste	4 egg whites
2 tablespoons apricot brandy	Chocolate Curls for garnish

1 Soak the apricots in water to cover for an hour. Cook until soft. Drain. Add sugar to taste and apricot brandy and purée the mixture in a food processor or blender until smooth.

2 Whip the cream until it forms fairly stiff peaks and fold half of it into the apricot purée. Chill.

3 An hour before serving remove from refrigerator. Just before serving beat the egg whites until stiff and fold them into the purée. Fold in the remaining whipped cream, barely mixing, so a nice marbelized effect results. Pile lightly in a cold serving dish and garnish with Chocolate Curls.

YIELD: 8 TO 10 SERVINGS

Chocolate Mousse

Easy to make and one of life's pleasantest rewards.

4 ounces semisweet chocolate	4 eggs, separated
1/4 cup rum or Grand Marnier	1/2 pint heavy cream, lightly
4 tablespoons butter or	whipped and lightly flavored
margarine	with sugar and liqueur

1 In top of a double boiler, melt chocolate with liqueur and butter. Cool. Beat in egg yolks with whisk.

2 Beat egg whites until stiff. Beat large spoonful of beaten whites into chocolate mixture, then fold in remaining whites. Put in serving dish and chill.

3 Serve with whipped cream.

YIELD: 4 SERVINGS

Lemon Pudding

When baked, this pudding forms a light, fluffy cake on top and a smooth, rich sauce on the bottom.

1 cup granulated sugar
3 tablespoons flour
3 eggs, separated
1 cup milk

juice and grated rind of 1
   lemon
1/4 teaspoon salt
1 cup lightly whipped cream

1 Preheat oven to 350°. Coat 1-quart soufflé dish with vegetable spray.

2 Combine the sugar and flour. Beat egg whites and yolks separately.

3 To sugar mixture, add milk, beaten egg yolks, lemon juice and rind, and salt. Carefully fold in stiffly beaten egg whites.

4 Pour mixture into prepared soufflé dish. Set dish in larger pan containing 1/2 inch of water. Bake about 35 minutes, or until toothpick inserted in center comes out clean. Serve warm with whipped cream.

YIELD: 4 SERVINGS

Bread and Butter Pudding

Serve with French Hard Sauce (p. 368), Brandied Apricot Sauce (p. 368), or both—or, if you prefer, with plain sweetened whipped cream.

1 cup milk
1 cup light cream
pinch of salt
1 vanilla bean
3 eggs
1/2 cup granulated sugar

6 slices white bread, crusts
   removed
2 tablespoons butter or
   margarine, at room
   temperature
1/2 cup white raisins, soaked in
   water, then drained.

1 Preheat oven to 350°. Coat 8-inch round baking dish with vegetable spray.

2 Bring to boil milk, cream, salt, and vanilla bean.

3 Beat together eggs and sugar. Add simmering milk and cream. Strain mixture.

4 Butter bread, cut slices into squares, and arrange squares in prepared

baking dish. Sprinkle raisins evenly over bread squares. Pour milk and egg mixture over all.

5 Place baking dish in larger pan of water and bake 30 minutes.

YIELD: 6 TO 8 SERVINGS

 ## Dr. Zabdiel Boylston's Honeycomb Pudding

This was a favorite of Dr. Zab-diel Boylston, who braved the threat of mob violence in 1721 in order to get Bostonians inoculated against smallpox.

1/2 cup flour
1/2 cup granulated sugar
1/2 teaspoon ground cloves
1/2 teaspoon ground cinnamon
1/2 teaspoon allspice
1/4 teaspoon salt
1/2 cup butter or margarine, melted
1/2 cup warm milk
4 eggs, beaten
1 tablespoon baking soda
1 cup dark molasses

Honeycomb Pudding Sauce

1 cup granulated sugar
1/4 cup butter or margarine, softened
juice of 1 lemon
1 egg, beaten
1/4 teaspoon salt
3 teaspoons cornstarch
1 cup boiling water

1 Preheat oven to 350°. Coat loaf pan with vegetable spray.

2 Sift together dry ingredients, then add remaining ingredients. Pour mixture quickly into prepared loaf pan.

3 Bake about 30 minutes.

4 Prepare Honeycomb Pudding Sauce. Cream sugar and butter, then add remaining ingredients and cook over low heat, stirring constantly, until thickened.

5 Turn pudding onto hot plate and serve with sauce. (When pudding is sliced, honeycomb will show.)

YIELD: 6 SERVINGS

Rice Pudding

 4 tablespoons long-grain rice
1 quart whole milk
granulated sugar to taste, about 2 tablespoons

handful of raisins
1 teaspoon vanilla extract
1/2 pint whipping cream

1 Wash rice and put in saucepan with 2 cups milk. Cook, tightly covered, over very low heat, about 1 hour. (You might want to use an asbestos pad to be sure not to scorch the milk.) Stir occasionally.

2 Add remaining milk, plus sugar and raisins, and continue cooking until pudding has firm, silky consistency.

3 Remove from heat, stir in vanilla, and chill.

4 When ready to serve, whip cream, flavoring lightly with sugar and vanilla.

YIELD: ABOUT 10 SERVINGS

VARIATION – Rice Pudding II

You can make rice pudding into a party dessert by spreading apricot jam mixed with 2 ounces apricot brandy over chilled pudding. Top with slivered almonds and whipped cream.

Caffé Espresso Jelly

 Light but rich, this is an excellent dinner party dessert.

3 tablespoons unflavored
  gelatine
³/₄ cup coffee liqueur
3 cups hot espresso coffee
³/₄ cup granulated sugar

pinch of salt
2 cups heavy cream, whipped
  until stiff
1 cup crème fraîche

1 Soften gelatine in coffee liqueur and dissolve in hot coffee. Add sugar and salt, then cool.

2 When mixture is syrupy, fold in whipped cream. Rinse 1¹/₂-quart ring mold with cold water, then pour mixture into mold and chill until set.

3 Unmold on serving platter, fill center with crème fraîche, and serve.

YIELD: 8 SERVINGS

Cousin Carrie's
Chocolate Pudding

 The old saying, "The sauce makes the pudding," is true in this case. The cake is on the dry side; the sauce is the "drencher." I found this recipe in the files of Elizabeth Throne Stamm. She said it came from an old Indian squaw in Brule, Wisconsin, who called it Pig Pudding— presumably because it had the same effect on northern woodsmen that the celebrated enchantress Circe had on Odysseus's men.

butter or margarine the size of
   an egg, about 3 tablespoons

1/2 cup granulated sugar

1/2 cup flour

1 teaspoon baking powder

pinch of salt

2 squares semisweet chocolate

1/2 cup milk

1 egg, well beaten

Pig Pudding Sauce

2 eggs, separated

1 cup granulated sugar

1 cup whipping cream,
   whipped 2 teaspoons vanilla
   extract

1 Preheat oven to 350°. Coat loaf pan with vegetable spray.

2 Cream together butter and 1/2 cup sugar. Sift together flour, baking powder, and salt. Melt chocolate squares in milk. Add egg, melted chocolate, and dry ingredients to creamed mixture.

3 Spoon pudding into prepared loaf pan and bake 20 minutes.

4 Prepare Pig Pudding Sauce. Beat egg yolks and whites in separate bowls. Add 1 cup sugar to egg yolks, then fold in whipped cream. Fold in egg whites and vanilla.

5 Serve cake hot with Pig Pudding Sauce.

YIELD: 6 SERVINGS

Chocolate Topsy-Turvy Pudding

Very easy, chocolaty, and good.

1 cup sifted flour

1/4 teaspoon salt

1 1/4 cups granulated sugar

2 teaspoons baking powder

4 1/2 teaspoons plus 6
   tablespoons powdered cocoa

2 tablespoons melted butter or
   margarine

1/2 cup milk

1/2 cup brown sugar

1 cup water

1/2 pint heavy cream, lightly
   whipped and lightly flavored
   with vanilla and sugar

1 Preheat oven to 350°. Coat 8-inch soufflé dish with vegetable spray.

2 Sift together flour, salt, sugar, baking powder, and 4 1/2 teaspoons cocoa three times.

3 Combine melted butter and milk and stir into dry ingredients. Pour into prepared soufflé dish.

4 In separate bowl, combine ¹/₂ cup granulated sugar and 6 tablespoons cocoa, plus brown sugar. Sprinkle over batter, then carefully pour water over all. Bake 40 minutes.

5 Serve with whipped cream.

YIELD: 6 SERVINGS

Cottage Pudding

An old-fashioned dessert that is good served a little warm. Vanilla Sauce (p. 370), Lemon Sauce (p. 371), or Strawberry Sauce (p. 371) goes well with Cottage Pudding.

1³/₄ cups sifted flour
2¹/₂ teaspoons baking powder
few grains of salt
¹/₄ cup melted butter or
  margarine

1 cup granulated sugar
1 egg, well beaten
¹/₂ teaspoon lemon extract
²/₃ cup milk

1 Preheat oven to 375°. Coat 8-inch-square Teflon pan with vegetable spray.

2 Sift together flour, baking powder, and salt three times.

3 Beat together butter, sugar, egg, and lemon extract. Add sifted dry ingredients and milk alternately, beating well after each addition.

4 Pour into prepared pan and bake 30 to 40 minutes.

YIELD: 9 SQUARES

Date Pudding

A fine party dessert, this is best prepared in the morning and served at room temperature, covered with cold, sweetened whipped cream. It is chewy and rich, and the recipe never fails.

1 cup granulated sugar
2¹/₂ tablespoons flour
1 teaspoon baking powder
2 egg whites, beaten stiff

1 cup nuts, coarsely broken
1 cup dates, chopped
2 tablespoons sour cream
2 egg yolks, beaten

1 Preheat oven to 400°. Coat 9-inch Pyrex pie plate with vegetable spray.

2 Combine all ingredients, adding egg yolks last.

3 Pour into prepared pie plate and set pie plate in larger pan of water. Bake 40 minutes.

YIELD: 8 SERVINGS

Date Apple Torte

 Serve hot or cold, with whipped cream or ice cream.

4 cups peeled and diced tart apples	1 tablespoon melted butter or margarine
1 cup granulated sugar	1 teaspoon vanilla extract
1/2 cup sifted flour	1/2 cup chopped nuts
2 teaspoons baking powder	1/2 cup chopped dates
1 egg	

1 Preheat oven to 400°. Coat 9-inch Pyrex pie plate with vegetable spray.

2 Combine all ingredients in bowl and stir until thoroughly mixed. Do not beat.

3 Turn into prepared pie plate and bake 40 minutes, or until apples are tender

YIELD: 8 SERVINGS

Indian Pudding

 A somewhat lighter, contemporary version of the old favorite. Still wonderful. Serve warm with cold whipped cream or a scoop of vanilla ice cream.

3 cups milk	4 eggs, well beaten
3 tablespoons butter or margarine	1/2 teaspoon ground ginger
1/2 cup cornmeal	1/2 teaspoon ground cinnamon
1/2 cup brown sugar	1/2 teaspoon ground mace
1/2 cup dark molasses	1/4 teaspoon salt
	1/2 cup sour cream

1 Preheat oven to 300°. Coat 2-quart soufflé dish with vegetable spray.

2 In double boiler, scald milk, add butter, and gradually beat in corn-meal. Stir until slightly thickened.

3 Remove from stove and add remaining ingredients, beating well after each addition.

4 Pour into prepared soufflé dish and bake about 2 hours.

YIELD: 8 TO 10 SERVINGS

 ## Baked Indian Pudding

As our new country became more prosperous in the 1800s, it attracted certain groups of wanderers who brought with them an atmosphere of mystery, a flair for colorful clothing, and a sorcerer's skill in extracting money from the pockets of the yokels.

These were the gypsies following a path that had started somewhere in northern India and that led them to the farm of the mother of Minnie Smith of West Franklin, New Hampshire. Among their gifts to her were a recipe and a story.

"When I was a small girl, my mother consented to let a band of gypsies pitch their tents on the lower part of her land. Toward morning, a young gypsy came to our door. He begged Mother to let him bring his young wife to our barn, as she was already in labor, and their tents leaked. My mother told him to bring his wife to the house.

"The gypsy girl was tucked up in Mother's bed, warm and comfortable, and tenderly cared for. Mother was obliged to act as both midwife and doctor. When daylight came, there was one more gypsy to join the band.

"The gypsies were so grateful to Mother for her kindness that they tried to do all kinds of helpful things. One of them brought her a dish of their own wonderful Indian pudding, made over their campfire. When they asked her what else they could do for her, she said that if they would give her the pudding recipe, that was all she could ask. So, years ago, she wrote down the rules given her by a grateful gypsy."

¹/₃ cup cornmeal
¹/₂ cup molasses
pinch of salt
3 cups scalded milk
1 egg, beaten
1 cup raisins
¹/₄ teaspoon ginger
¹/₄ teaspoon cinnamon
¹/₄ teaspoon nutmeg
1 cup cold milk

Mix well the cornmeal, molasses, and salt. Pour over the mixture 3 cups scalded milk. Let stand 5 minutes. Add the well-beaten egg, spices, and raisins. Put in baking dish and place in oven. In 10 minutes, after it starts to bake, add 1 cup of cold milk. Stir. Bake 2 hours.

YIELD: 6 SERVINGS

Prune Icebox Cake

2 egg yolks, beaten
1 can (15 ounces) sweetened
  condensed milk
1/2 cup lemon juice
1/4 teaspoon salt

1 1/2 cups cooked, chopped
  prunes
2 egg whites, beaten stiff.
18 graham crackers

1 Coat small soufflé dish with vegetable spray. Beat egg yolks until light and stir in condensed milk, lemon juice, and salt. Fold in prunes and beaten egg whites.

2 Place mixture in prepared dish, alternating with layers of graham crackers, and chill overnight.

YIELD: 6 SERVINGS

Steamed Cranberry Pudding

Serve with Hard Sauce (p. 368).

1 cup sifted flour
2 teaspoons baking powder
1/2 teaspoon salt
1/2 cup breadcrumbs

1/2 cup brown sugar
2/3 cup finely chopped suet
1 cup fresh cranberries
1/3 cup milk

1 Coat 2-quart pudding mold with vegetable spray. Sift together flour, baking powder, and salt.

2 In separate bowl, combine breadcrumbs, sugar, suet, cranberries, and milk. Add dry ingredients and blend well.

3 Pour mixture into prepared mold, filling two-thirds full. Cover tightly.

4 Place mold on rack in kettle containing 1 inch of boiling water. Steam 2 hours, using high heat at first, and then, as steam escapes, lowering heat. Add more water if necessary.

YIELD: 6 SERVINGS

Our recipe came from Grandma Lane, who lived in Midlands England without suspecting that her progeny would migrate to a place called "New England" and be known as "Yongsees." And her basic instructions are simple, because she never dreamed there would come a time when housewives would need to be told how to tie off a pudding bag.

Assuming that somebody will care to revive this lost and ancient delight, the precepts should begin by urging great care and attention. The first time around is critical—in after years, the process will be routine. Go, first, to a department store (Grandma Lane, of course, went to the draper's shop) and buy a square yard of unbleached cotton cloth. Harder to find, but it can be done, is a length of stout cord—not ordinary grocer's twine (which grocers no longer use) but something like a boy's top whip, if you can remember what that was. It needs to be a hard-twist string that will support 8 to 10 pounds, at least. You now own a pudding bag.

Christmas Bag Pudding

8 eggs
1 pound beef suet (ground)
1 pound white flour
1 pound raisins, seeded or
    seedless
1 pound currants
1 cup granulated sugar
1 tablespoon freshly grated
    nutmeg
1 teaspoon ground ginger
1 tablespoon salt

Use an extra cup of flour to flour the fruits well—this will hold the fruits in suspension in the mixture while cooking. Break the eggs into a bowl and whisk them. Don't beat them and don't whisk them to a froth. Just make them smooth in the bowl. Because the eggs are the only rising material in the mixture, this maneuver is better underdone than overdone.

Then mix everything together well in a big container. As the mixture may be difficult to combine with a spoon, there is no objection to going in with your hands and really giving it a larruping. This done, turn your attention to the pudding bag.

Soak the cotton square in warm water and wring it relatively dry. Lay it flat on the kitchen table and flour the top side well. This will form a moist coating of flour on the cloth that is essential to removing the pudding from the bag later. Shake off excess flour. Now dump the pudding mixture in the center of the cloth. The mixture will not be too loose and will remain pretty much upright in a blob.

Gather the corners and edges of the cloth up around the mixture to form the "bag" around the pudding, and, while somebody holds the folds, tie off the pudding-bag string. Make allowance for some rising (the eggs) and some swelling during cooking. In short, don't tie the bag completely tight about the mixture, but leave a small emptiness between the string and the pudding. If you do it right, the ultimate pudding will have the form of a flattened orb, swelling to the precise size you have left in the bag. If you leave too much space, the pudding will sag.

Leave a loop in the string so you can thrust in the handle of a long wooden spoon to retrieve the finished pudding from the boiling water. Everything is going to be wicked hot when the time comes, and the loop is a must. Also, tie the knot around the bag so it can be easily untied. (I suggest a bowline on the end of the cord and a clove hitch around the bag.)

An ordinary canning kettle is ideal—you are dealing with a pudding nearly the size of a basketball. Make a judgment as to how much water will last 4 hours and have it boiling when you lower the pudding by its loop. (It is all right to add water during the cooking, but don't let the boiling stop at any time.) After the pudding has absorbed the heat, you can lower the heat, but keep the boil going all 4 hours. You will want a "kivver" on the "kittle."

If possible, plan so that the 4 hours will be up just as the family sits down to dinner. The pudding is now removed from the heat and left to linger in the hot water until time for the final dessert. When that time comes, lift the bag from the big kettle and lower it onto the platter. Best way is to have two people lift on the wooden spoon handle through the loop, and have a third person shove the platter home as soon as the kettle rim is cleared. Untying the pudding needn't be difficult if 'twas tied right at first. The pudding will roll forth all fine and dandy. Top it with a sprig of holly.

Serve the pudding with brandy poured over it and set alight—or not, as you choose. Slice it, and pass around hard sauce (p. 368) and Christmas pudding sauce (p. 369)—both should be available, and those who take both are what we know as the "Wise Men." And what they do not eat that Christmas night will last sometimes into March (unless, of course, it is eaten sooner), which is pretty good mileage for Christmas.

Be careful tying the string, and don't fret the eggs too much.

Yankee Christmas Pudding

1 loaf stale bread with crusts, crushed into crumbs

1/2 pound chopped, mixed candied fruit peel

1/2 pound suet, chopped

1/3 cup finely chopped pecans or walnuts

2 cups currants

2 cups raisins

grated rind of 1 lemon

1 tablespoon ground cinnamon

1 1/2 teaspoons ground ginger

1/2 teaspoon allspice

1/4 teaspoon ground mace or nutmeg

1 cup granulated sugar

1/2 cup cherry jam

1 teaspoon salt

1/2 cup brandy or rum

6 eggs, well beaten

1 Coat 2-quart pudding mold (or two 1-quart molds) with vegetable spray. In large bowl, combine ingredients in order given. Turn batter into prepared mold. Place on rack in kettle containing 1 inch of boiling water. Cover and steam 4 to 5 hours, adding more water if needed.

2 Remove mold to wire rack, uncover, and allow to cool.

3 Invert mold on rack and wrap cold pudding in plastic wrap or aluminum foil. (You can store it for several weeks in the refrigerator.)

    When you are ready to use Christmas pudding, return it to mold, cover, and steam 30 minutes. Unmold pudding again on hot platter, decorate with some cherries and pour heated brandy or rum over it. Touch a match to the pudding and serve it encircled with blue and orange flames. Pass Hard Sauce or French Hard Sauce (both on p. 368).

YIELD: 16 SERVINGS

PIES

A few versions of New England's very favorite food. Eaten hot or cold—with cheese, heavy cream, or ice cream—pie is delicious from breakfast to bedtime.

Basic Pie Crust

Recently I have discovered the Perforated Pie Pan, a professional utensil now available to home bakers. Twenty-four tiny holes in the bottom of the pan allow moisture to escape and heat to enter, producing a far crisper crust. It's wonderful.

With practice, it is easy to make a good pie crust, but if you are inexperienced or in a hurry, the commercially prepared crusts are excellent too. Shake a little sugar on the lower crust to form a coating that will keep the pie's juices from sinking in.

Mrs. Armande Madore of St. Johnsbury, Vermont, bakes the finest pie I have ever tasted. It melts in your mouth. Here is her basic recipe.

2¼ cups flour	¾ cup shortening
1 teaspoon salt	¼ cup cold water

1 Sift together 2 cups of the flour and the salt onto board or marble surface. Cut in shortening with pastry blender or 2 knives until mixed thoroughly and the consistency of coarse sand. Combine remaining flour with water to make a paste and add quickly and lightly with a fork. Shape dough into ball, cover, and chill thoroughly.

2 When chilled, divide dough into 2 unequal portions. Larger portion will be for bottom crust, smaller portion for top crust.

3 On lightly floured surface, roll out both portions very carefully and lightly, going from center to edges until larger portion is somewhat larger than a 9-inch pie plate.

YIELD: CRUST FOR ONE 2-CRUST 9-INCH PIE OR TWO 9-INCH SHELLS

Rhubarb Pie

 So welcome because it is the first fruit pie of spring, rhubarb pie stands with cherry, blueberry, and apple as one of New England's permanent favorites.

Basic Pie Crust (above)
1¼ cups plus 2 tablespoons
  granulated sugar
¼ cup cornstarch
¼ teaspoon salt
1 bunch (1 pound) rhubarb, cut
  in 1½-inch pieces
2 teaspoons grated orange rind
  (or 1 teaspoon grated lemon
  rind)

juice of 1 orange
drop of red food coloring
  (optional)
2 tablespoons butter or
  margarine
milk

1 Preheat oven to 400°.

2 Divide pastry dough into 2 unequal portions. Roll out larger portion and fit into 9-inch pie pan. Trim pastry ¹/₂ inch beyond rim of pan. Roll out remaining pastry to ¹/₈-inch thickness and cut into strips about ³/₄ inch wide.

3 Combine sugar, cornstarch, and salt. Add rhubarb, rind, and orange juice and toss until well mixed. Tint pink if desired and turn into pastry shell. Dot with butter.

4 Arrange pastry strips over pie in lattice pattern, securing strips firmly to shell and fluting shell and strips together to form high rim. Brush pastry with milk and sprinkle sugar over all.

5 Bake 50 to 60 minutes, or until filling has bubbles that do not break.

YIELD: 9-INCH PIE

A Pair of Pumpkin Pies for Thanksgiving

Pumpkin pie is as traditional as turkey for Thanksgiving, so here are two variations, each a little different.

Basic Pie Crust (p. 352)
³/₄ cup chopped dates
2 McIntosh apples, cored, peeled, and sliced very thinly
3 tablespoons cornstarch
1¹/₂ cups granulated or brown sugar
¹/₂ teaspoon ground cinnamon
¹/₂ teaspoon ground ginger
¹/₂ teaspoon ground nutmeg
1 can (14¹/₂ ounces) stewed pumpkin
¹/₄ cup molasses
2 eggs, beaten
1¹/₂ cups milk
¹/₂ teaspoon vanilla extract
1¹/₂ tablespoons melted butter
lightly whipped cream

1 Preheat oven to 400°.

2 Line two 9-inch pie plates with pastry. Build up and flute the edges.

3 Scatter chopped dates into bottom of one pie, and spread apple slices into bottom of second pie.

4 Prepare remaining filling for both pies. Into a large bowl, sift together cornstarch, sugar, cinnamon, ginger, and nutmeg. Add molasses, eggs, milk, and vanilla and stir well. Add melted butter and beat mixture with egg beater.

5 Pour filling immediately into pie shells, making sure pumpkin mixture coats all of the fruit. (The apples will rise to the top and the dates will remain on the bottom.)

6 Bake about 45 minutes, or until filling is firm. Serve on Thanksgiving Day—"palm warm," with lightly whipped cream.

Strawberry Pie

1 8-inch flaky pie shell, baked
1 1/2 quarts strawberries
    (reserve a few for garnish)
1 package (8 ounces) cream
    cheese
2 tablespoons sour cream

3/4 cup granulated sugar
3 tablespoons cornstarch,
    softened in small amount of
    water
1/2 pint whipping cream 10 or
    12 mint leaves

1 Wash, hull, and dry strawberries.

2 Soften cream cheese with sour cream and spread in pie shell. Reserving a few for garnish, arrange 1 quart whole berries on cream cheese.

3 Cook 1/2 quart berries with sugar over low heat. Bring to boil, then put through fine strainer. Add cornstarch and cook a few minutes, until clear. Cool.

4 Pour strawberry sauce over fresh berries. Cover pie with whipped cream and garnish with reserved berries and mint leaves.

YIELD: 8-INCH OPEN PIE

Fresh Fruit Pies or Tarts

This recipe may be used for making blueberry, raspberry, gooseberry, cherry, peach, and other fruit pies. Use recipe for Basic Pie Crust (p. 352). If you prefer a lattice top, cut the smaller portion of the pie dough into narrow strips, fit them over the pie, and secure the ends by moistening and crimping them firmly to the bottom crust.

1 to 1 1/2 cups granulated sugar
1 or 2 tablespoons cornstarch
1/4 teaspoon salt
3 to 4 cups prepared fruit

1 tablespoon butter or
    margarine
milk

1 Preheat oven to 450°.

2 Combine sugar, cornstarch, and salt, adjusting amount of sugar and cornstarch according to sweetness and juiciness of fruit. Add to prepared fruit and mix thoroughly.

3 Fill pastry-lined pie pan with fruit and dot with butter. Arrange top crust or lattice. Brush top with milk and sugar.

4 Bake 10 minutes, then reduce heat to 350° and bake 20 to 30 minutes more.

Apple Pie

Armande Madore's apple pie. Gravensteins, Rhode Island Greenings, Roxbury Russets, and Cortlands are among the traditional Yankee cooking apples. The familiar McIntosh is as good as any of these. Serve hot with Vermont cheese.

4 to 5 cooking apples, depending on size
Basic Pie Crust (p. 352)
3/4 cup plus 1 teaspoon granulated sugar (if you like tart pie)

ground nutmeg and ground cinnamon (optional)
milk

1 Preheat oven to 400°.

2 Peel, core, and slice apples, mix with 3/4 cup sugar, and place in unbaked pie shell. If desired, sprinkle with nutmeg and cinnamon. Cover with top crust and crimp edges firmly. Make several slits in top to allow steam to escape. Brush top with milk and sprinkle with 1 teaspoon sugar.

3 Bake 10 minutes, then reduce oven temperature to 350° and cook 50 minutes more.

YIELD: 9-INCH PIE

Hot Apple Dumplings

Basic Pie Crust (p. 352)
6 cooking apples
6 tablespoons granulated sugar
6 teaspoons butter or margarine

6 ounces raisins (optional)
cinnamon, sugar, to sprinkle
butter or margarine, to dot

1 Preheat oven to 400°.

2 Roll out pastry to 1/8-inch thickness and cut into 6 squares.

3 Peel and core apples and place one on each square of dough. Fill hollow of each apple with 1 tablespoon sugar and 1 teaspoon butter (and, if you like, a few raisins). Bring edges of pastry upward and fold over each apple, pressing edges together.

4 Place dumplings in shallow baking pan, sprinkle with cinnamon and sugar, and dot with butter. Bake 30 to 40 minutes.

5 While still warm, serve with heavy cream or Hard Sauce (p. 368). If you have strong guests, you may also pass Brandied Apricot Sauce (p. 368) with the hard sauce.

YIELD: 6 SERVINGS

Deep Dish Pear Pie

 A delicate change from apple pie. Very good indeed.

6 large pears, not too ripe, sliced
1/2 cup granulated sugar
2 tablespoons flour
1/2 teaspoon ground cinnamon
1/2 teaspoon ground nutmeg

1/2 cup butter or margarine
3 tablespoons lemon juice
Basic Pie Crust (p. 352)
whipped cream, flavored with sugar and 1 drop of kirsch

1 Preheat oven to 400°. Coat 1 1/2-quart casserole or soufflé dish with vegetable spray.

2 Plunge pears in boiling water so skins will peel off easily. Slice into prepared dish alternately with sugar, flour, spices, butter, and lemon juice.

3 Cover with pastry crust and slash crust in several places.

4 Place on lowest shelf of oven and bake 45 to 50 minutes, until pears are tender and surrounding syrup is caramelized. (If crust browns too quickly, cover with aluminum foil.)

5 Serve warm with whipped cream.

YIELD: 6 SERVINGS

Pecan Pie

3 eggs
1 cup granulated sugar
1 cup dark corn syrup
2 tablespoons butter or margarine, melted

1 teaspoon vanilla extract
1/8 teaspoon salt
8-inch pastry shell, unbaked
whipped cream

1 Preheat oven to 400°.

2 Beat eggs lightly, then add sugar, corn syrup, melted butter, vanilla, and salt. Pour into unbaked pie shell.

3 Bake 10 to 15 minutes, then reduce oven temperature to 350° and bake 30 to 35 minutes more. Cool.

4 Serve with whipped cream.

YIELD: 8-INCH OPEN PIE

Lemon Meringue Pie

1 cup plus 4 tablespoons granulated sugar

1/2 cup flour

1/2 teaspoon salt

1 1/2 cups boiling water

2 eggs, separated

juice and grated rind of 1 lemon

1 tablespoon butter or margarine

1 8-inch baked pie shell (preferably baked 1 or 2 days ahead)

1 Preheat oven to 400°.

2 Mix 1 cup sugar with flour and salt in heavy saucepan or double boiler. Add boiling water. Stir and cook over low heat until mixture boils and looks clearer.

3 Beat egg yolks lightly with fork. Spoon small amount of hot mixture over yolks and stir. Then add yolks to mixture in saucepan and cook 2 minutes.

4 Add lemon rind and juice and butter. Stir, then cool slightly before pouring into baked pie shell.

5 Prepare meringue by beating egg whites until stiff, gradually adding 4 tablespoons sugar. Spread beaten egg whites over top of pie.

6 Bake 3 to 4 minutes, until meringue is light brown.

YIELD: 8-INCH OPEN PIE

Chess Pie

1 1/3 cups firmly packed light brown sugar

1/3 cup melted butter or margarine

3 eggs, lightly beaten

1/3 cup water

1 teaspoon vanilla extract

1/2 cup coarsely chopped nuts (pecans or walnuts)

2/3 cup raisins

1 unbaked 9-inch pastry shell

1 Preheat oven to 375°.

2 Beat together brown sugar and butter until well blended. Add eggs, water, and vanilla and beat again. Stir in nuts and raisins.

3 Pour into unbaked pie shell and bake 45 minutes. Cool to room temperature before serving with whipped cream.

YIELD: 9-INCH OPEN PIE

 ## Mincemeat

If you make this during the hunting season, you can grind up the venison neck meat and use that instead of beef. This makes enough for 10 medium-size pies and keeps forever improving with age. It is the best mincemeat you ever tasted.

2 pounds ground beef
1 pound suet
5 pounds apples
5 pounds raisins
2 pounds currants
3/4 pound citron
2 1/2 pounds brown sugar
2 tablespoons ground
cinnamon

2 tablespoons ground mace
1 tablespoon ground cloves
1 tablespoon salt
1 teaspoon ground nutmeg
1 quart sherry
1 pint brandy

1 In large kettle, cook all ingredients together slowly, uncovered, about 1 1/2 hours, or until mincemeat reaches right consistency.

2 Can while hot in sterilized jars or store in earthenware crock in cold place. (Mincemeat will be protected by a coating of suet.)

Coconut Pie Crust

 This is good filled with vanilla ice cream and hot chocolate sauce or with Silk Pie filling (below).

2 cups shredded coconut

1/3 cup melted butter or margarine

1 Preheat oven to 350°.

2 Combine coconut and melted butter and press into 8-inch pie plate. Bake 15 minutes.

YIELD: 8-INCH PASTRY SHELL

Silk Pie

1/2 cup butter or margarine,
  softened
1/4 cup granulated sugar
1 square unsweetened
  chocolate, melted
1 teaspoon vanilla extract

2 eggs
Coconut Pie Crust, baked
  (above)
1/2 pint heavy cream, whipped
  and flavored with vanilla
Chocolate Curls (p. 334)

1 Cream butter and sugar until light and fluffy. Blend in melted chocolate and add vanilla.

2 Add eggs, one at a time, beating 5 minutes after each addition. Turn into baked coconut crust. Chill 2 or 3 hours.

3 Serve with whipped cream and chocolate curls.

YIELD: 8-INCH OPEN PIE

Arundel Rum Pie

1 9-inch graham-cracker pie
  shell
2 tablespoons unflavored
  gelatine
1/2 cup cold water

6 egg yolks, well beaten
3/4 cup granulated sugar
1 pint cream, stiffly beaten
1/2 cup rum

1 Bake graham-cracker pie shell according to package directions and cool.

2 Soak gelatine in water, then bring to boil.

3 In mixing bowl, combine beaten egg yolks and sugar. Stir gelatine into yolks. Fold in whipped cream and rum.

4 Pour mixture into baked pie shell and chill. Serve topped with more whipped cream. (This does seem, really, to be gilding the lily!)

YIELD: 9-INCH OPEN PIE

Baked Bananas in Rum

 Allow 1 or 2 bananas more than the number of people to be served. If you want to make this dish very festive, flame it with some heated rum when you serve it.

6 bananas	¹/₂ package Butter Buds
dark rum	brown sugar (optional)
¹/₂ teaspoon lemon juice	

1 Preheat oven to 350°.

2 Peel bananas and split lengthwise and crosswise.

3 Combine rum, lemon juice, and Butter Buds.

4 Arrange banana sections in ovenproof dish and pour rum sauce over them. Bake 15 or 20 minutes. Serve. Sprinkle with brown sugar if you desire.

YIELD: 4 SERVINGS

Grapefruit Soufflé

2 grapefruit	¹/₂ cup strawberries, halved
granulated sugar to taste	2 egg whites

1 Halve grapefruit and remove sections of fruit with sharp spoon. Squeeze juice over sections. Remove and discard membrane from shells, reserving shells. Chill shells until needed. Mix fruit with sugar and strawberries and chill.

2 When ready to serve, preheat oven to 400°.

3 Beat egg whites to stiff peaks, adding small amount of sugar.

4 Divide fruit sections among 4 chilled shells and top with meringue, making sure meringue adheres to edges of shells.

5 Place shells on small baking sheet and bake until meringue is puffed and golden, about 6 to 8 minutes (watch carefully!).

YIELD: 4 SERVINGS

Oranges Orientales

4 large navel oranges
$^{1}/_{2}$ cup water
$^{1}/_{2}$ cup rosewater

$^{1}/_{2}$ cup granulated sugar
1 maraschino cherry, thinly
  sliced

1 With vegetable peeler, remove outer skin (orange zest) from oranges—
   cut pieces as large as possible. Cut zest into long, thin slivers.

2 In saucepan, bring water, rosewater, and sugar to boil. Add orange
   slivers and simmer over low heat 10 to 15 minutes. Shake to separate
   pieces. Chill.

3 Peel oranges, removing all the white pith. Over bowl to catch juices,
   slice oranges as thin as possible. Remove seeds.

4 Arrange orange slices in chilled compote in circular pattern to resemble a rose. Sprinkle candied rind in center and garnish with cherry
   rings.

YIELD: 4 SERVINGS

Macaroon-Stuffed Peaches

4 firm but ripe peaches
4 stale macaroons, crushed
  with rolling pin or in blender
$1^{1}/_{2}$ tablespoons granulated
  sugar

6 tablespoons unsalted butter
  or margarine, softened
2 egg whites, lightly beaten
1 tablespoon kirsch

1 Preheat oven to 375°. Coat 8″ x 10″ baking dish with vegetable spray.

2 Blanch peaches, two at a time, in boiling water for about 20 seconds.
   With slotted spoon, lift out peaches and plunge into cold water. Peel
   off skins with sharp knife.

3 Cut peaches in half and remove pits. Scoop out enough pulp from each
   half to make a deep space in center. Add pulp to crushed macaroons,
   then stir in sugar, butter, beaten egg whites, and kirsch. Stuff peach
   halves with mixture.

4 Arrange peach halves in prepared baking dish and bake about 25 minutes. Serve immediately.

YIELD: 8 SERVINGS

Mixed Fruit in Raspberry Sauce

1 package (10 ounces) frozen
   raspberries, thawed
1 tablespoon framboise liqueur
1/2 pint raspberries

1/2 pint blueberries
2 kiwifruit
2 egg whites, beaten stiff and
   sweetened to taste

1 Purée raspberries and put through fine strainer to remove seeds. Mix with liqueur and chill.

2 Wash and dry raspberries and blueberries; peel kiwifruit. Chill.

3 At serving time, pour raspberry purée on individual serving plates. Arrange three piles of fruits on each—raspberries, blueberries, and sliced kiwifruit—and put a dollop of egg white in center of each plate.

YIELD: 4 SERVINGS

Raspberries Romanoff

A great dessert when raspberries are in season, and nowadays that's nearly all year. (Strawberries may be prepared the same way.)

1 pint raspberries
1/4 cup confectioners' sugar
1 ounce Cointreau
3/4 cup whipped cream

few slivers of orange rind for
   garnish
chopped pistachio nuts for
   garnish

1 Rinse berries and dry thoroughly. Combine carefully with sugar and Cointreau, then fold into whipped cream.

2 Place mixture in serving dish and garnish with slivers of orange rind and chopped pistachios.

YIELD: 4 SERVINGS

Strawberries Jupiter

1 1/2 quarts fresh strawberries
1/4 to 1/2 cup granulated sugar
1 package (10 ounces) frozen
   raspberries
1 tablespoon orange liqueur

1 teaspoon lemon juice
chopped pistachio nuts for
   garnish
fresh mint sprigs for garnish

1. Wash and hull strawberries and dry on paper toweling. Slice, sprinkle with sugar, and chill several hours.

2. Purée raspberries in blender or food processor and put through fine strainer to remove seeds. Add orange liqueur and lemon juice and chill.

3. Just before serving, ladle raspberry sauce over strawberries and garnish with pistachios and mint sprigs.

YIELD: 6 SERVINGS

Wine Jelly

Serve with Cool Whip or lightly whipped, sweetened cream.

2 envelopes unflavored gelatine	$^1/_2$ cup orange juice
2 cups sherry	$^1/_3$ cup lemon juice
1 cup boiling water	1 cup granulated sugar

1. Rinse 3-cup mold with cold water.

2. Soften gelatine in $^1/_2$ cup sherry and add boiling water to dissolve. Add remaining sherry and other ingredients and stir.

3. Pour mixture into mold and chill until firm.

YIELD: 6 SERVINGS

ICE CREAM

A freezer of ice cream on Sunday all through the summer was as necessary to the American way of life a generation ago as firecrackers on the Fourth of July and band concerts on warm Saturday evenings.

Smooth ice cream and sherbet can be made in an old-fashioned ice cream freezer, in an electric one, or in the freezer compartment of a refrigerator. If you opt for the latter, it is convenient to freeze the mixture in a round plastic quart container saved from when you have bought commercial ice cream. Freeze until nearly solid, then remove from the freezer and beat vigorously for several minutes with a hand beater or electric beater or at top speed in a blender. The latter method will produce the lightest texture. The ice cream will increase in bulk by about one-fourth. Return it to the freezer until solid.

Vanilla Ice Cream

4 cups light cream

1 cup granulated sugar

pinch of salt

1 1/2 teaspoons vanilla extract

1 Heat 1 cup cream very slowly (do not boil). Stir in sugar and salt until dissolved. Add vanilla and chill.

2 Remove from refrigerator, add remaining cream, and freeze.

YIELD: 1 1/2 QUARTS

VARIATION – Peach Ice Cream

Add 3/4 cup granulated sugar to 1 1/2 cups peach pulp; decrease vanilla extract quantity to 1 teaspoon and add 1/2 teaspoon almond extract. Mix well. Add to ice cream mixture and freeze.

VARIATION – Strawberry Ice Cream

Add 3/4 cup granulated sugar to 1 cup crushed strawberries and let stand 1 hour at room temperature. Add to ice cream mixture and freeze.

VARIATION – Banana Ice Cream

Mash 3 ripe bananas with silver fork and beat until smooth. Add to ice cream mixture and freeze.

VARIATION – Maple Ice Cream

Substitute maple sugar for granulated sugar. If you wish, stir 1 cup broken nut meats into ice cream just before it solidifies.

SHERBETS

Sherbets make a refreshing finish to many meals when a heavier dessert might seem too filling. Lemon, orange, and raspberry are fairly usual, but it is easy to concoct other, more surprising flavors.

Blueberry Sherbet

½ cup granulated sugar
2½ cups boiling water
juice of 1 lemon

1 cup puréed fresh or frozen
    blueberries
2 egg whites

1 Boil together sugar and water. Add juice and puréed berries and freeze until nearly solid.

2 Beat egg whites until stiff. Remove sherbet from freezer and beat together with egg whites. Return to freezer.

YIELD: 1 QUART

Lemon or Lime Sherbet

3 cups water
1½ cups granulated sugar

⅔ cup lemon or lime juice
2 egg whites

1 Boil water and sugar together until sugar is dissolved. Add fruit juice, cool, and freeze until nearly solid.

2 Beat egg whites until stiff. Remove sherbet from freezer and beat together with egg whites. Return to freezer.

YIELD: 1 QUART

Fresh Strawberry Sherbet

¾ cup granulated sugar
1 cup boiling water
juice of half an orange
juice of half a lemon

2 cups puréed fresh
    strawberries
drop of red food coloring
2 egg whites

1 Boil together sugar and water. Add juices and puréed berries and food coloring and freeze until nearly solid.

2 Beat egg whites until stiff. Remove sherbet from freezer and beat together with egg whites. Return to freezer.

YIELD: 1 QUART

Cassis Sherbet

3/4 cup granulated sugar

1 cup boiling water

1 tablespoon lemon juice

2 cups fresh or frozen
  raspberry purée

1/2 cup crème de cassis

2 egg whites

1 Boil together sugar and water. Add lemon juice, raspberry purée, and cassis and freeze until nearly solid.

2 Beat egg whites until stiff. Remove sherbet from freezer and beat together with egg whites. Return to freezer.

YIELD: 1 QUART

Bombe Cassis

I think this dessert is divine—devastating—delectable.

1 quart vanilla ice cream

1 quart Cassis Sherbet (above)

1 jar (12 ounces) blackcurrant
  preserves

4 ounces crème de cassis

1 Fill 2-quart mold with vanilla ice cream, covering sides and leaving a hollow in the center. Fill hollow with cassis sherbet. Freeze until very hard and firm.

2 In bowl, beat together blackcurrant preserves and créme de cassis. Refrigerate until ready to serve.

3 At serving time, unmold bombe on chilled serving dish and surround with sauce.

YIELD: 8 TO 10 SERVINGS

Maple Mousse

4 egg yolks

3/4 cup maple syrup

2 cups heavy cream, whipped

1/2 cup finely chopped walnuts
  or almonds

1 Beat yolks until they form light ribbons. Set aside.

2 Heat maple syrup in top of double boiler. Add small amount of syrup

to beaten eggs and mix well. Then add eggs to hot syrup and stir over low heat until thickened. (Do not allow mixture to boil.) Cool.

3 Fold in whipped cream and pour into wet 1-quart mold rinsed with cold water and freeze.

4 When ready to serve, unmold mousse and sprinkle with chopped nuts.

DESSERT SAUCES

Hard Sauce

 ½ cup butter or margarine, at room temperature
pinch of salt
1 cup confectioners' sugar

1 teaspoon vanilla extract
freshly grated nutmeg, to sprinkle (optional)

1 Beat together butter, salt, and sugar. Add vanilla and, if desired, sprinkle with nutmeg.

YIELD: 1½ CUPS

French Hard Sauce

 ½ cup butter or margarine, at room temperature
1½ cups confectioners' sugar

1 egg yolk, beaten
3 tablespoons brandy or rum

1 Beat together butter and sugar in small bowl of electric mixer at high speed until light and fluffy. Stir in egg yolk and rum. Chill.

YIELD: 1½ CUPS

Brandied Apricot Sauce

 Good with various steamed puddings. For Christmas pudding, you can serve this along with Hard Sauce (above).

1 jar apricot jam	²/₃ cup brandy

1 Combine jam and brandy over low heat. Serve hot.

YIELD: 1½ CUPS

Fluffy Sauce

 For Christmas pudding.

1 egg	1 tablespoon rum
2 cups confectioners' sugar	½ teaspoon vanilla extract
1 cup heavy cream, whipped	pinch of salt

1 Beat egg until thick and lemon colored. Gradually add sugar and salt and fold in whipped cream and flavorings.

YIELD: ABOUT 2 CUPS

Christmas Pudding Sauce

 The best of all. Serve with flaming Christmas pudding.

¼ pound sweet butter	2 tablespoons apricot jam
2 cups confectioners' sugar	½ pint heavy cream, beaten
2 eggs, well beaten	stiff
2 tablespoons brandy or rum	

1 Beat together butter, sugar, and eggs in double boiler over hot water until frothy and thick (like zabaglione).

2 Stir brandy, jam, and whipped cream into warm sauce.

YIELD: 2 CUPS

Hot Fudge Sauce

2 cups granulated sugar	2 tablespoons butter or
2 squares semisweet chocolate	margarine
³/₄ cup milk	dash of salt
	½ teaspoon vanilla extract

1 Combine all ingredients except vanilla and cook in top of double boiler, over rapidly boiling water, about 15 minutes, or until 1 drop forms a very soft ball when dropped in cold water.

2 Stir in vanilla and serve.

YIELD: 2 CUPS

VARIATION – Chocolate Mint Sauce

Follow directions for Hot Fudge Sauce, omitting vanilla and substituting $1/2$ teaspoon peppermint extract or $1/4$ cup crushed peppermint candy.

Butterscotch Sauce

$3/4$ cup brown sugar
1 cup light corn syrup
$1/4$ cup butter or margarine

1 cup light cream
dash of salt

1 Boil sugar, syrup, and butter, stirring constantly, about 5 minutes.

2 Add cream and salt and return to boiling point. Serve hot or cold.

YIELD: 3 CUPS

Caramel Sauce

1 cup brown sugar
1 cup butter or margarine

1 cup heavy cream
1 teaspoon vanilla extract

1 Combine sugar and butter in top of double boiler over low heat. Add cream slowly, stirring well.

2 Remove sauce from heat and stir in vanilla.

YIELD: $2^1/2$ CUPS

Vanilla Sauce

$1/2$ cup granulated sugar
2 tablespoons butter or
    margarine
1 tablespoon cornstarch

pinch of salt
1 cup boiling water
1 teaspoon vanilla extract
pinch of ground nutmeg

1 Mix together sugar, butter, cornstarch, and salt. Gradually stir in boiling water. Boil, stirring continuously, until smooth and thick, about 5 minutes.

2 Stir in vanilla and nutmeg.

VARIATION – **Lemon Sauce**

Follow directions for Vanilla Sauce, but omit vanilla and substitute 2 tablespoons lemon juice and 1 teaspoon grated lemon rind.

Maple Syrup Sauce

Good on puddings or on unfrosted cake.

$^1/_3$ cup butter or margarine, softened	1 egg, separated
1 cup confectioners' sugar, sifted	$^1/_2$ cup maple syrup
	$^1/_2$ teaspoon vanilla extract
	$^1/_3$ cup heavy cream

1 Cream butter, gradually add sugar, and beat until blended.

2 Add egg yolk and beat well, then add maple syrup and vanilla. Beat until creamy.

3 Beat egg white until stiff. Whip cream until stiff. Fold egg white and whipped cream into syrup mixture.

YIELD: ABOUT 2$^1/_2$ CUPS

Strawberry Sauce

$^1/_3$ cup butter or margarine	1 pint strawberries, mashed
1 cup confectioners' sugar	1 egg white, beaten (optional)

1 Cream together butter and sugar. Add strawberries and, if desired, beaten egg white.

YIELD: ABOUT 2 CUPS

Baked Alaska

And, finally, from New England, a tribute to our fiftieth state. Baked Alaska—easy to prepare and festive to serve—provides a light, flattering end for a special-occasion dinner. Children love it, too, and a few candles make it into a birthday cake.

There are countless combinations for the flavors filling a Baked Alaska. Children love peppermint-stick ice cream topped with fudge sauce. Peach ice cream topped with cherry jam and a jigger of kirsch pleases a more sophisticated palate, as does coffee ice cream with marrons glacées and a tot of Cognac or crème de cacao.

We suggest using a Baked Alaska pan, about 10 inches in diameter, now readily available in specialty stores.

1 layer (8 inches) angel-food or sponge cake	1 quart round container of ice cream (6 inches in diameter), frozen solid
6 egg whites	jam, fruit, marrons, or liqueur (optional)
1/4 teaspoon cream of tartar	chopped nuts (optional)
2/3 cup granulated sugar	

1 Make room in freezer or freezing compartment of refrigerator for storing finished cake.

2 Cut layer of cake 1 inch thick. (If there is a hole in the cake, fill with "plug" of cake.) Place layer in Baked Alaska pan.

3 Beat egg whites until stiff and add cream of tartar. Little by little, add sugar. Beat until very stiff.

4 Unmold ice cream on cake, leaving 1-inch margin all around. (Work quickly.) If desired, make a hollow in center of ice cream and fill with jam, fruit, marrons, or splash of liqueur.

5 With spatula, cover entire block of ice cream to 1-inch thickness. (Be sure there are no gaps in meringue, for heat must not get through.) If desired, decorate meringue with sprinkling of nuts. Return dish to freezer—it can wait several hours.

6 When ready to serve, preheat oven to 500°. Set shelf low in oven.

7 Place Baked Alaska in oven and bake about 5 minutes, until meringue is slightly browned. Serve immediately. Cut into wedges.

YIELD: 8 TO 10 SERVINGS

Index